I0813821

If I Can Get Home This Fall

If I Can Get Home This Fall

A Story of Love, Loss, and a Cause in the Civil War

TYLER ALEXANDER

Potomac Books { *An imprint of the University of Nebraska Press* }

Manufactured in the United States of America.

For customers in the EU with safety/GPSR concerns, contact:
gpsr@mare-nostrum.co.uk
Mare Nostrum Group BV
Mauritskade 21D
1091 GC Amsterdam
The Netherlands

Library of Congress Control Number: 2024054324

Frontispiece: Company D, Sixth Vermont Infantry, Camp Griffin, Virginia, February 1862. Library of Congress.

Set in Monotype Fournier by A. Shahan.

In memory of my father, Edwin E. Alexander (1953–2022). Like Dan Mason, he was a brave, honest man who cared about and loved his country. His grave is just uphill from Mason's.

CONTENTS

CONTENTS

ILLUSTRATIONS

PREFACE

On Father's Day in 2007, I spent the day touring around the Northeast Kingdom of Vermont with my father, Edwin Elijah Alexander. We visited our family's camp in Wheelock, had lunch, then drove north along VT Route 16 to the town of Glover, where we planned to fish the Barton River. Before we began fishing, we pulled off the road at Westlook Cemetery, about a mile south of Glover Village. We visited the grave of my grandfather, whose headstone—a giant slab of granite that had once been a boulder on his property—includes a whole family genealogy on one face. It was a perfect, sunny, quiet, early summer day. While we were there, we walked through the cemetery, where many of my ancestors going back two centuries are buried, now including my father himself, who succumbed to a long struggle with pancreatic cancer in the winter of 2022. He made a specific point of showing me a particular headstone that stood out prominently: the gravesite of a Civil War soldier named Dan Mason. On one face of Mason's grave is etched the following inscription:

> Capt. Dan Mason was mustered into U.S. service, Oct. 15, 1861, & while in active service was engaged in the following engagements.
> Apr. 16, 1862, Lee's Mills.
> May 5, 1862, Williamsburg.
> June 27, 1862, Golden's Farm.
> 29, Savage Station.
> 30, White Oak Swamp.
> Sept. 14 & 17, Antietam.
> Dec. 12. Fredericksburg.
> May 3, 63, Mayres Heights Fredericksburg.
> 4, Banks Ford.
> June 6, Franklin's Crossing.

July 2, 3, & 4, Gettysburg.
July 10, Funkstown.
Oct. 13, Rappahannock.
    20, Skirmish on the Warrenton Pike.
Nov. 7, Rappahannock Station.
July 30, 1864, Petersburg.

I'm not sure how my father knew that this grave existed, but I imagine that he had seen it earlier, perhaps with his own father, and it had clearly made an impression on him. He said to me something to the effect of, "I've always been amazed at how many battles he took part in. Can you imagine being at all those places?" My father was a math teacher, not a historian, but he always had a keen interest in American history, particularly the Civil War. He, like millions of other Americans, had been enraptured by the airing of Ken Burns's Civil War series on PBS in 1990. We visited Gettysburg the next year, one of my first exposures to the Civil War. He read the novel *The Killer Angels*, and then we watched the movie *Gettysburg*, which is based on the novel, over the course of three nights (July 1, 2, and 3 to be exact, to correspond with the sequence of the actual battle). It was no surprise then that he would have taken an interest in Mason's grave and was able to appreciate the significance of that one face of his headstone. And Mason's grave was not alone. Throughout that one cemetery in one small town in one small corner of one small state lie numerous other headstones of Civil War soldiers, identified by small American flags waving from GAR markers, including that of my ancestor Elijah Stone, who served in the same unit that Mason did: Company D of the Sixth Vermont Volunteer Infantry, Second Brigade, Second Division, VI Corps, Army of the Potomac. On that tranquil summer day, as we wandered the cemetery alone, far removed from the time and place where these men fought, one could not help but feel a strange connection to the past and imagine the circumstances that lead so many young men from a rural town not far from the Canadian border to Virginia and points south in the 1860s. For what? Why? How did the war transform their communities and their families? What did they bring home with them? The town from which they came, Glover, had a population of 1,244 residents according to the 1860 census. The population of the town has never been as high. In 2020 there were only 1,114 residents, over 100 residents fewer than there were in 1860. It would be an oversimplification to state that nothing in Glover (or the Northeast Kingdom of Vermont) has changed since the nineteenth century. But if one momentarily overlooks the traces of modernity that have come to town (paved roads, electric utility poles, automobiles, and the like), it isn't too difficult to imagine the town as it once was. Many of the same homes built in the nineteenth century, mostly Cape-style homes and modest farmhouses, still stand. Stone walls and abandoned cellar holes still dot the landscape. Although once-cleared fields have now reverted to forest, many hillsides are still actively managed as agricultural land. If one wants to picture what nineteenth-century rural America looked like, then towns like this are a good place to start. The residential, industrial, and commercial development that has transformed so much of the nation since the end of the Civil War, including many Civil War sites, has largely eluded this area. I'm not sure if there is a description for it—somber reflection, seeing ghosts, an awe-inspired marveling at the turmoil that previous generations of Americans have endured in extraordinary times, a good dose of patriotism, or something else—but I have experienced this kind of *feeling* many times in places like Westlook Cemetery, and certainly at places around the nation where the crucible of war burned hottest.

We crossed the road, walked a short way across a hay meadow, then descended a wooded bank until we reached the Barton River, where we fished throughout the afternoon. The stream is not more than a few feet across, but we had good luck. I caught several trout, including a particularly nice one that I had to work for, feeding my line underneath a tangled thicket of speckled alders that hung over the stream until it reached a nice, deep, shaded pool where a respectable trout was lurking. I reeled it in, excitedly hustled downstream to where my father was fishing to reveal my catch, knowing that he would be happy. He was. Did any of the soldiers buried across the road ever fish this same reach of river 150 years earlier on a quiet summer day like this before leaving for war? Or maybe some came here after the war, losing themselves in the river's current the way Hemingway's protagonist Nick Adams does in "Big Two-Hearted River," a momentary escape from the trauma of World War I?

About a decade later, in trying to find out more about my own Civil War ancestor, I spent an afternoon at the Vermont Historical Society Library in Barre, Vermont. I learned that Dan Mason's Civil War letters were housed in a collection there, and knowing that Mason was in the same unit as my ancestor, I thought I might learn something about him by reading Mason's letters: the campaigns that the unit participated in, the conditions of camp life, and so on. It didn't take long for me to realize that I was looking at a remarkable collection of a whole war's worth of letters. Although countless volumes of Civil War letters have been published and Civil War soldiers were known for their prolific letter-writing, still, this collection seemed worthy of publication.

Mason wrote to his sweetheart turned fiancée turned wife, Harriet Clark, over the course of four years. The letters are elegant, candid, uncensored, graphic, humorous, full of romantic longing and relationship strife, and offer a good deal of insight into the factors that compelled so many off to war and sustained them throughout. Mason enlisted in Company D of the Sixth Vermont Volunteer Infantry as a corporal, then was promoted to sergeant. His closest friends were other noncommissioned officers from Glover and its surrounding towns who also left a rich, detailed record of their service. Their writings, together with Mason's, allowed me the great privilege and honor to piece together the story of one company within the famed Vermont Brigade, the Union brigade that was destined to suffer more casualties than any other.

In early 1864, after much deliberation, Mason reenlisted as a captain in the Nineteenth United States Colored Troops (USCT), an all-Black regiment made up mostly of formerly enslaved men from Maryland, which he served in for the duration of the war. I have attempted to the best of my ability to tell the story of this unit as well. Although the enlisted troops were largely illiterate, pension records, slaveowners' compensation claims, widows' pension claims, Freedmen's Bureau reports, casualty reports, newspaper coverage, court-martial records, regimental records, and the letters of their white officers offer a great deal of insight into the experiences of Black troops, especially those from border states such as Maryland.

Mason's letters reveal that he was motivated to serve for a variety of reasons: a genuine sense of patriotism, a belief in maintaining a republican government by crushing the rebellion against it, and, on several occasions throughout his letters, a strong desire to blot out the institution of slavery. An overwhelming amount of evidence suggests that his antislavery convictions were not the exception to the rule, at least in Vermont. Beginning with the development of the Lost Cause narrative after the war and continuing through the present with ongoing culture wars and battles over school curricula, many have sought to minimize slavery as the ultimate cause of the war. Mason knew better. Despite the presence in Vermont of an outspoken minority that opposed the revolutionary impulses of the war (and frequently drew the ire of Mason and his comrades), most people in his unit and community knew even before the war started that slavery was the wellspring of the rebellion and that the war could not be won without bludgeoning it out of existence. Indeed, Vermont supported Abraham Lincoln more than any other state in the election of 1860, and though far removed from the seat of war, the Yankee hill folk of this tiny state were absolutely conscious of the centrality of human bondage as the war's root cause and spared no words in denouncing it as the nation's original sin. The institution of slavery and the inequalities it generated were fundamentally at odds with the kind of dignified, honest free labor that Vermonters have long celebrated.

Mason also made it clear that, although he believed in making soldiers of Black Americans, a commission as an officer in a Black regiment was appealing because of the much higher pay that it offered. He praised the troops under his command numerous times and indicated his pride in them for their discipline, effectiveness as soldiers, willingness to withstand hardship, and knowledge about the political questions of the time. Despite this he at times used language that by any definition would be considered racist. This juxtaposition was hardly uncommon at the time. I've made no effort to conceal or sanitize such comments made by Mason or other white officers that he served with, although at a time when millions of white Northerners were unwilling to emancipate enslaved people, much less arm them or lead them into battle, Mason showed no doubts about such measures and was *personally* willing to take part in the transformation of the war's purpose.

In the final year of the war, Mason's thoughts turned increasingly to his biggest concerns: getting married and coming home. There is no question that he was exhausted and ready to return to civilian life, though he felt compelled to continue to serve "as long as there is war in the land" and admitted that there was something "wild and exciting about military life" that made it difficult to leave the army.

He used language characteristic of the romantic, Victorian era that he lived in. In many cases, his thoughts were lofty, high-minded, and altruistic. In a handful of instances, he came across as self-serving, especially when he became an officer and admitted that he enjoyed the taste of power that came with his new rank. He often admitted vulnerability on many levels, especially when he spoke of having "the blues" several times. He was so shaken by his near-death experience at the Battle of the Crater on July 30, 1864, that he contemplated leaving the service dishonorably, though his fiancée, Harriet, encouraged him to stay on. He was concerned about saving money to buy a farm when he returned home. He planned all the details of his wedding and honeymoon over the course of several exchanges of letters. He spoke ill of his fellow troops at times, condemning them for their cowardice or debauchery. He had no patience for those who were critical of the war effort, avoided service, or begrudgingly entered the ranks only after being drafted. He was infatuated with Harriet, especially after his marriage. In short, his letters form an intensely human account of the full lived experience of one person trying to survive the deadliest, most traumatic, most polarizing event in American history.

Although he was human (by his own admission) and made comments that were troubling, it is hard not to admire the conviction, endurance, and faith that he exemplified for four terribly long years. The Union's victory in the Civil War was incomplete, especially considering the rise of new forms of racial discrimination that became rooted in American life after the war or the fact that the Confederate flag (or "filthy rag" as the men of the Sixth Vermont called it) was hoisted in the halls of the Capitol Building 156 years after Appomattox, but it nevertheless was a significant victory and a watershed moment in American history. It preserved the constitutional system of republican government, it made possible the addition of three new constitutional amendments that many historians have referred to as a "second founding," it demonstrated to the world that democracies were viable and could govern themselves at a time when most nations were still dominated by minority forms of government, and it did, to a degree, offer four million people freedom and new possibilities. It took military force to do this, and those who, as Mason said, fought "for the right," deserve praise. It would be difficult for me, as someone who has never served his country in wartime, to minimize the idealism and bravery that everyday Americans like Mason demonstrated. We are in desperate need of stories that remind us that positive change can come at all levels, that men and women who have demonstrated remarkable moral courage and incomprehensible sacrifices are the true patriots whom we should seek to emulate today, and that "the better angels of our nature" can prevail again.

Countless volumes by prominent historians have been written that offer great insight into the lives, motives, and experiences of soldiers and civilians, men and women, Northerners and Southerners, and those free and enslaved during the war. This is just one story of millions that could be told. I will not attempt to draw major conclusions and generalizations about the experiences and beliefs of all those who lived through the war from one soldier's writings, nor is my goal to analyze the minutiae of every military campaign that Mason served in, but Mason's words, and those of others that were associated with him, will speak for themselves. At a time when our nation faces dangerous divisions, many of which can be traced back to the Civil War and its aftermath, when democratic governance is under renewed assault, and when questions about national identity and what it means to be an American generate intense, often violent, reactions, it is worth remembering what some were willing to give so "that that nation might live." And perhaps we may even honor Dan and Harriet Mason by finding it within ourselves to "strive on to finish the work" that they, and countless other men and women of their generation who shared their struggles, "so nobly advanced."

ACKNOWLEDGMENTS

I am indebted to numerous individuals and organizations who have helped me tell Dan Mason's story—and those of others whom he was closely associated with. This has been a project years in the making, and it would not have been possible without support from many friends, colleagues, and family members.

First of all I would like to thank my aunt Joan Alexander for her invaluable assistance. Nobody has devoted more time to researching, documenting, and writing about the history of Glover, Vermont. Her familiarity with Glover's nineteenth-century residents is unsurpassed. Her commentary on Mason's letters, the documents, photos, anecdotes, and stories she shared with me, and her enthusiasm for the project were all a great source of support for me.

I was incredibly fortunate to have been able to speak with the descendants of the two major figures in the book, Dan and Harriet Mason. Harriet Borland, a direct descendant of her namesake, generously allowed me to borrow a scrapbook her mother kept, which included original newspaper clippings, letters, pages of diaries, photographs, and poems that were written by or to Dan and Harriet themselves. I also had the great pleasure of speaking to June Wardell Mason, a nonagenarian who shared with me fascinating details of Mason family history, including her own life story and that of her late husband, John Mason, a World War II veteran. June and John's donation of Dan Mason's letters to the Vermont Historical Society in 1989 made my project possible.

I owe a debt to John Kimball, a Californian and a descendant of Fred Kimball of the Sixth Vermont, who generously made available a great deal of source information from his noble, eloquent ancestor that allowed me to learn much about the intimate, human details of soldiering in the regiment.

The Vermont Historical Society (VHS), which houses Mason's letters in their beautiful library, was a pleasure to work with. Special thanks go to

Marjorie Strong, who helped me access Hobart Bliss's diary, census records from the 1860s, and photographs in the VHS collection.

Additional support in my research came from the staff at the Old Stone House Museum in Brownington, Vermont, especially Bob Hunt and Darlene Young, who provided me with access to numerous items in their collection, including bound volumes of the *Orleans Independent Standard*, which were a priceless resource. I am also grateful to Senator Peter Welch's office, particularly Ally White, for helping to secure a research appointment at the National Archives building in Washington DC, where I was able to uncover much of the history of the Nineteenth U.S. Colored Troops. The staff at the American Antiquarian Society in Worcester, Massachusetts, also offered great assistance in providing access to the letters of James Rickard, a friend and fellow officer of Mason's in the Nineteenth USCT.

Learning about the American Civil War has been a lifelong interest of mine that pre-dated my work on this project. For teaching me much about the daily life of the Civil War soldier, I am grateful to the Vermont Civil War Hemlocks, who take great pride in the authenticity of their impression and have done much to honor the sacrifices and memory of the men of the Old Vermont Brigade.

For almost two decades I have been a member of the Northeast Kingdom Civil War Roundtable of Newport, Vermont. I have met many friends who share my interest in learning about the Civil War. I have so enjoyed hearing countless stories over the years from some of the finest men and women in Vermont's Northeast Kingdom, many of whom have served in uniform themselves. I have learned so much from all the speakers who have generously visited us over the years, often making long drives up to the Canadian border from hours away for little or no compensation.

To my friends, colleagues, and students at North Country Union High School: it was an enormous privilege to work with you and get to know you. Thank you for your friendship, kindness, and support for me and my family. I will always be a Falcon in spirit.

Most importantly, I want to thank my wife, Aimee, a fellow history teacher, who has very patiently supported me throughout my project, willingly endured the financial costs associated with this work, and has been interrupted hundreds of times, often late at night, as I discovered a particular gem in my research or felt like expounding with long monologues on the election of 1864, the details of life on the home front, the Gettysburg campaign, the Battle of the Crater, Lincoln's assassination, the politics surrounding the recruitment of Black troops, or any number of other related issues. How lucky I am to have a spouse who actually cares about and is interested in (most of the time) such light bedtime conversation.

If I Can Get Home This Fall

Introduction

"The Sum of All Villainies"

The news of the Confederate attack on Fort Sumter on April 12, 1861, like the news of the Japanese attack on Pearl Harbor eighty years later, came as a shock to Americans of that time and meant that life would never be the same. President Lincoln immediately called up seventy-five thousand volunteers for a period of ninety days to suppress the rebellion, which was then followed by the secession of additional four Southern states from the Union, most notably Virginia. In Vermont, Governor Fairbanks called a special session of the state legislature in response to recent events. Fairbanks described the situation:

> Unprincipled and ambitious men have organized a despotism and an armed force for the purpose of overthrowing the Government which the American people have formed for themselves, and of destroying that constitutional frame-work, under which we have enjoyed peace and prosperity, and, from a small and feeble people, grown and expanded to a rank among the first nations of the earth. The enormity of this rebellion is heightened by the consideration that no valid cause exists for it. . . .
>
> No act of oppression, no attempted or threatened invasion of the rights of the revolting states, has existed, either on the part of the General Government, or of the loyal states; but the principle has been recognized and observed, that the right of each and every state to regulate its domestic institutions, should remain inviolate.
>
> The inception and progress of this rebellion have been remarkable; and characterized, at every stage, by a total absence of any high honorable principle or motive in its leaders.[1]

The governor's call to arms was typical of similar proclamations that were made throughout the nation in the weeks following the fall of Fort Sumter:

a condemnation of secession as treasonous, a vow to uphold the Constitution and its republican form of government, and a strong patriotic appeal to the loyal citizens of the Union. Invoking the memory of the American Revolution and the patriots of 1776 was also commonplace in the North—and in the South—in the first heady days of war. In Vermont references to the spirit of '76 inevitably made mention of the Green Mountain Boys of Revolutionary War fame. However, Fairbanks's message only contained an oblique reference to slavery, without a mention of the word itself. The governor repeated the policy of the Lincoln administration, which had made it clear that the federal government had no authority to interfere with the "domestic institutions" of the Southern states. President Lincoln, in his first inaugural address, delivered just over a month before hostilities began, made this policy abundantly clear and even promised to do his part to return fugitive slaves. Despite the hesitancy among many Northern politicians to acknowledge slavery as the cause of the war, as Lincoln admitted four years later during his second inaugural address, "these slaves constituted a peculiar and powerful interest. All knew that this interest was somehow the cause of the war. To strengthen perpetuate and extend this interest was the object for which the insurgents would rend the Union even by war while the government claimed no right to do more than to restrict the territorial enlargement of it."[2]

Slavery had been the most divisive issue in the nation since its founding and was, as Lincoln later said, "the cause of the war."[3] By the election of 1860, Abraham Lincoln—and the Republican Party—had made their opposition to the spread of slavery westward their central platform. Opposition to the spread of slavery on moral grounds did not equate to a call for immediate emancipation though, nor certainly to advocacy of racial equality. But by 1860, a majority of Northerners, as evidenced by the fact that every Northern state voted for Lincoln in the election of 1860, had accepted the argument that slavery was a moral wrong at odds with both Christianity and the ideals expressed in the Declaration of Independence. Antislavery agitation, and the consequent full-throated defense of slavery, had precipitated such events as "Bleeding Kansas," the formation of the Republican Party in the mid-1850s, and John Brown's Raid at Harpers Ferry, Virginia.

No state supported Lincoln more than Vermont, where he won an astounding 76 percent of the popular vote in 1860. No other state came close to matching this percentage. By contrast Lincoln won adjoining New Hampshire with 57 percent of the vote, New York with 54 percent of the vote, his home state of Illinois with 51 percent of the vote, and New Jersey with 48 percent of the vote. In Orleans County, Vermont, the percentage was even higher: 81 percent of residents there voted for Lincoln. Only Addison County voted for Lincoln by a higher margin.[4] In Orleans County, which consisted (and still does) of a number of lightly populated, remote towns and villages near the Canadian border where the vast majority of citizens were engaged in small-scale agriculture, the fact that slavery was the cause of the war seemed to be lost on no one. In town after town, as "war meetings" were held to rally public support for the war effort, denunciations of treason and secession were common, but attacks on slavery also took center stage. According to the main organ of news dissemination at that time in Orleans County, the *Orleans Independent Standard*, a weekly newspaper published in the town of Irasburg, antislavery sentiment ran deep. In Irasburg a reverend claimed that "18,000,000 of people armed in the sacred cause of liberty, and with untold wealth and the respect of the civilised world to back them, ought certainly to be a match for 8,000,000 of people equipped in defence of slavery, the most heinous and unblushing crime the world has ever seen."[5] Such meetings usually involved a grand display of pomp and ceremony, complete with speeches, music, feasts, prayers, readings of the Declaration of Independence, the firing of cannon, and the unfurling of flags and often concluded with the enlistment of new recruits. The "ladies" of each town often played a symbolic and ceremonial role. In Irasburg, for example, the newspaper reported that "the patriotic ladies" of the town "have engaged to make up the uniforms and any necessary clothing for the volunteers. The stars and stripes were run up over the court house, and another flag, made by the ladies of Irasburgh, was run up at the hotel, amid the salutes of cannon, and as they shake their beautiful folds in our pure mountain air, they admonish us that we still have a country to defend, a flag to Uphold, and thousands of patriotic sons and daughters ready to share in the honors and perils of the fight."[6]

In Craftsbury, on April 25, "the stars and stripes were flung to the breeze from the flag staff on Craftsbury Common, and received such a salute as those of the present generation never before offered to their country's flag. The ladies hailed it with joy, and one of the prominent citizens of that place proposed that 'the man that refuses to salute it be pelted with rotten eggs till he will.'"[7] In Newport "the utmost unanimity and harmony of sentiment prevailed, and all, of whatever political faith, seemed to unite with each other in expressions of attachment to the Constitution and Union. . . . Convincing evidence was not wanting that the spirit of freedom which animated our forefathers in 'the times that tried men's souls' still lived in the hearts of the 'Green Mountain Boys.'"[8] In Glover "much enthusiasm prevailed, several declaring themselves ready to march against the rebels at any time. At the close the Band played 'Hail Columbia,' and the meeting broke up with three cheers for 'The Flag of the Union,' three for 'Honest Old Abe,' and three for the ladies."[9] Josiah Grout, who later became a governor of Vermont, recalled:

> The first patriotic outburst I recall was at Glover, where I was attending school. When the news of the surrender of Sumter reached that place, the post office was crowded with students and residents awaiting the arrival of the mail. When it came one of the fathers read from the *Boston Journal* that Fort Sumter had surrendered to the Confederacy. Following the reading there was deep silence. Finally one of the parties seized a broom, mounted the counter, and said, "Boys, let us give three cheers for the old flag!" The cheers were given with a zest, repeated with a tiger, and the crowd moved out of doors for a better opportunity to shake off the spell. One of the company said that he could not see why we cheered, that he felt more like crying over such news. The one who wanted to cry did not enlist.[10]

On April 21 in Derby Line, the Reverend John Fraser preached a lengthy sermon, all of which was reprinted in the local newspaper. He began by acknowledging that "I am a peace man and pray for peace; and therefore, paradoxical though it may seem, preach for this war." Less than two weeks after the firing on Fort Sumter, Rev. Fraser, in a town located directly on the Canadian border, devoted most of his sermon to a withering attack on the institution of slavery:

> As trees grow from seeds and streams flow from fountains, so the fruitful cause of this war with all its attendant train of horrors is slavery. It has long been a root of bitterness and bone of contention. . . . I will not insult your understandings by showing that it is an evil, socially, politically, and morally—only evil, and that continually. . . . The wise and good men who formed the Constitution found slavery existing . . . treating it as an evil which the measures they took would, they trusted, in time remove.

Offering forgiveness to the founders for sidestepping the issue of slavery, which many knew contradicted the ideals of the revolution, Reverend Fraser then alluded to an attempt by Congress to insert a Thirteenth Amendment into the Constitution that would protect slavery—again, without mentioning the word—where it currently existed. The amendment, a last-ditch effort to ensure peace, passed both the House of Representatives and the Senate by the necessary two-thirds margin. It was then submitted to the states, where only Ohio and Maryland ratified it.[11] Four years later the word "slavery" finally appeared in the Constitution, but a very different Thirteenth Amendment would abolish it everywhere, not protect it. Fraser continued:

> The attempt is now made to insert the accursed thing [into the Constitution]. And when we see the abomination that maketh desolate standing in the holy place where it ought not, it is high time for us not to flee but to fight. Fight the traitors who would make that temple of justice and sanctuary for all nations a den of thieves that steal mints and arsenals, and sell, not oxen and sheep, but the bodies and souls of men and women.

He then referred to the fact that previous generations of Southerners, especially the revolutionary generation, at least acknowledged the hypocrisy of maintaining slavery in a land of purported freedom. But as the abolitionist fervor intensified in the decades leading up to the Civil War, so too did the defense of slavery. Slaveowners, most notably Senator John C. Calhoun of South Carolina, began describing slavery as a "positive good" that was sanctioned by the Bible and by the Constitution. The Fifth Amendment to the Constitution, which states that "no person shall . . . be deprived of life, liberty, or *property* without due process of law," was often cited as a legal sanction protecting slavery and indeed was the basis for the Supreme Court's opinion in the notorious *Dred Scott v. Sandford* ruling in 1857, which seemed to imply that Southerners could take their *property* anywhere they pleased, including into the western territories, and even revisit Northern states:

> Slavery has at length assumed a new phase. . . . Whilst it was regarded at the South as an evil there was hope. . . . But now that they have repudiated not only their public and private debts, but every moral obligation, it is for God to levy an execution on them. . . . If there are many antichrists, this, the great heresy of our age, with its intolerance, its inquisition, and selling the bodies and souls of men, is undoubtedly one of them.

The reverend then turned toward a more class-conscious argument that echoed the themes of the "free labor" ideology. The fact that a disproportionate majority of the nearly four million enslaved people in 1860 were owned by an elite planter class was the most glaring example of the contradiction between America's self-image as an egalitarian, democratic land of opportunity where there was more social mobility than anywhere else in the world at the time, and the reality that slavery lead to massive wealth inequality, a lack of social mobility for all people, Blacks as well as whites, and the development of a hereditary upper class that, as Jefferson admitted in his *Notes on the State of Virginia* in 1787, corrupted slaveowners as well as the enslaved. In a message that echoed Walt Whitman, Frederick Douglass, William Lloyd Garrison, and the Old Testament, Fraser continued:

> I am proud to be a working man and to belong to the working class. God has given me a head, and heart, and hands. I am descended from the mud-sills of society, for my ancestors earned their bread by their sweat and served their country with blood. . . . The laborer is made a coworker with God to create, to command and bless.—And if I have any authority over my fellow men, it is by addressing and developing all that is noblest in their nature. It is not by sinking them to the level of

> beasts and chattels, but raising them to the dignity of men and Christians. I am one of those they would enslave, for the question is not of freeing the Blacks but of enslaving the whites. For the present they seek only to shackle our souls. They would poison our free atmosphere. The vial is to be poured into the air. They would merely gag the pulpit, fetter the press, and take from us the spirit of freedom. I would rather fight amid the stifling heat of Sumter than live at large under such a sense of bondage. . . . And all of us working men know how to labor and know how to die; But we know not, nor can they teach us, how to be slaves. Do they imagine that those whose free and generous natures scorned the scepter of kings would bow before the lash of slave drivers?

In a remarkably prophetic statement that anticipated Lincoln's Gettysburg Address two and a half years later and his second inaugural address four years later ("The Almighty has His own purposes"), Fraser accurately predicted what the war would achieve:

> As it was not for us to begin this war with slavery, it will not be for [them to end]. Man knows the beginning of strife, but God only knows the end thereof. But this much we may know, for all history teaches it, that war when protracted passes beyond the designs, and out of the power of those first directing it, and often assumes a new and unexpected nature. There need be no new modeling of our army, but there may be of the object for which we contend. Let the south see to it, for it is not unlikely to become a war of emancipation. . . .
>
> We are finishing the work of the revolution. One man or age doesn't complete a revolution. Moses was unable to lead the chosen tribes into the land of promise. . . . So the leaders in our revolution saw the good land, and were ready to enter, but the people were not. God, we must confess, is just and making us both chairs and instruments in the punishment of slavery, because of our complicity in the sin.

Finally, in a rousing, militaristic conclusion that would be nearly impossible to resist, given the spirit of the times, Fraser implored the young men in his congregation to take up the sword:

All that a man hath will he give for his life and he ought to give for the life of his country. And you, young men and bold, go forth to fight in the high places of the field. . . . Give yourselves first to the Lord and then to your country in his service . . . and with a passion strong as that of the ancient Christians for the martyrs crown seek on the battlefield a short way to heaven glorious as Elijah's chariot and horses of fire.

Alas, that as this spring opens so many of the young, and noble, and good must be laid in the ground as the seed from which the future ages shall reap the rich harvests of freedom and peace!—Are you worthy to die for your country? I urge you not. If any need to be urged they ought not to be allowed to go.—If any are fearful and faint hearted, if any have not heard the voice of God in their country already sounding so loud and clear, let them stay at home. There are enough of brave men without them. . . .

Go, then, and the Lord grant that you may return in victory and peace, for the work of righteousness shall be peace, and the effect of righteousness, quietness, & assurance forever. . . . And many shall go and say come ye and let us go up into the mountain of the Lord, to the house of the god of Jacob, and he will teach us of his ways, and we will walk in his paths. And they shall beat their swords into plowshares, and their spears into pruning hooks; And nation shall not lift up its sword against nation, neither shall they learn war any more.[12]

The intensity, fervor, and righteousness of this sermon were by no means unique at that time or place. The editor of the *Orleans Independent Standard*, Araunah A. Earle, often condemned slavery in a similar manner. Beginning with the first issue of the newspaper, published on January 1, 1856, the masthead of the newspaper proclaimed: "No More Compromise with Slavery." Earle's editorials were staunchly in support of the Republican Party, he was scathing in his criticism of Northern Democrats, and he fully supported abolitionism, even before the war began. Although one must be cautious in claiming that the views of highly literate newspaper editors or clergy members represented public opinion at large in Orleans County, there was clearly strong antislavery sentiment throughout the region, as evidenced by the fact that 81 percent of voters in Orleans County had cast their ballot for Abraham Lincoln in 1860. In the spring of 1861, Earle defended the language of his masthead:

> "NO MORE COMPROMISE WITH SLAVERY"
>
> This is our motto, and this is our position. By it we do not mean that we will occupy a post of neutrality or be indifferent to the great interests of humanity. This we have no desire to do and could not if we would, for we believe that in this as in every moral question, "he that is not for is against." . . . We have long thought that the founders of our republic committed a great error when they made any admission in favor of human slavery. How ever much we revere their memory in this work, we are now satisfied they entailed upon us a terrible evil. They vainly imagined that the monster, after he had attained strength to do as he chose, would willingly consent to die and leave the land for freedom—for social, civil, and religious liberty. It seems they did not realize the deep and damning depravity of the slaveholder's heart.

Again here was a condemnation of the "deep and damning depravity of the slaveholder's heart" in strong, Calvinist terms that Americans who came of age during the Second Great Awakening would surely understand. This was a blistering criticism of the political and religious hypocrisy that slavery engendered and although, generally speaking, the founders of the republic should be admired, Earle believed they made a "great error" in allowing a "terrible evil" to exist. Ever since the conclusion of the Civil War, apologists for slavery contend that it is unfair to judge individuals of the past by values of the present or seek to create a kind of moral equivalence between North and South by claiming that Southerners were defending their "home," their "way of life," their "states' rights," and their land against an "invasion" by an overly powerful federal government. But it is ever so clear that the values of the "present" were shared by countless Americans in the nineteenth century, or even earlier. It is not just a politically correct, "woke," modern idea to argue that slavery was morally wrong or that the founders did not create a perfect union. From the pulpits, in the press, at the ballot box, and in the actions of ordinary Americans who lived in the nineteenth century, including those living in small hill towns near the Canadian border far removed from the cotton kingdom of the South, there is no doubt that slavery was widely regarded as an evil that had blotted the soul of the nation since its founding. Earle had much more to say on the subject:

> In our opinion, the church and state have too long connived with one of the greatest evils that ever arose to prevent the triumph of truth, and only in the positive overthrow of this "sum of all villainies" can we see hope for the future. We do not believe that as a nation we can advance in the path Providence has opened before us unless we throw off this mighty incubus which has for many years been our curse, and a disgrace to our flag throughout the world. . . .
>
> We will have no more to do with such a work. The partnership of wrong must be dissolved. On our part there shall be no more compromises with this stupendous system of iniquity. It has called for war, and now our war cry will be, "War to the death of the foul system of American slavery." Let the contest be carried until a universal jubilee is proclaimed through the length and breadth of the land. In obedience to the commands of the slave power we have "sown the wind and are now reaping the whirlwind." But truth and right must prevail, und we are more than ever hopeful—the storm will do its work and we are confident the political and religious atmosphere will become purified.[13]

Of course, not every Northerner was such a vehement critic of slavery or supported a policy of immediate emancipation at the war's commencement. The Democratic Party as a whole, with its origins in the South as the party of Jefferson and Jackson, both slaveowners, was reluctant to make emancipation a war aim. The Republican Party was hardly united on the question of slavery either. But by 1861, those seeking to destroy slavery were not just a radical, outspoken, fringe minority. A woman from Albany, Vermont, wrote a letter to the editor in June addressed to "The Ladies of Orleans County." Far from only playing a ceremonial role as men marched off to war, women exercised their political leverage by circulating petitions calling on state governments and the Lincoln administration to use the war as an opportunity to abolish slavery:

Mr. Earle: permit me to say a few words through your paper to the ladies of this county. I wish to interest them, if they are not already interested, in behalf of the four millions of slaves in the United states. Long has this curse blotted our land, until we have become a byword and reproach among nations for our "boasted freedom." Our forefathers did not expect that slavery would live to see this day, but instead of being done away with as our nation has grown stronger it has grown with the nation—yes, and the slaveocrats would have it swallow up the whole land. . . . The time has come when slavery *must* be extirpated or reign supreme and we must submit to that tyranny; and instead of being a free and intelligent nation we shall become slaves and barbarians. . . . The great cry has been, "Slavery is Constitutional." Be that as it may, they have waged war upon the Federal Government without a just cause, and the government has a right in case of war to confiscate the property of the rebels. . . . Does not justice demand that the slaves be freed?

If the slaves were declared free, they would aid in putting down the rebellion. . . . Now, ladies, what I wish to say to you is, that you will petition to the president for the abolition of slavery—that the great cause of all this political commotion may be extirpated. Although the president has made no great pretension to anti-slavery principles, yet he is an honest man. He is the representative of the people, and I doubt not will be ready to promote universal liberty wherever his constituents instruct him so to do. . . . I have been expecting to hear of the circulation of petitions by the gentlemen of our county, but if we ladies start they will not be far in the rear. . . . This is the means we are to employ to reach the president, and there should be immediate action that petitions may go up from every town throughout the free states. Let us who believe "that all men are created *equal*, that they are endowed by their creator with certain inalienable rights, that among these are life, liberty, and the *pursuit of happiness*," make a mighty effort. Now is the time to act; And as we love freedom ourselves, and as we would have others do unto us—yes, as we love our country, let us work for its safety, work for its deliverance from "that sum of all villainies the vilest that ever saw the sun." Then shall our nation stand forth as a beam of light to the world and we each can exclaim with pride, "I am an American."[14]

What is astounding is that all of these remarks were made in the spring and early summer of 1861, before the First Battle of Bull Run, before Congress passed any Confiscation Acts, over a year before Lincoln issued his preliminary Emancipation Proclamation, and during a period where most Americans expected that the war would last ninety days or less. After the Union's defeat at the First Battle of Bull Run in July, the illusion of a ninety-day war was shattered, and the Union mobilization effort took on a new life. Calls from the Lincoln administration to the states for more recruits—this time for a period of three years or the duration of the war—flooded telegraph wires throughout the nation. It was in this context that millions of young men volunteered to take up arms, including thousands in the small state of Vermont. On September 27, 1861, a statement appeared in the *Orleans Independent Standard* that read: "Now is a good time to enlist; There is ample opportunity to do so, as there are two additional regiments being raised in this state—one of cavalry and one of infantry—which are called for *immediately*. The sixth regiment of infantry must be raised by the first of October, now close at hand. . . . There are several in this town who talk of going,—*Talk* no more; *Enlist*; Now is the time; The country has need of your services."[15]

Two weeks later the newspaper announced that the ranks of the latest infantry company from Orleans County had been filled and listed the names of the recruits, including Corporal Dan Mason. It is impossible that Mason, who would later write numerous letters to the editor during the war, who was often mentioned in the newspaper himself, who made frequent references to "The *Standard*" in his letters, and who addressed the editor as "Friend Earle," had not seen or read any of the news and opinions that appeared in the paper in the months following the attack on Fort Sumter. Newspapers in the nineteenth century were widely circulated and voraciously read, full of local news and gossip, human interest stories, partisan rancor, and the latest reports from the front. The unit he joined would become Company D of the Sixth Vermont Infantry, Second Brigade, Second Division, VI Corps, Army of the Potomac. The historian Bruce Catton referred to the Vermont Brigade as "one of the two or three best in the army" with "soldiers as cool and as tough as any."[16] It would also have the distinction of having a higher casualty rate than any other brigade in the Union Army.

One can only imagine the psychological anguish that new recruits—and their families, friends, and communities—experienced as they wrestled with the decision to enlist. The factors that motivated young men to march off to war likely included a powerful combination of forces; personal honor, peer pressure, economic incentives, romantic ideals of chivalry common to the Victorian era, a genuine sense of patriotism, a moral or religious conviction that their cause was just, a masculine sense of duty, and a desire to take part in a historic event. While many of these motives are timeless and common to all wars, the Union cause in the American Civil War was certainly an idealistic one, arguably the most idealistic cause for which the nation has ever gone to war, and this was reflected especially in the uncensored, candid letters that soldiers from that war wrote to their loved ones at home. Regardless of whichever motives influenced individual soldiers, the final goodbyes, the uncertainty about what the future held, the departure from home (especially for those who had never been very far away from home), the possibility of injury or death, the substitution of the comforts of home for the rigors of military life, and the major upheaval to daily life for all parties involved could not have been anything less than heart-wrenching, agonizing, and scary, to say the least. And in the case of Company D of the Sixth Vermont, leaving the hills of northeastern Vermont in full autumn splendor could only have emphasized the transition from one world to another. Grain was cut and shocked, barns were full of hay, potatoes were dug and stored in the root cellar, apple trees were bare as their fruit had been picked and pressed into cider, the first frost had undoubtedly occurred, the days were getting shorter—the summer's work was over. It was time to go to war. How many fathers "carried" their young sons to the nearest train station (in this case, to the depot at Barton), shook hands or embraced as they said goodbye, and then rode back home into the hills alone with misty eyes, a swollen throat, a heavy heart, a numbed body and soul, a love and a pride never felt so deeply before, a something having died within, and one less helping hand to tend to the evening chores? This is the story of a soldier and his community from what Winston Churchill called "the noblest and least avoidable of all the great mass-conflicts of which till then there was record."[17]

{ 1 }

"The Wildest Enthusiasm Prevails" (Winter 1861–62)

Dan Mason was born on April 27, 1839, during the presidency of Martin Van Buren, to Moses Hibbard Mason and Olive Ballou. The Masons lived on a farm in Glover, Vermont, high up in the hills above Glover Village. Though the farm has long since been abandoned, the fields have reverted to forest, and the house no longer stands, evidence remains of the life that the Masons once lived. A stone house foundation is still visible, as are stone walls, a barn foundation, the walls of what appears to have been an icehouse, and ancient sugar maple trees that the Masons likely tapped each spring. A daughter, Emily, was born in 1844. Little is known of Mason's early life, though his pastor, Reverend Sidney Perkins, later said that he was

> the grandson of Rev. R[euben] Mason, the first pastor of the Congregational Church in Glover. I am told by those who witnessed it, that that venerable man took a deep interest in the welfare of his young grandson, and helped the relationship between them, being most kind and friendly, to form his correct views and habits as they often conversed and read together.
>
> There was also that confiding intercourse between Capt. Mason, when a youth and young man, and his father . . . which is so exceedingly desirable and profitable, but which is very rare in our day. Besides these most happy sources of influence, Capt. Mason was a constant attendant upon public worship, having a prominent place in the choir, and whoever else might be absent from the Sabbath school-class, I expected to find young Mason there. It should be added also, that he was a successful scholar as well as instructor in our public schools.
>
> It was not strange that a young man thus educated should have many of the qualifications thus specified in this discourse, nor that when his

> country called for men to see that the republic received no detriment, he should be among the first to volunteer his services. Accordingly in September, 1861, he enlisted and became a member of the same company to which several from this town belonged.[1]

Mason's mother, Olive Ballou, died in 1857 of consumption (or tuberculosis) at the age of thirty-nine. His father remarried the following year and with his new wife had two more sons, William, born in 1859, and Reuben, born in 1864. In the 1860 census, Dan, now twenty-one, was still living with his father and stepmother. The Masons owned $2,500 worth of real estate.[2] Their farm consisted of eighty acres of "improved" land and twenty acres of "unimproved" land, with $100 worth of farming implements and machinery, 2 horses, 6 milk cows, 2 working oxen, 6 "other cattle," 10 sheep, 1 hog, 27 bushels of wheat, 21 bushels of "Indian corn," 50 bushels of oats, 27 pounds of wool, 100 bushels of "Irish" (white) potatoes, 10 bushels of buckwheat, 1,300 pounds of butter, 100 pounds of cheese, 40 tons of hay, 2,000 pounds of maple sugar, $10 worth of "homemade manufactures," and $50 worth of animals slaughtered.[3] This was a fairly typical farm for northern Vermont at the time in terms of the amount of acreage, diversity of products, and overall value.

At the time Vermont had public "common schools" that usually were in session for only six months of the year, but public high schools did not yet exist. The closest equivalent to high schools were private academies, often associated with a religious denomination. As the historian James McPherson has pointed out, "New England led the world in educational facilities and literacy at midcentury. More than 95 percent of its adults could read and write; three-fourths of the children aged five to nineteen were enrolled in school."[4] Mason and others in his community certainly benefited from this culture of democratic learning and literacy. Mason attended the Orleans Liberal Institute in Glover, a Unitarian-affiliated school founded in 1852, which was described at the time as producing graduates that were "honorable as citizens and as teachers, and who are highly esteemed wherever they have found a home."[5] Students attended from throughout northern Vermont and New Hampshire and boarded with local families, though Mason continued to live at home, since the school was within walking distance.[6]

At some point before the war, Mason began a courtship with Harriet Betsey Clark, a farmer's daughter from West Glover. She was born on August 27, 1842, the third of five children born to John and Elizabeth (Lyman) Clark. Harriet lost a one-year-old sister, Hannah, in 1851, and then an older brother, John, who died at age twenty-two in 1860 of typhoid fever. Her older sister, Eleanor, and younger brother, Alson, survived to adulthood. In 1860 the Clarks owned a three-hundred-acre farm with 1 horse, 9 milk cows, 2 oxen, 60 sheep, 1 hog, 30 bushels of wheat, 100 bushels of oats, 200 pounds of wool, 1,200 pounds of butter, 30 tons of hay, and 300 pounds of maple sugar.[7] The Clarks and the Masons lived five miles away from one another. How, when, or where Dan and Harriet met is not clear, but opportunities abounded for young people to meet: at church, corn huskings, fairs, Independence Day celebrations, lectures, lyceums and debating societies, and numerous other townwide activities and social events. In a letter that he wrote to her on January 29, 1865, he referred to their "6 years Courtship," which suggests that their romance began sometime in 1858 or 1859.[8]

The letters that follow are those that Dan wrote to Harriet throughout the course of the war. Not a single letter from Harriet to Dan survives, since he burned them all, for fear that his fellow troops might discover them. Despite that, something can be learned of Harriet through his letters: her character, sentiments, experiences on the home front, and more. The first letter in the collection details Mason's journey from Glover to Montpelier, where the Sixth Vermont was mustered into service.

Camp Smith Oct[ober] 11th 1861

Dear Hattie

It is with pleasure that I seat myself pen in hand for the purpose of writing you a few lines.

I am enjoying good health at the present time the rest of the Glover boys ditto. This is truly a great blessing & I hope these few imperfect lines will find you enjoying the same blessing. I dont feel just right about leaving you in the manner that I did but it hardly seemed possible for me to do differently under the existing circumstances. Friday we were full of business all day we had to be inspected by the Surgeon Dr Skinner of Barton to ascertain if we were sound & healthy quite a number were declared unfit for service some appeared very much disappointed so much so as to shed tears. We then elected our Officers which was quite a delicate piece of business to do & suit all. We at last succeeded in electing the following list of Officers viz Capt[ain] O[scar] A Hale 1st Lieut[enant] Geo[rge] H Phelps 2d Carlos W Dwinnell I will not name all the non commissioned Officers Fred M Kimball is 1 of the Sergeants E[lbert] H Nye Alex Davis & myself Corporals from Glover. We did not get away from Barton until quite late Friday evening so you see it was almost impossible for me to visit you. But I trust that the noble disposition which I know you to be possessed of will cause you to forgive me. There is scarcely an hour passes but what I think of you but this we know to be impossible at present. But we can converse with each other by aid of the pen which is a source of great enjoyment to me.

Perhaps a short sketch of our journey from Barton to this place will be interesting to you. We left Barton Saturday morning at 8 oclock. We arrived at White River Junction at noon marched to the Hotel & took dinner at 2 Oclock we took the cars for Montpelier we arrived here at 6 Oclock took supper at Burnhams Hotel we then marched to the Fair Ground a distance of half mile up two or three clay hills made muddy by recent rains. We arrived at the encampment about 9 Oclock. We there received two blankets each 1 oil cloth & 1 wool blanket—we found 87 tents pitched to protect us from the storm these tents are large enough to accommodate from 12 to 20 men the bottom of each tent is covered with straw this with our blankets makes a good place of rest—I rest well nights feel well in good spirits during the day. Our rations though not of the finest quality consist of good substantial food such as Beans Bread & Beef Pork Tea or Coffee with the trimmings. My appetite never was better. We have received our uniforms mostly. We have received 2 coats each 1 over & 1 dress coat—1 hat our hats are ornamented with a small piece of brass in front in the form of a bugle on the left side with an eagle. We expect the rest of our uniforms tomorrow. It is quite doubtful about my going to Glover before leaving for Washington the Capt[ain] has no power to give us permission to go home some of the boys are mad about it but we must submit to the rules & orders of military discipline. We have some fine boys in our Co[mpany] & some that are not so fine. Nearly all the boys that enlisted from the towns of Glover Albany Barton & Browning-ton have signed a pledge thereby pledging themselves to abstain from the use of all intoxicating liquors as a beverage also not to indulge in the use of profane language this I think is a fine thing. I tent with Glover boys except two & they are good likely fellows. Before leaving Glover Mr Perkins gave each of us a Testament & we make a practice of using them every evening before retiring to rest—We expect to leave for Washing-ton some time next week cant tell the day. In regard to me being Corpo-ral it is no great honor but I shall not have to stand out on guard—this I should not like to do. I get 22 doll[ar]s per month. A private gets but 20 doll[ar]s per month. The Regimental Band is full so I shall have to go to fight for my country. I will now draw this scroll to a close by wishing you peace and happiness. Hattie please excuse all mistakes for I have written this on a rudely constructed table in my tent surrounded by 8 or 10 jolly boys & all the noise & confusion of the tented field.

Yours in haste from your
affectionate lover Dan Mason

PS. Please write all the news you can get on receiving this

After a brief stay in Montpelier, the regiment headed south on October 19, a Saturday morning. G. G. Benedict, who wrote the official state his-tory of Vermont in the Civil War, described the scene thus: "It was a rainy morning; but the whole population of Montpelier, and hundreds of fathers, mothers, wives and friends from the neighboring towns, turned out to see the boys off and bid them Godspeeed. Not a man was left behind. The usual patriotic demonstrations greeted the regiment all along the route through Vermont and down the Connecticut Valley. At Springfield, Mass., refresh-ments were provided for the men by the mayor and citizens."[9]

At New Haven, Connecticut, the regiment boarded a steamer, which carried them to Jersey City, New Jersey, then reboarded a train, which made stops in Philadelphia and Baltimore, where the troops dined and lodged. Finally, they reached Washington, where the regiment encamped on Capitol Hill.

Washington Oct[ober] 24th 1861

Dear Harriet

It is with pleasure that I seize the pen of correspondence to converse with the object of my affections for a few moments though hundreds of miles stretch between us we can communicate by aid of the pen. This I deem a great privelege. But it would be a much greater one to converse face to face but this is impossible.

I am now in the city of Washington enjoying good health happy as a fish in high water. I have not seen a sick hour since I enlisted. The rest of the Glover boys ditto. Our reg[imen]t left Montpelier Saturday morn Oct[ober] 19th 9 oclock. We arrived at Springfield Mass at 10 in the evening we were there furnished with a good supper by citizens of that place free of charge thanks to them. We arrived at New Haven Conn[ecticut] Sunday morn at 4 oclock we took the steamboat *Elm City* bound for Jersey City—I enjoyed riding on the salt water very much. We sailed up through Long Island Sound the day was pleasant the water was dotted here and there with vessels of all shapes and sizes the sea fowls were flying in every direction the Steam Boats blew their shrill whistles men and boys were cheering as we sailed near the shore the ladies waved their handkerchiefs every one seemed filled with excessive joy. We sailed through what is called Hells Gate this is a narrow channel between New York City & Brooklin we sailed within a stones throw of each city the shore was lined with masts & sails. I saw some of the most beautiful farms & houses surrounded by the most beautiful groves on Long Island that I ever saw. The Steamer *Elm City* is a first class steamer of the largest size I should judge it to be more than 20 rods in length finished & furnished nice as any parlor. . . . I rode on the upper deck most of the time where I had a fair view of the surrounding country the scenery was beautiful words fail to describe my feelings at that time. . . . We arrived [at Washington] at 9oclock Monday evening. Tuesday we were removed ¾ ths of a mile from the city. On Wednesday rather Tuesday we remained in the city. I visited the Capatol buildings. I went up on to the marble steps in front—the doors were locked but there was a great deal to be seen on the veranda and outside. It is made of marble carved

& worked in the most beautiful manner. There are quite a number of beautiful marble statues standing in front which look as natural as life. Since I commenced writing our reg[imen]t has been marched into Virginia a distance of 11 miles from W[ashington]. . . . We came by the way of Chain bridge this is a bridge across the Potomac river. . . . Virginia is a rougher colder place than I expected to find it—we had a very heavy frost last night—though I have seen but a small portion of it. Our friends tell us there is no rebel encampments within ten miles of us. There are a good many Federal troops encamped in sight of us as I write there is a Brass Band playing the nicest music but a few rods from me. Soldiers are practicing target shooting others are pitching tents some are killing oxen for food that have been taken from the rebels. Yesterday a Company of Cavelry brought in 8 rebels 7 hogs & 1 horse. I must now close by asking you to excuse all mistakes and accept my best wishes

from Dan

The regiment then marched from Washington to Camp Griffin in Virginia, where it spent its first winter. The acclimation to camp life was not easy. Lieutenant George Phelps of Company D, an Albany man, wrote on November 2:

> There is no more playing soldier, for the stern realities of camp life are upon us. We are truly launched upon the tempestuous sea for war; and though there may be "breakers ahead," yet we must meet them as they come. . . . The general health of the regiment is very good indeed. Not one of us all is confined to his bed by sickness, I believe. If we should remain here long, however, I fear our sick list would increase, for the climate is most unhealthy. The days are fine, but the nights would chill a Laplander. There is little rain, but when it comes it seems as if all the unbridled powers of AEolus, the wind god, were let loose at once, and were bound to blow away forever the southwest side of creation. Such is the condition of things while I write. Nothing can be heard but wind; nothing can be seen but mud—I mean Virginia mud. It resembles a clay pit sprinkled with ground brick, and the depth depends mostly upon the amount of stirring power applied.[10]

The general health of the regiment did not remain very good for long. Months before seeing any combat, the regiment confronted its first killer: disease. Phelps himself succumbed to typhoid fever two months later. According to Benedict, "Before the end of November, nearly a third of the men were unfit for duty, and they were falling sick at the rate of forty a day. . . . In the first two months in Virginia 27 men died from disease. The frequent death and prevailing sickness caused a general seriousness and much religious reflection among the men, and the prayer-meetings, held every evening, were numerously attended." By March forty-seven men in the Sixth Vermont had died, "among the saddest of which was that of Lieutenant Geroge H. Phelps, of Company D., a favorite young officer."[11] Mason remained healthy during the first weeks at Camp Griffin (he had previously had the measles before the war so likely had developed immunity), but he acknowledged that "there is considerable sickness in our reg[iment]t at the present time."

Camp Griffin Nov[ember] 17th 1861

Dear Harriet

It is with pleasure that I seize my pen to acknowledge the reception of your worthy letter. I had been anxiously looking for one for a number of days. I feared that my letter had been lost or miscarried, but I was happily disappointed on receiving an answer. I was sorry to learn of your ill health you must be careful of yourself & get well as soon as possible. Obey your Mother & be a good girl. If she says take medicine you must take it. Remember Mother knows best.

I am well & enjoying myself firstrate at the present time. I have enjoyed very good health most of the time since I enlisted. I have gained 11 lbs in flesh since I enlisted I think the climate is going to agree with me. I like Virginia much better than when I wrote you last. Since that I have been out in to the surrounding country & I like it much. I think it a fine country for farming. The surface is smooth & the soil appears productive. There is considerable sickness in our reg[imen]t at the present time. The prevailing disease is measles. Quite a number of the Glover boys are sick with them, viz, Edward Ufford, Hobart Bliss, Zebina Y

Bickford & Alex Davis. Davis & Bickford are just coming down. Ed & Hobart have been in the Hospital about a week they have been quite sick they are now able to walk out if they dont take cold they will soon be able to perform duty. I am glad that I had [the measles] when I did in fathers house. It is bad enough to be sick under the best of care surrounded by kind friends. The boys complain some of their treatment in the H[ospital] but I think they were treated as well as could be expected in camp life. We are having some cold bleak weather now. We have had very beautiful weather most of the time since I came here the ground froze slightly night before last for the first time. I was out on Picket Guard duty the air though not very freezing was very chilly. I was stationed on what is called a reserve. . . . In the night no one is allowed to sleep. . . . I have not seen a rebel since I came here our Pickets have not been troubled for a long while. I felt perfectly safe. . . . Pickets build cabins of rails & bushes & then line them with straw if they can get it. . . . Pickets start from camp at 3 in the morn & return about 7 the next morn. We carry our provision with us in our haversacks something similar to a leather satchel made of oil cloth. . . . We have bought us a large sheet iron baker & we now have a plenty of nice bread & good beef & pork as a general thing to go with it we have boiled rice & molasses twice a week we have beans & pork 2 a week or rather 2 meals in a week we have had a number of messes of doughnuts since we came here we miss the butter & cheese pies & cakes & such dainties but we manage to grow fleshy on what Uncle Sam furnishes. I should like to call at your house some of these frosty mornings & get a piece of your warm punkin pie or warm potatoes & meat would not go bad with fried eggs for trimmings. In regard to our bed[d]ing we have ticks filled with husks from rebels cornfields we use our blankets & coats for covering & our knapsacks for pillows we have under ground trenches or arches covered with flat stones to warm our tents with. In this manner we sleep very well. I commenced this Sunday & today is Tuesday. Sun[day] night one of Co[mpany] F died in the Hospital of the measles this is the first death in the Reg[imen]t. He has not been buried yet. There has been 16 deaths in the Vt 5th Reg[imen]t. They came here in the month of Sept[ember] when the days were very warm & the nights cold & foggy this caused a good deal of fever. I am now seated on my knapsack in a pine grove about 3 miles from camp with a reserve our whole Reg[imen]t is on Picket guard today. I will now draw this dirty scroll to a close by asking you to excuse all mistakes & remember me to all the friends & receive this from your true lover Dan

PS I am now going out scouting to see what I can find. Some of the boys bring in milk in their canteens that they milk from rebels cows. I dont think they always ascertain whether she is owned by a rebel or not. Of course I would not do any such thing. Of course I would not. Though a little warm milk would go well with our cold bread. Of course it would.

Write soon & oblige Dan

Diseases, particularly measles, continued to take their toll. Fred Kimball, a Glover man and friend of Mason's, wrote on December 6:

> As regards health—our greatest boon on earth—I am pained to write that there is much sickness in the Vermont regiments, particularly in the new ones. . . . In ours, the 6th, there now are on the sick list two hundred and fifty soldiers. Eleven have gone to their long homes. "Peace to their ashes." The last one who died belonged to our company, D. He was Charles Santan, of Westfield, the first from our number. It was imposed on me to see to the digging of his grave, and with three privates I went and did the sad task. That duty was new to me, yet a soldier can dig a soldier's grave. The muffled drum beat the mournful dirge as his fellow soldiers followed his remains to their Virginia grave. Only a soldier's tear was shed.
>
> As yet, during our six weeks in Virginia, nothing exciting or of much importance has occurred in camp; But the keen desires of the Vermont boys are that we may be led on to battle, meet the accursed traitors to our country, and illustrate to them that the same spirit which demanded Fort Ti[conderoga] in the name of the Great Jehovah and the Continental Congress, is today as powerful as then. . . .
>
> Alas! Since writing the above another of our company, Edson Fairbrother, son of Thomas Fairbrother of Barton Landing, has died, and I

record the sad intelligence. His father reached his bedside only in time to see him die. He had hope in the blessed Savior of the world.[12]

Lieutenant George Phelps, who would die in less than a month, wrote the following day:

As I previously predicted, our sick list has rapidly increased, and what is worse still, we have had several deaths. Some ten have died in our whole regiment. Two from our company have paid the debt of life and fallen, not by the sword, but by disease—away from home and its sweet consolations, but among brothers and friends whose watchful care cheered and supported them till the last spark of life had gone out, and whose sympathy and respect shown in the tearful eyes that followed one to a soldier's grave in the enemy's land, and the other away to be buried beside his fond mother in his native state. If, as some claim, it is a weakness for a soldier to weep, we must acknowledge that weakness, for we really mourn the loss we have met.[13]

Mason's next letter described the joy of receiving a "care package" from home, just in time for Thanksgiving, as well as a detailed account of a tour of Washington DC:

Camp Griffin Va Dec[ember] 10th 1861

Dear Harriet

This morning as I came into camp from picket duty I received your worthy letter which was a very welcome visitor. I had not heard from Glover for sometime except a few lines that I received from Emily inside of the box of clothing & eatables concerning the contents. All of the Glover boys received a bundle of clothing & eatables. I received 1 p[ai]r of boots 1 p[ai]r of gloves & a quarter of an excellent cheese. Some of the boys received cakes & cheese some butter pie & sugar cakes. As it arrived the night before thanksgiving we were able to have quite a thanksgiving. There was great rejoicing over the contents I assure you. . . . I will venture to tell you that I have gained 17

½ lbs since I enlisted or the scales lie. I weigh 165 ½ lbs in my dress coat minus a vest—7 lbs more than I ever weighed before. I have not been sick any length of time since I came here. . . . We slyed off to a deserted habitation & found 3 Percimmon trees well laden with fruit. This fruit is sweet & good to eat it resembles frozen apples in outward appearence some of them are nearly as large as hens eggs there are a number of large seeds in each one (I will enclose a number please plant them next spring). We ate all we wanted & brought some into camp in our haversacks. We started for camp about sun down we arrived at camp about 7 ½ in the eve with about 70 wagon loads of hay corn &c the result of our expedition. We are having some of Vt Sept[ember] weather here now for it has been uncomfortably warm for several days past—the soldiers were out minus coat & vest & plenty warm. Yesterday when on drill I should have been glad to get into the shade. Today it is quite cool. I cant realize that you have good sleighing in Vt but according to all accounts you have upwards of a foot of snow. I dont care about walking on your snow paths but I should like to take a sleigh ride some of these moonshiny evenings with Miss H.B.C by my side firstrate well. We have not had any snow except a few scattering flakes 2 or 3 times just enough to say snow not enough to make any show on the ground. A week ago last Saturday E.H. Nye & I obtained passes to go to Washington city our Capt[ain] went with us & as he was acquainted there he took us to see the fine sights. We went on foot to Georgtown. We there took an omnibus for W[ashington] city a distance of 4 miles [one] can ride through to the Capitol for 6 cts or if he rides but 10 rods it is the same. We went into the treasury building where Uncle Sam keeps his money it is a very large marble building finished in splendid style. We also went to the Presidents house this is a beautiful marble house surrounded by a beautiful yard full of fine shade trees. We went into the great celebrated east room this room is furnished in the most splendid manner imaginable. The carpet curtains & furniture was much nicer than any that I ever saw. There were mirrors set in the sides of the room larger than 1 side of your kitchen. I should judge there were quite a number of chandeliers as much nicer than the one in the meeting house at Glover village . . . as you can imagine. In fact I cannot describe the splendor of it in a letter. Of the green room as it is called ditto. We did not see Old Abe.

Mason also toured the Patent Office, Post Office, Smithsonian Institution, and Capitol Building, where he climbed to the top of the rotunda (then unfinished) and "had a splendid view of the surrounding country. We could see the whole city & a good many little white villages the habitations of soldiers."

While Vermonters were dying of disease at Camp Griffin, Araunah Earle, the editor of the *Orleans Independent Standard*, called for immediate emancipation on December 6:

> We wish that the president, his cabinet, and all in authority, would cease their foolish palaver about the "constitution," look things squarely in the face and strike a blow as becomes the occasion. . . .
>
> The South is trying to break away from the union for the sake of founding a government whose cornerstone shall be slavery, and the north is forcing the South to enjoy a constitution which recognizes, (as we believe) the same thing. . . .
>
> Suppose that in one or two years hence the rebellion is crushed, the constitution fully maintained, and slavery still the black jewel in our crown of shame.—What then? Will the country be less liable to the attack of traitors than before the rebellion? No. Why not? Because slavery, the great first cause of all our woes, will still exist, and our country will be liable to the same scenes now witnessed south of the Potomac, and in all the rebel districts. Remove the cause, we say, while traitors offer us an opportunity. . . .
>
> We believe that this is a holy war, one that will terminate in a crusade against slavery. We believe the almighty is making instruments of the slaveholders to administer their own punishment for their sins against those in bondage.—And when that happy day to our country shall arrive that all shackles are struck, the old "Liberty Bell" that has hung in silence and in shame since the stormy days of the revolution, because it fulfilled not its mission, will joyfully obey the behest of its creator and "Proclaim Liberty through all the land and to all the people thereof."[14]

On December 20 the Anti-Slavery Convention of Orleans County met and adopted the following resolutions:

> *Whereas*, The Rebels promptly declare that their rebellion is to sustain and perpetuate slavery, and we can see no other course for it. And *Whereas*, liberty and slavery are irreconcilable enemies, and cannot live at peace under the same government, and *Whereas*, human rights are the same in all ages and places, therefore,
>
> *Resolved*, 1st. That the principles of our Declaration of Independence demand the liberation of every slave. 2d. That as our constitution was adopted to establish justice, and secure liberty, its principles are opposed to slavery, and if enforced would destroy it. 3d. That the rebels have by their treason forfeited not only their lives, but their property, and the government has a right to use that property for the overthrow of rebellion. 4th. That justice, mercy and expediency demand that the government restore to the slaves their inalienable right, and employ them in crushing the rebellion of their masters.

A petition was then sent to the Vermont General Assembly:

> To the honorable Senate and House of Representatives assembled:
>
> We, the subscribers, inhabitants of Orleans Co., Vt., believing that slavery is the sole cause and main strength of the rebellion, and that by treason the rebels have forfeited all their property, do hereby respectfully petition your honorable body as an act of self-defense and justice long delayed, to restore to the slaves their inalienable rights and employ them in crushing the rebellion of their masters.[15]

A motion was then made and approved to meet in four weeks' time at West Glover. Meanwhile, at Camp Griffin, Oliver Stiles, another friend of Mason's, described the daily routine of soldiering:

> We have the same routine of drill and guard duties to perform, but it is very seldom we have anything exciting to do to keep up our spirits. We have the drum call for everything: in the first place, we have reveille, at

six o'clock, P.M.; roll call at six A.M.; breakfast at half-past seven; guard mounting at eight; company drill at 9; ke call at 10; squad drill at 11; ke call at 12; dinner at half-past twelve; brigade drill at half-past one, P.M.; dress parade at half-past four; supper at half-past five; roll call at eight; taps at half-past eight—the taps are for the lights to be put out in the tents. . . .

Well, to commence with company D., as far as the health of the company is concerned it is in a very bad state indeed. We have now on the sick list about 40; five have died in our company, 2 of them died last night; one of them was from Albany, his name was Seth Bumps; the other was a corporal from Troy, he was a very fine fellow and he will be missed by the company very much; he is going to be sent home—he will start today.[16]

Mason closed out the year of 1861 by telling Harriet that "I had an ill turn that lasted two days," but that he felt better after consuming "hot sling" and "flapjacks." He optimistically concluded, "Other Reg[imen]ts from Vt that have been here long enough to get acclimated are tough & rugged & I think that we shall be equaly so after we get naturalized." On New Year's Day, 1862, Mason's friend and tentmate Fred Kimball wrote:

The health of the Vermont brigade is improving. The sick list in our regiment has decreased nearly one half, from most four hundred to about two hundred, still the fell destroyer, Death, has often reminded us of the frailty of man and the uncertainty of life. More than thirty of our companions have fallen his victims, including five of our company—noble fellows, they have given their life in defense of their country and their memories will live. Lieut. Phelps is very sick, but we trust he will soon be restored to health and again be among us. Another year has rolled away and numbered itself with time that was but is not, and a new year has dawned upon creation and finds our country in a perilous and distracted state, but ere it closes may peace be restored and the goddess of liberty again be enthroned. "Let slavery perish and freedom smile." A happy new year to all.[17]

Lieutenant Phelps died the next day. Kimball wrote, "Our noble Lieutenant . . . has been snatched away by the unrelenting grasp of death. Yesterday morning, at fifteen minutes to one o'clock A.M., he breathed out his young and ambitious life calmly and without a struggle, and his spirit has gone, we trust, to dwell with God who gave, yet we as a company of soldiers are left to mourn over the sad and irreparable loss which is ours to suffer. . . . His remains have been sent to his early home to be interred."[18]

Mason's first letter of 1862 began by "scolding" Harriet for innuendo that he perceived in her letters. References to "sugar" and "apples" appeared often in his. He also alluded to the impatience of many of the soldiers to see action. John Moodie, a Scottish-born member of Company D from Craftsbury, said, "There has [been] nothing of any great importance occurred in camp lately. However, the keen desires to meet the enemy are as fresh in the hearts of the Vermont boys as ever. Give them a chance to meet the rebels, and you would hear them shout till their voices would echo over the hills of their own Green Mountain homes."[19] Fred Kimball also complained that "we, and also the whole grand Army of the Potomac, are laying seemingly idle upon our oars; and why is it? Why should we remain so inactive?—Our force is sufficient; our *will* is adequate to meet whatever resistance the enemy can command. Then why not move forward?"[20] The reality was that any large movement of an army in the winter was logistically impractical. Mason expressed faith in the wisdom of General McClellan's strategy and expressed a naive hope that the war would end by year's end.

Camp Giffin Va Jan[uary] 12th, 1862

Dear Harriet

As I came in off Picket this morning I received your worthy letter bearing date Jan 7th with the pleasing news that you were enjoying good health which was the best news you could have written. I am blest with the same enjoyment. The rest of the Glover boys ditto. I fear that you are getting to be a disobedient girl. Who would have thought that you so pure & guileless would ever stray from the path of virtue so far as to go to the sugar tub in the absence of your parents & steal sugar & melt to cool on snow & eat, & even go so far as to say that if your lover would come & visit you when the folks were gone you would treat him on the stolen sweets. Only think of it. If that is not old Eve right over again I am no judge. I suppose that you are surrounded with a beautiful carpet of white snow & the cold bleak winds which Vt is noted for in Jan. We do not have to plod around in the snow here in Va but we have plenty of Va mud which is very friendly so much so that it is hard parting with it. It is very adhesive. We have had but little snow yet. The most we had was about 2 inches or a little less Jan 5th. Since that we have had a thaw which carried of[f] the snow & took the frost out of the ground. . . . We have seen no rebels yet some of the boys are quite impatient & find considerable fault with the Gen[era]ls because they dont order an advance but I think they know this business best. At least they ought to know better about Government affairs both civil & military than we youngsters do. I have a good deal of confidence in Gen[eral] McClellan. . . . I will now close this great epistle by wishing you health & happiness. Give my respects to your Mother & all the friends.

Receive this from
your lover Dan

After the new year, the death toll from disease began to decline in the Vermont Brigade, though by no means was the epidemic over. For the rest of the winter at Camp Griffin, no major military operations occurred. Mason continued to report on the daily routines of camp life, reassuring Harriet that "I have not played a game of cards since I enlisted no not for 2 or 3 years previous. I see a great deal of card playing & gambling on a small scale in the Reg[imen]t. Many foolish boys lose their entire wages in this way or if not all in this manner the Sutler gets the remainder for little dainties which are very injurious to their health." He also expected "to be Regimental Bugler. I dont know how much pay I shall get. Some say I shall get more than I now do & some say I get the same. . . . It is considered quite an honer to be Bugler for a reg[imen]t."

Mason, like so many others, had no idea about the duration or scale that the war would assume. Indeed, the news in early 1862 was mostly positive, especially from the western theater, where U. S. Grant's victories over Confederate forces at Forts Donelson and Henry boosted Northern morale and contributed to the illusion that the war would be of short duration. Upon hearing the news of Grant's successes, Fred Kimball wrote on February 21: "Our entire camp became wild with joy. Long and loud cheers ascended heavenward, such as give token of loyal hearts, and the soul-stirring strains of music from the many bands were such as could but arouse the most dormant spirit."[21] The next day Mason wrote to Harriet and looked forward to accompanying her to the Independence Day celebration that summer.

Camp Griffin Va Feb[ruary] 22 1862

Dear Harriet,

I take this opportunity to answer your worthy letter bearing date Feb 12th. As usual it was a welcome visitor. I experienced much pleasure in perusing its contents. . . . I considder you about perfect or as near to it as any one. I know you to be the possessor of true Patriotism. This you have proved by your actions. I honor & admire you more yes love you more if possible than I did previous to your being brought to the test. I am afraid that you are staying at home this winter from parties & social gatherings on my account. If so you are not doing right—I want you should go every chance that you can get to go with likely fellows & I know you to be to[o] pure to accompany any that were not. I am not afraid to trust you. I have perfect confidence in you. I believe your love to be as pure & lasting as ever kindled in womans heart. I long for the time to arrive when peace shall be declared throughout the land & the grand army of the Potomac & all the union forces shall be disbanded & return to their respective homes. I long to grasp your loving hand & steal a kiss from your loving lips. I want you to make preparations to go some where with me to celebrate next 4th of July. I honestly expect to go to Vermont before 4 months shall pass away. One month has wrought a great change. Our army has been successful at every point. Many Forts & important places with thousands of rebel prisoners have been taken by our gallant troops. As you will get the news in the papers long before this reaches you I will not give the particulars here. The daily newspapers (which are brought from Washington every day by little news boys) are filled with cheering news. Our arms are crowned with success at every point. Camp Griffin is often made wild with joy on receiving the glorious news loud hurrahs rend the air. It is deafening to hear the shouts of the excited soldiers. The wildest enthusiasm prevails. I dont see much prospect of our advancing at present—it is so very muddy now (& has been for the last 6 or 8 weeks) that it is impossible to move heavy artillery & the baggage waggons which must necessarily attend the advance of an army. Some think that we shall never see any fighting. It is reported in the newspapers that Manassas Junction is being evacuated by the rebels according to all accounts the rebels feel very much disheartened they think their ca[u]se a doubtful one. This Afternoon I went over to Gen[eral] Smiths head quarters to see 7 rebel prisoners that the Penn[sylvania] Cavalry captured & brought in this morning. I saw 3 of them they were dark complexioned long haired dirty inferior looking chaps. They had no uniformity of dress. One had on an over coat that was taken from the Maine 7th Reg[iment] at the Bull run fight last July. In regard to Bugling I am not prepared to say much about it. Our Col[onel] has been to Boston to visit his friends he returned night before last he was gone 15 days. It has been so muddy for several weeks that we have not drilled any to speak of except in firing blanks or target shooting. I expect the mud will dry up before long & then we shall drill in skirmishing & then I shall be able to tell you something about it. I have got the calls all learned. I will now close by wishing you health & happiness.

receive this from Dan

As the weeks at Camp Griffin dragged on, Mason wanted Harriet to know just how lovesick he was. After having been gone for only just over four months without seeing any real action yet, Mason told Harriet, "The longer I am absent from you the more perfect you seem to me" and hinted at the possibility that she might eventually become his "better half."

Camp Griffin March 7th 1862

Dear Harriet

Your ever welcome letter bearing date Feb 28 came to hand last evening & was perused with the usual degree of satisfaction. How miserable I should be if I could not hear from you. Though we can not converse face to face at the present time we can by aid of pen correspond to each other (though hundreds of miles stretch out between us) & convey ideas that are interesting & pleasing especially to one in my situation in an enemys country far from the object of my affections. I experience a great deal of real enjoyment in perusing your letters. I have often heard said that lovers lose or were apt to lose their love to some extent when absent from each other any great length of time. This saying does not fit my case, for the longer I am absent from you the more perfect you seem to me. I thought when at home that I loved you as much as possible for one to love, but I am aware of the fact that the longer I am absent from you the dearer you seem to me. There is scarce an hour passes but what I think of you. In your letter you seem to think that I estimate your perfection to[o] highly, but I think not. I dont suppose that you are exactly perfect in the strict sense of the term but I think you come as near to it as anyone that I know. I wish that I was as perfect as you are. I am surrounded by all kinds of vice but I intend to return to my home with as good morals as when I left. I know that if my morality becomes impaired that I shall not merit your loving hand which I hope to possess it at some future day. At all events I am willing to acknowledge you my better half. Oh excuse me I am a little to[o] fast I mean that I hope to be able to some future day to call you so. I know that your generous disposition will compel you to overlook my little imperfections & wrong saying. . . . You know that this loving business is a little delicate in its first stages especially to one of my temp[e]rament, but enough of this. I am enjoying very good health at the present time I never enjoyed such perfect health. . . . I enclose this ring for you not because I think it anything very nice or beautiful, but it is one of my own manufacture wholly so. I whittled it out of cocoa nut shell & by the aid of a file I cut a piece from a 3 cent piece & filled it in to the top as you see. I have made 3 rings one that I intend to send to Emily one that I wear & this one that I send to you. Our boys have made a good many & sent home. In regard to slavery I think it will receive a death blow before peace is declared. Mr. Lincoln advocates the gradual emancipation of the slaves.

Receive this from your lover Dan

This was the first letter where Mason referred to the politics of slavery. His remark that "I think [slavery] will receive a death blow before peace is declared" offers some insight into his views. The Lincoln administration was nowhere close to calling for emancipation at this point in the war, though many enslaved people forced the issue by escaping into Union lines. These "contrabands" of war presented Union authorities with thorny political and legal questions about their status. The Vermont Brigade welcomed contrabands, who "always found a safe refuge in the camps. One night in February, twenty-seven colored fugitives came in, were fed, and sent to Washington by General Brooks."[22] The same day that Mason wrote his letter of March 7, it was reported that the Orleans County Anti-Slavery Convention had met again and adopted additional resolutions condemning slavery. One of the resolutions stated that "it is the duty of the government in self-defense and self-preservation to proclaim immediately universal emancipation,—in the rebel states by confiscation, and in the loyal states with provision for a reasonable compensation." This resolution was controversial, not because it was too aggressive, but because it was too lenient, as it allowed for compensating slaveowners. It was rejected and replaced with a substitute: "That it is the duty of the government in self-defense and self-preservation to proclaim immediately the universal emancipation of all the slaves." Later that evening the convention announced a declaration of rights, borrowing from the language of the Declaration of Independence, as virtually every movement to expand equality in American history has done:

> We hold these truths to be self-evident:
>
> 1st. The right of man as man is sacred and inviolable without distinction of race.
>
> 2d. Property in man is impossible, as being without grant from the Creator and equally contrary to natural rights and to revealed religion.
>
> 3d. The system of American slavery and the practice of slave holding is essentially sinful and anti-Christian . . .
>
> 7th. The abolition of the vast system of American slavery to be accepted as the Providential mission of the American people of this generation.[23]

Enslaved people themselves, Union soldiers, and sympathetic citizens back home in Orleans County and around the nation were growing more impatient by the day with the Lincoln administration's cautious approach to blotting out slavery.

{ 2 }

"The Final Blow to Secession Will Be Struck Here" (Spring 1862)

After five months of relative inactivity at Camp Griffin, the Vermont Brigade—and the Army of the Potomac—began to move in the spring of 1862. The long-awaited order to move came at midnight on March 9, 1862. Confederate forces under Joseph Johnston had spent the winter encamped at Manassas, Virginia, about twenty-five miles from Camp Griffin. Union forces moved once again toward Manassas only to discover with great disappointment that Johnston had retreated southward across the Rappahannock River with a force of only forty-five thousand troops, far fewer than the number that Union general George McClellan had estimated. Several days later the brigade began a march eastward toward Alexandria, where it awaited transport ships that would take it down the Chesapeake Bay toward Fortress Monroe. Mason encountered his first taste of a long march with full gear while camping in the field.

Headquarters 6th Vermont Regiment
Company D
Camp Near Newport News
March 31st 1862

Dear Harriet, I have not received an answer to the letter that I wrote you 3 weeks ago yesterday. Perhaps you have not received it, or if you have received & answered it it has not reached me yet. It is rumored that there is no mail matter allowed to leave Washington for a certain number of days. This is to prevent the rebels from knowing the movements of our army. The next day after I wrote you the Great army of the Potomac advanced about 10 miles in the direction of Manassas. We encamped about 3 miles from Fairfax Court House. It was quite rainy in the A.M. which made it muddy & hard walking & as we were each well loaded with a knapsack filled with 1 heavy wool blanket 1 rubber blanket 1 over & 1 fatigue coat 1 shirt 1 p[ai]r drawers portfolio & some other little trinkets, 2 days rations in haversack, canteen, Cartridge box & belts with 40 rounds of ball cartridges & a gun & bayonet, we were somewhat fatigued when we got to our journeys end. We are provided with small linnen tents 1 for every 4 men they are in 2 pieces which button together at the top. When stuck up they resemble the roof of a house. They make quite a comfortable shelter to crawl under in a climate like this. We stopped there untill the next Saturday. When we started toward Alexandria by way of Fairfax Court House, it commenced raining when we were at F[airfax] C[ourt] H[ouse] waiting for other reg[imen]ts to pass. It rained most of the time during the day & night. After marching about 1 ½ miles we turned into a piece of pine woods for the night—were thoroughly drenched with rain. I was wet through long before we halted. About the time we stopped it rained harder than ever my boots were full of water & I felt cold & chilly. Others were in as bad or even worse condition than I was. Some were inclined to curl up by a tree they did not seem to care whether they lived or died (it was a cold rain). I knew that I must do something to stir my blood so I went with several others to get some rails when I got back with my rails I felt better. It was hard starting a fire but we succeeded in doing so after a while. We mixed our rails with green logs as large as 3 or 4 of us could carry in a little while we had a regular log heap fire our shanties were open in front so that the fire could shine in & dry our clothes. As the ground was level the soil is such that the water was 3 or 4 inches deep all over the ground. We cut pine poles 3 or 4 inches in diameter for a floor to our hovel & covered them with brush we then spread our blankets & sought natures kind restorer sleep. I slept soundly several hours. When I awoke the steam was rising from my wet clothing in large quantities. I felt much refreshed & strange to say I didn't take cold, but few of comp[any] did. Sunday the 23d we marched to Alexandria & went on board the Steamboat *Catskill*. Thousands of soldiers embarked that day. Thousands went the week before. I have not time to give the particulars of our voyage but Tuesday morn when we awoke we found ourselves ankored near Fortress Monroe. We ran up to the wharf by the fort & stopped some time but did not get off. The old Fortress is a strong costly looking Institution with many heavy guns mounted on the top & judging from the large number of port holes in her massive walls she has a large number of guns inside. The Union & Floyd guns are on the outside elevated on heaps of sand they are monsters to behold. . . . This is a beautiful country very level & free from stone. I think the soil is very fertile & productive though many beautiful fields have been poorly cultivated & has become somewhat exhausted. I think if it could be cultivated like our New England soil it would yield a bountiful reward. Peach trees are in blossom here & have been for several days. . . . Day before yesterday I went over to Newport News I saw the wrecks of the *Congress* & *Cumberland* which were sunk by the rebel Steamer *Merrimac*. They are but few rods from shore. . . . I must draw this piece of pencil marks to a close. I fear you cant read all of this, but as I have no ink I have to use a pencil.

Receive from your lover Dan

General McClellan had devised a plan to attack Richmond from the southeast. He would land his forces at Fortress Monroe, Virginia, then move up the peninsula formed by the York and James Rivers toward Richmond. Although Lincoln viewed the plan as risky, since it left Washington vulnerable to an attack, McClellan argued that the route to Richmond via the peninsula was shorter, with fewer river crossings than the direct overland route from Washington. He hoped that he could catch the rebel forces off guard, even capture Richmond before Johnston's army could rush back to defend it. Moreover, McClellan thought that he could maneuver his army in such a way as to occupy a defensive position and force Johnston to attack him. His supply lines would be secure as well, given the Union's complete naval supremacy. By late March the massive amphibious force had landed at Fortress Monroe and was ready to begin its march up the peninsula.

As the Union Army approached the old Revolutionary War battlefield at Yorktown, Virginia, thirteen thousand Confederates under General John Magruder had entrenched themselves and, by employing a variety of theatrics, had convinced McClellan that their force was much stronger than it actually was. McClellan insisted that the only way to take Yorktown was by siege and awaited the arrival of siege artillery and additional reinforcements. Lincoln, a Republican, already distrustful of McClellan, a Democrat, urged McCellan to attack at once: "By delay the enemy will relatively gain upon you—that is, he will gain faster, by *fortifications* and *re-inforcements*, than you can by re-inforcements alone. . . . It is indispensable to *you* that you strike a blow."[1]

South of Yorktown ran the Warwick River, which empties into the James River and presented the advancing Union Army with a significant obstacle. The river had been dammed by Confederate forces (who employed over one thousand "negro laborers"), widening and deepening it, and had been fortified on its western bank with numerous earthworks and rifle pits. Still the Union forces had overwhelming manpower advantages, and with an aggressive, well-coordinated attack as Lincoln had urged, the rebel defenders would not have held for long. Union commanders lacked sufficient information about the enemy's strength along the Warwick River, however, so McClellan issued cautious orders to IV Corps commander Erasmus Keyes to occupy the enemy's works if practicable, while avoiding a general engagement. McClellan said that "the object of the movement was to force the enemy to discontinue his work in strengthening his batteries, to silence his fire, and gain control of the dam existing at that point."[2] Brigadier General William Farrar Smith, a Vermont native who commanded the second division of the IV Corps, was tasked with carrying out McClellan's orders. The Third Vermont began the attack in the afternoon on April 16, supported by four batteries of artillery, drove out the defenders, and for a brief period occupied the Confederate works. Due to poor communication, the rest of Smith's division did not follow up the initial breach of the rebel lines, the Third Vermont was soon exposed to a deadly crossfire from a Confederate counterattack, and the order to retreat back across the Warwick River was given. By this point the rebel lines had been strengthened, and the river was swollen by the closing of a dam below the scene of action. Regardless, the attack was renewed two hours after the initial attack had begun. At this point, Mason and the other men of the Sixth Vermont "saw the elephant"—a Civil War term for experiencing combat for the first time.

CAMP IN WOODS NEAR LEE'S MILLS
ABOUT 4 MILES FROM YORKTOWN
Warwick Co[unty] April 24, 1862

Dear Harriet

You have doubtless heard of the engagement that the Vt troops have had with the enemy near this place long ere this, & as a matter of course this first account that reached your ears was highly magnified. I can well imagine the painful uneasyness that you & many other near & dear friends (in the Green Mountain State) had to experience on receiving the first exagerated report. Though the sad event which happened a few days since has made many weeping Mothers sisters & lovers it is not near as bad as at first reported. Wednesday Apr[il] 16th was a beautiful day the sun arose in a cloudless sky. It shed its smiling ray on many a gallant youth for the last time. But I must be brief. The Vt Brig[ade] had orders the night before to prepare 3 days rations. This we all knew indicated a movement but where we knew not. We have got used to sudden moves so that we don't lose any sleep in framing conjectures what is going to happen tomorrow. I should sleep soundly if I knew that I should go in to battle tomorrow. We had been encamped about 1 & ½ miles from the rebel Fort—for several days. On the morn of the 16th our Regt marched about ¾ of a mile toward the F[ort]. We were stationed perhaps 60 rods from Cap[tain] Motts Battery to support it—we were behind a piece of pine woods which hid us from the enemy a heavy cannonading was kept up for about an hour when the enemy made no reply. At first the rebels threw several shells near M[ott]s but which exploded in fair view of us. The first only doing damage which exploded under a cannon killing 3 & wounding 4 of M[ott]s gunners. I saw 1 of the killed & several of the wounded which was a sad sight. As the En[emy] made no reply the firing was suspended for several hours during which Gen[eral] Mcclellan & staff rode by near us. About half past 2 P.M. Motts Ayers Wheelers & Kenedy's Bat[terie]s moved up several hundred yards nearer the F[ort]. Our Reg[iment] was placed at the right & left of the B[atterie]s to support them if charged on by the rebels. The part that I was in was stationed on the right in the edge of the woods about 30 rods from the cannons, the firing now comenced in good earnest. The deafening roar of Artillery mingled with the bursting of shells the crashing of falling trees as they were slivered to atoms & the sharp vollies of musketry fired by skirmishers & sharp shooters made a scene very impressive. It was terrific but grand. About 4 oclock that part of our Reg[iment] on the right double quicked it across the field at the rear of the Bat[terie]s until we got behind a piece of woods. We then marched toward the Fort. We found several Co[mpanie]s of the 3d Vt Reg[iment] waiting, 3 Co[m-panie]s of their Reg[iment] which had crossed the creek which runs in front of the F[ort] which is 12 or 15 rods in width. As they had heard considerable firing on the other side they feared their companions had been overpowered & killed or taken prisoners. But soon after our arrival they came back but their ranks were greatly thinned. They had waded through water waist deep many of them wetting their cartridges. They told us that we were going into an awful place. They bid us good bye & with a hearty God bless you as we passed we sprang into the water holding our cartridge boxes as high a[s] possible to prevent them from getting wet. As we jumped into the water our Col[onel] told us that every man of us should sleep in the Fort that night but he was mistaken. We crossed the stream amid a shower of leaden hail, part of the time in the water nearly to our arms. Just as we stepped on dry ground on the further side Chandler E Colburn of Troy fell back in the water dead but 2 or 3 steps from me. A ball had pierced his brain. About this time the rebels poured a volley into us that seemed to fill the air with balls they being concealed in their rifle pits in great numbers judging from the great amount of musketry fired at us. We done the best we could but as their pits were concealed by vines & shrubery so that we could not get a good sight at them but we fired at them as often as we could get sight at them. They poured one continued volley into us the poor boys fell in ever[y] direction. Our Officers seeing that we were fighting against fearful odds on very unequal footing gave us orders to retreat. This we done without any panic or confusion carrying of[f] our wounded we did not go back as fast as we went over. Gen[eral] Brooks who commands the Vt Brigade complimented us highly on the coolness & bravery exhibited by us under a deadly fire. As we retreated the enemy continued to pour a deadly fire in among us until out of their reach. The trouble was the enemy was intrenched much stronger than they supposed. Our Co[mpany] lost 1 killed which was the one spoken of above. Our 2d Lieut[enant]—C F Bailey of Troy badly wounded the hip. Orderly Sergeant M[artin] W[arner] Davis of Brownington wounded in side. W[illiam] Livingston of Albany wounded in arm. A[listine] Sabine of Hardwick wounded in arm. John Robinson of Brownington wounded in foot. Lewis Talbot of Troy wounded in bowels badly died next morn. Our Reg[iment] lost 12 killed & 77 wounded. Among the killed was Capt[ain] Reynolds Co[mpany] F. Several commissioned officers were wounded. The 3d Reg[iment] lost more killed than ours did but not as many wounded the other Vt Reg[imen]ts did not suffer much. I think there will not be any more fighting for some time. Our army is strengthening its position every day & night. We do a great deal under cover of darkness. Very heavy siege guns are being mounted every day. Many think that Mcclellans plan is to not make an attack until Gen[eral] Banks & Mcdowell march down behind them & surround them. Many think the final blow to secession will be struck here. When you hear of a fight here you may expect to hear it greatly enlarged. Our Officers have seen the folly of trying to drive them out of their dens with Infantry. It has got to be done principally with heavy siege guns. I am enjoying good health. You must be car[e]ful of yourself & dont borrow any trouble about me. None of the Glover boys were hurt. Direct as before.

From Dan

The Battle of Lee's Mills was a mismanaged affair. General Smith stated, "The moment I found resistance serious and the numbers opposed great I acted in obedience to the warning instructions of the general-in-chief, and withdrew the small number of troops exposed from under fire."[3] Despite the efforts of Smith and McClellan to downplay the loss of "skirmishers" during a "reconnaissance," the loss of lives was great; 44 Vermonters died, 148 were wounded, and 21 of the wounded eventually died of wounds received. There was speculation that General Smith was drunk during the battle, which prompted a Congressional investigation into Smith's conduct.

Ultimately Smith was exonerated of blame. G. G. Benedict later stated that the Battle of Lee's Mills was "one of the most useless wastes of life and most lamentable of unimproved opportunities" of the war.[4] The men who saw war up close for the first time were shaken. Alex Davis recalled: "Such a sight never again met my gaze during the war. Wounded men, on reaching the old bed of the stream sank with cries of despair, to be found later in the swamps down the stream, where their bodies had lodged. I saw two men ahead of me carrying a wounded man, when they were struck by rebel bullets and one or both sank. I saw two others assisting a wounded man, when a bullet passed through the latter's head and he pitched forward and was gone. The muddy water literally boiled with bullets."[5] Fred Kimball said,

> As we came upon the opposite bank the enemy poured a perfect shower of bullets upon us from their rifle pits, and also in a cross fire from the fort killing and wounding many. . . . One poor fellow of our company was left upon the enemy's shore shot through the brain, though his, with the remains of others who were killed, have since been recovered by a flag of truce and received a soldier's burial. . . . Our color-bearer was wounded and fell, dropping the colors, but they were caught up and brought out pierced by ten balls. Sergt. Holston, of company I, has the honor of bringing out the colors.[6]

The bodies that were returned to the Vermont Brigade three days later under the flag of truce were "blackened by decay and despoiled of shoes, buttons and valuables."[7] McClellan, in his report to the War Department, said, "The purposes of crossing the skirmishers was to ascertain the real state of the case on the enemy's side. There was no other way of obtaining the information. The loss sustained in accomplishing this is to be regretted, but was small in comparison with the importance of the object in view. . . . It was the fortune of Mott's Battery (Third New York Artillery) and the Vermont regiments (Brooks' brigade), particularly the Third, Fourth, Fifth, and Sixth, to be especially exposed. Their conduct was admirable and worthy of veterans."[8]

For weeks following the attack on Lee's Mills, the Vermont Brigade remained encamped on the east bank of the Warwick River. McClellan spent precious weeks bringing up his siege artillery to position it around the Confederate defenses at Yorktown. Meanwhile, as Lincoln predicted, the Confederates strengthened their fortifications around Richmond. As soon as McClellan's guns were in position, though, Confederate General Joseph Johnston began a retreat under the cover of darkness and his own cannonade on May 3, rather than submit to the pounding of the Union guns. His retreat up the peninsula was slowed by recent rains, however, so as pursuing Union cavalry and infantry threatened his escape, Johnston dispatched General James Longstreet with a full division to act as a rear guard. Longstreet battled his future foe at Gettysburg, Winfield Scott Hancock, at Williamsburg, Virginia, on May 5. Hancock's brigade of Smith's division had moved upon the enemy's flank in a strong position, but for want of reinforcements and better coordination among Union officers, Hancock was unable to press his attack further, so by day's end, Longstreet had escaped, buying the main Confederate body additional time to continue its retreat toward Richmond. General Brooks, who commanded the Vermont Brigade, and General Smith, who commanded the division to which the Vermont Brigade was attached, were both furious about the lost opportunity. The Vermont Brigade remained close enough to the fighting on May 5 to witness it directly, but despite Hancock's repeated pleas for reinforcements, the brigade never went into action.

After Williamsburg the Army of the Potomac moved closer to Richmond, both by land and water, though heavy rains meant little fighting until the end of May. There was plenty of optimism about the prospects of capturing Richmond. Oliver Stiles, a soldier in Company D, wrote, "If you could see the army of the potomac as they move along, you would know, if you stopped to think what a glorious cause we were engaged in, that there was no force, however large, that was fighting against a government so glorious as ours has proved to be in times past, that could defeat us, or at all impede our progress as we go marching on. The rebel army is much demoralized . . . hoping that *God* will preserve the right, and *men* hang the leaders of this accursed rebellion."[9] On May 31 the armies clashed at the Battle of Seven Pines (or Fair Oaks), where Confederate general Joseph Johnston was wounded in the shoulder. Command of the Army of Northern Virginia thereafter went to Robert E. Lee. As the Battle of Seven Pines began, Mason penned his next letter to Harriet.

Camp in the woods near Chickahominy
river about 6 miles from Richmond
air line & 8 to go the road
May 31st 1862

Dear Harriet

I received your every welcome letter (bearing date May 22 & 23d) this morning. As it was mailed the 27th (today being the 31st) you perceive it was not long on the road. I was highly gratified to learn that you was enjoying good health which is the best news that an absent lover can hear from the object of his affections. I am enjoying the same great blessing & I doubt not that you will be equally gratified to learn this from me. The Glover Boys are all well except Fred [Kimball] & Orange Williams. Fred is with the Co[mpany] but is not able to do duty. I think he is having a run of the jaundice which is quite common among the soldiers lasting generally several days. Symptoms loss of appetite an unnatural desire to sleep complexion very yellow. Orange is also with us getting better of the same disease. Z[ebina] Y Bickford died the last day of Apr[il] of typhoid fever. His parents live in Greensborough he was cousin to Orange W[illiams]. Perhaps you have seen him. . . . He tented with me last winter. He was a good fellow & it seemed hard to leave him so far from his friends in a strange land. His burial was a solemn duty to perform.[10] As I stood by his grave & saw his remains lowered to their final resting place I was reminded of the poetry composed before the burial of Sir John Moore "No useless coffin enclosed his breast, but he lay like a warrior taking his rest with his blankets wrapped around him."[11] We sent home his Overcoat portfolio testament & memorandum book in a box. . . . As it is quite warm & I am tired of writing I will close hoping to hear from you as soon as convenient.

receive from Dan

{ 3 }

"We Had a Pretty Rough Time" (Summer 1862)

As the Army of the Potomac approached Richmond's doorstep, McClellan characteristically overestimated the enemy's strength and repeatedly asked Washington for reinforcements. He wired the War Department on June 25, preemptively placing blame on the Lincoln administration for any defeats that he might suffer: "The rebel force is stated at 200,000. . . . I regret my great inferiority in numbers, but I feel that I am in no way responsible for it, as I have not failed to represent repeatedly the necessity of re-enforcements. . . . If the result of the action, which will probably occur to-morrow, or within a short time, is a disaster, the responsibility cannot be thrown on my shoulders; it must rest where it belongs."[1] Lincoln replied that McClellan's telegram, "suggesting the probability of your being overwhelmed by 200,000, and talking of where the responsibility will belong, pains me very much. I give you all I can, and act on the presumption that you will do the best you can with what you have, while you continue, ungenerously I think, to assume that I could give you more if I would. I have omitted and shall omit no opportunity to send you re-enforcements whenever I possibly can."[2] For reasons that have long confounded historians, McClellan, despite his oversized ego, insubordination, and tendency to shift blame to others for defeats, remained very popular with his troops, as is reflected in Mason's letter to Harriet on June 21. In addition to praising McClellan as "active vigilant and brave," Mason also commented on courtships back home.

Camp Lincoln June 21st 1862

Dear Harriet

I received your ever welcome sheet this morn. It gave me great pleasure to learn of your good health. I am enjoying the same great blessing. The Glover boys are all well & in good spirits. It is very healthy throughout the Reg[imen]t. Since I last wrote you our Divis[ion] has moved across the Chickahominy river. . . . Doubtless you Vermonters think Mcclellan very slow. But he is active vigilant & brave. You must remember that great wheels move slow & military ones doubly so. At least he has the confidence of his men. As he rides along the lines wild cheers rend the air hats handkerchiefs & flags are swung & the wildest enthusiasm prevails. He is with us & plans the work. We are now strongly entrenched on the west side of the Chic[kahominy] riv[er] & Richmond is destined to be ours at some future day but perhaps not for several weeks. I think that Mcclellan[s] plan is to first strengthen his position by means of reinforcements forts &c so that the rebels cannot drive us across the C[hickahominy] riv[er] & then close in slowly but steadily driving the enemy from his outside fortifications by means of Artillery which we have a great supply & cut of[f] the rebs supplies & capture the main rebel army & give secesh its final death blow. At least it has that appearance & that is the prevailing opinion here. The weather is quite warm here most of the time though we have some quite cool days. . . . I should like to meet you in your fathers parlor tomorrow night & stop a few hours I think I could pass the time from 9 till 2 or 3 oclock very pleasant. What do you say Miss Harriet? . . . It gives me pleasure to ponder over the happy hours passed in your fathers house when all sensible folks were asleep. But you & I little fools were sitting up trying to make ourselves agreable laughing at each others little witticisms whether they were cunning or not, but such is love, we enjoyed it, & its nobodys business but our own. I am sorry that Guy & Jane do not get along better I never thought it a suitable match. I think that Guys money bought her for she could not have loved him it is impossible it is not natural for a young & blooming girl to fall in love with an old red nosed toothless old hunchbacked dried up old Bacheldor twice her age if he has [not] got money. Our boys are nearly all on Picket—as but one non Commissioned officer is detailed from each Co[mpany] it dont come my turn very often. Corporal E[lbert] H Nye is Corp[oral] out this time. I will now wind up this scrip of scribbling by wishing you good health & a long life of happiness hoping to be spared to enjoy the same blessings with you. Give my respects to your Mother & all friends.

receive from your lover Dan

Three days later Mason wrote a long letter to the editor of the *Orleans Independent Standard*, where he vigorously defended McClellan, repeating nearly verbatim many of the same thoughts he had expressed to Harriet:

> Methinks I hear some of your readers say, "how slow Gen. McClellan is," but, reader, you must recollect that great wheels move slow in civil life, and doubly so in military. At least they appear so to those who do not comprehend the magnitude of the great work of suppressing this wicked rebellion. Civilians who lay back out of harm's way, enjoying all the embellishments of civilized life, worshipping your hoarded treasures of old rusty dollars, do not growl and grumble about Gen. Mcclellan's slow movements, for you know nothing about it. I can see where the shoe pinches; you are afraid you will have to shell out some of those little idols to the tax gatherers, and by grumbling about McClellan's inactivity, you virtually say that the loss of a few thousand men, by rushing on to the foe without taking advantage of him, aiming only to gain the victory, regardless of human life, is better than to take a few more months time, and a few more of the rusty coin, and save the great effusion of blood. You thereby show a little, contracted mind, besides making asses of yourselves.—But I tell you Gen. McClellan is not slow. I believe him to be active, vigilant, and brave. He has the confidence of his men, as he rides along the lines, the greatest enthusiasm prevails; loud cheers rend the air, hats and handkerchiefs are swung, and all goes to indicate the great degree of confidence placed in our leader. We believe that he has a great work to do; we also believe that he has a great mind, and is competent for the task, and it will take more than the slurs and jeers of a New York newspaper General to make us think differently. . . . The boys are in the best of spirits, and are ready and willing to go into danger when our beloved Chieftain gives the word.—To quote from one of our patriotic songs, "Mcclellan is our man." I must now close hoping that the defenders of the old flag will be enabled to return to their respective homes and dear friends before many months.[3]

On June 25, with McClellan's army just outside of Richmond, Robert E. Lee, at the urging of Jefferson Davis, launched a series of counteroffensives designed to relieve pressure on the rebel capital. In what became known as the Seven Days' Battles—seven engagements fought in seven days from June 25 to July 1—the Union Army was mostly on the defensive as it was driven away from Richmond. The price of going on the offensive was steep for the Army of Northern Virginia; it lost nearly twenty thousand men killed or wounded, about twice the figure for the Army of the Potomac. Nevertheless, Lee had driven McClellan's force back down the peninsula, and Richmond was saved, which proved to be a strategic victory for Lee and a major blow to Northern morale. After the Battle of Gaines' Mill on the third day of the Seven Days' Battles, McClellan angrily telegraphed Secretary of War Stanton and fumed,

> I have lost this battle because my force was too small. I again repeat that I am not responsible for this, and I say it with the earnestness of a general who feels in his heart the loss of every brave man who has been needlessly sacrificed today. . . . In addition to what I have already said, I only wish to say to the President that I think he is wrong in regarding me as ungenerous when I say that my force was too weak. . . . I know that a few thousand more men would have changed this battle from a defeat to a victory. As it is, the Government must not and cannot hold me responsible for the result. . . . If I save this army now, I tell you plainly that I owe no thanks to you or to any other persons in Washington. You have done your best to sacrifice this army.[4]

Lincoln's response was blunt: "I have not said you were ungenerous in saying that you needed re-enforcements. I thought you were ungenerous in assuming that I did not send them as fast as I could."[5]

The Vermont Brigade was engaged heavily in the Seven Days' Battles. When it became apparent that McClellan's plan was to retreat down the peninsula, Lee ordered additional attacks on McClellan's army. On the morning of June 29, at Savage's Station, the retreating federals torched "piles of hard bread as large as houses, and immense quantities of flour, sugar, coffee, and pork." In addition, "a long train of cars was loaded with powder and shells, the cars set on fire, and the train started down grade to the river, filling the air with exploding shells and fragments of shattered cars as it held its fiery way, till it crashed through the blazing railroad bridge, when, with a grand explosion, train and bridge disappeared together."[6] Later that afternoon the Vermont Brigade was part of a rearguard action that bought the Union forces precious time to escape. As the sound of gunfire grew louder on the north bank of the Chickahominy, it became apparent that the rebels were on the move. As Alex Davis recalled, "The now increasing and continuous roar of musketry, warned us that grim-visaged war was assuming for us a rougher aspect. We spoke less, laughed not at all, and our then young faces bore an anxious look." Soon the rebel force attacked the Vermonters. The brigade suffered heavy casualties, but held its ground, and continued its retreat at 10 p.m. after hours of fighting in dense woods, leaving the dead and wounded behind. Among the wounded was Alex Davis, who languished on the field throughout the night and into the next morning. Davis said, "By daylight, the 30th, my thirst was intense. . . . My suffering of body and mind was intense, for the prospect of a rebel prison, with all its horrors, was before me and yet the agony of those around me was far in excess of mine, told only feebly by the groans of wounded and dying men which filled the air." Davis was captured later that morning by the advancing rebels. On his way to Libby Prison in Richmond, he encountered "a tall lieutenant from a New York regiment, terribly wounded by a shot through the body, yet with only an occasional groan, walking erect, manfully," he moved along with the procession of prisoners before dying. En route to Richmond, Davis was taken to a hospital, where the suffering "far exceeded anything I ever witnessed, for the reason that it was a sick and wounded resort, and all of the worst cases 'went out' in a short time, amid piteous groans, insane callings for wives and mothers, while the sick were tortured by the dense swarms of flies."[7]

The survivors of the fight at Savage's Station marched all night, then fought another rearguard action the following day at White Oak Swamp, holding off a strong attack by Stonewall Jackson. Again, after the day's fight, the brigade began a night retreat at 11 p.m. toward the main Union body at Malvern Hill. As both armies were exhausted after seven days of continuous fighting, Lee did not continue his attacks, and McClellan retreated to

Harrison's Landing on the James River, where a large fleet of transports waited to take the bruised Army of the Potomac back up the Chesapeake Bay. The final march of the Vermont Brigade to Harrison's Landing was described as "the saddest and weariest march of its length in the history of the brigade. The rain poured in torrents; the wagons and artillery had poached the roads into canals of mud; the stouter men could hardly drag one foot after another; and the weaker fell out by hundreds, some to die of their exhaustion."[8] Colonel Wheelock Veazey of the Third Vermont recalled the sights of the march:

> Stragglers sick and dying, arms of every description, stores of all kinds. Abandoned wagons, broken down horses and mules, mud so deep that no bottom could be reached. All these at every step; and then add the sickening feeling of defeat and retreat, and the momentary expectation of a rear attack, and no help within reach. Weary, hungry, exhausted, sick, what torment could be added, except the loss of honor? . . . But fortunately everything has an end; and more dead than alive we found the end of that march at last. But it was only to find a bivouac in water and mud, without fire or rations until the next day.[9]

Fred Kimball wrote, "We marched through drenching rain, and about six inches of mud, to Harrison's Landing, probably a distance of 6 miles. Thus our army arrived, jaded and fatigued, yet with firm confidence in Gen. McClellan and the final success of our arms."[10] After such an ordeal, no wonder Mason's description of the Seven Days was relatively brief. An understatement, Mason simply explained that "we had a pretty rough time."

CAMP ON JAMES RIVER
July 6th 1862

Dear Harriet

As there has been some unexpected movements in our army since I last wrote you I thought I would just drop a line to you & state the facts in regard to them. You have doubtless heard many reports that were false as usual when the public mind is excited. Saturday June 28th we commenced to retreat or rather fall back toward James river. Thursday before the right wing of our army had a great battle with the rebels & drove them back with great slaughter. The rebel papers admit 20,000 loss killed wounded & missing. The next day the rebs were greatly reinforced & our men were compelled to fall back but McClellan had made calculations for this & sent his stores away to a safe place. It is said that Beauregard & Braggs armies are in the vicinity of Richmond if so it was much better to concentrate our forces on the James river under the protection of our gunboats until we can raise more troops than to fight them as long as we could & then perhaps lose all our cannon & baggage. Our Artillery & baggage trains are now safe & all we want is more men. The rebs have staked their all on Richmond & we must have a great force & crush the rebellion at this point. I am well the Glover boys are all well. Our Divis[ion] covered the retreat & guarded the baggage train we had a pretty rough time. The enemy made several attacks on us but we always repulsed him. Sunday night the 29th we had a fight with the rebs & drove them. The 5th reg[imen]t was pretty badly cut up. Our reg[imen]t lost quite a number killed & wounded. Alex Davis had his 2d toe shot off & we had to leave him at a house with the rest of the wounded we left a surgeon with them they will have good care taken of them. I presume Alex will go home within a month on parole of honor he is now of course a prisoner. I have not received an answer to my last letter which I wrote you I expect one every day. E[lbert] H Nye & I have been promoted to Se[r]geants which will increase our pay to $24.00 per month. I must now close for the mail will soon leave & I want this to go this morn

Direct as usual

yours with much love
Dan

The Peninsula campaign was over. The Vermont Brigade had suffered greatly. The first drive to Richmond the previous summer had ended in disaster for the Union at Bull Run, and now, a year later, the war's end was nowhere in sight. It had only just begun. The Union's defeat—and the growing realization that the war would not end soon—led to a growing chorus of calls to wage the war more aggressively, including increasing manpower through conscription and depriving the rebels of their greatest source of strength: the forced labor of four million enslaved persons.

On July 1 Lincoln issued a call for 300,000 additional troops for three years' service, with Vermont's quota established as 4,898. On August 4 a call was made to the states for another 300,000 troops for nine months' service, with the threat that if quotas were not filled, the federal government would implement a draft. As an extra incentive, volunteers were promised town bounties. Following Lincoln's call in August, numerous towns in Orleans County once again held "war meetings" to encourage enlistment. At Troy, Vermont, for instance, a series of resolutions were adopted, one of which alluded to the real possibility that additional Union setbacks would lead to the recognition of the Confederacy by European nations.

> *Resolved*,—That as we are engaged against an unholy rebellion, we as citizens and patriots pledge our lives, our property, and our sacred honor to put it down.
>
> *Resolved*,—That while the aristocrats of England and France, are rejoiced to see our government endangered, we are rejoiced to hope and believe that it will be sustained and perpetuated, and that the star-spangled banner, untarnished and untorn, shall long be, as it has heretofore been, the pride of freemen and the terror of tyrants.
>
> *Resolved*,—That we desire at this time to express our unqualified contempt for the whole race of humanity termed *Skedaddlers* and sneaks, who run away in this, the time of our country's need, and endeavor to hide their cowardly heads, ostrich-like, in some hole in Canada.
>
> *Resolved*,—That it should be the pride of every son of Old Vermont that her quota of men be furnished without resort to draft.[11]

The editor of the *Standard* asked,

> Why is it that scores of brave and hardy men are not flocking to the recruiting office daily, when the government which has cherished and protected every citizen calls for assistance? It is because the men of wealth and influence, the property holders will not come forward and don the uniform. . . . Farmers and mechanics, merchants and professional

men of Orleans County! Does your property need the protection of the government? If it does, come forward and enlist in the army of noble soldiers that has pledged to uphold and defend the constitution that has made you all you are.[12]

Fred Kimball wrote to the editor that "if the North will but keep step with the spirit of the federal army, and send to our aid volunteer reinforcements . . . ere the autumn's frosts this unholy rebellion may be known as a thing that was. . . . I hope the historian will never have to record that men had to be drafted from the Green Mountain State."[13] Mason also predicted that the arrival of three hundred thousand additional troops would hasten Richmond's fall.

Camp near Harrisons Landing Va
July 27th 1862

Dear Harriet

I seat myself on a piece of secesh chair pen in hand to do what I ought to have done several days ago. . . . Today is Sunday I have been to Church in a brick church but a few rods from our camp. It is called Westover church it is quite a nice church we have services in it—ever[y] Sabbath. We have quite good singing. There is an Organ in it, & the Orderly Sergeant of our Co[mpany] plays it. As there is plenty of Hymn books & singing books in the house, we have good times singing, but we miss the soft harmonizing tone of womans voice, & will you believe me there was not a woman there. . . . We are stopping near where we were when I last wrote you. We have built Forts & rifle pits so that we have no fears of an attack from the enemy. I think we shall stop here during the hot weather. By that time the 3 hundred thousand troops called for will be in the field & then Richmond must fall. We have some very warm weather & some quite cool cloudy days. We have a good many terrific thunder showers accompanied by furious gales of wind. We have plenty of good Cold spring water by going a few rods. We have not heard directly from Alex Davis since he was taken. But as there was 2 boat loads of sick & wounded soldiers passed down the river from Richmond under a flag of truce some of them Vermonters, it is quote probable at least possible that Alex was aboard. I should not be surprised to hear any day that he was at home. . . . I hope Sammy & Josie will enjoy each others company as doubtless they do. But Josie is to[o] good for the miserable deceptive drunken scamp & though he is capable of appearing quite glossy & slick she will find that all is not gold that glitters. I hope in your next you will put in a line concerning Jack & Ellen. I must now close hoping to hear from you soon

receive with much love from Dan

At last the Vermont Brigade was transported from the peninsula up Chesapeake Bay to Alexandria, Virginia. The units surrounding Washington had been organized as the Army of Virginia under General John Pope. Lincoln hoped that McClellan's forces would unite with Pope's, though Pope and McClellan resented each other. The Vermont Brigade, now assigned to the VI Corps, marched toward the old battlefield at Manassas, Virginia. As Stonewall Jackson's forces clashed with Pope's army at the Second Battle of Bull Run on August 29 and 30, the VI Corps was held in reserve. McClellan did not support Pope despite Pope's urgent pleas for reinforcements. Before the battle McClellan wrote to his wife that "I have a strong idea that Pope will be thrashed during the coming week—& very badly whipped he will be & ought to be—such a villain as he is ought to bring defeat upon any cause that employs him. . . . I think the result of their machinations will be that Pope will be badly thrashed within two days & that they will be very glad to turn over the redemption of their affairs to me."[14] Northern morale reached a new low after the Union's second defeat at Second Manassas. The *Orleans Independent Standard* expressed the mood back home, which included a growing disenchantment with George McClellan:

> For several months past we have heard much about "new lines of defense," "new bases," "falling back to safer positions," and like phrases. Our readers, many of them, have doubtless wondered at these expressions, and have accepted them as masterly maneuvers in that system of "profound strategy" of which our general-in-chief is such a master! It is about time we think that these mystifying dispatches are put into homely

English, so that hereafter if we hear of "new lines of defense," we can understand without further explanation that we have been compelled to evacuate, to back out and skedaddle. And when we hear of "falling back to a safer position," after a hard fight, because the ground chosen was "untenable," let us understand the exact truth at once, that our army has been whipped because we could not help it. We shall then have a clear knowledge of the facts without waiting for the truth to break on us a little at a time for months afterward. Let us know the truth, the full truth, the terrible truth—if it be terrible—at once, and we shall be prepared sooner to meet it. But no more soft words for hard facts. It is time that things are called by their right names. "Washington is safe," is once more the stereotyped telegram, and "all is quiet along the Potomac," we suppose. How that *does* sound after looking daily for months to see the thrilling announcement of "Richmond taken!" We are now invaded instead of being the invaders.[15]

After another victory at Second Bull Run, Lee decided to attempt his first invasion of the North. His goals were numerous: to demoralize the Northern public before the midterm elections in the fall, amplify the voices of the Peace Democrats, gain European recognition of the Confederacy as a sovereign nation (which was not a remote possibility in the summer of 1862), encourage Maryland—a slave state with a significant number of Confederate sympathizers—to secede from the Union, carry the war out of Virginia and into the enemy's country during harvest season, and provide for his army by foraging off of the rich farmlands of Maryland and Pennsylvania. Although Lincoln's cabinet urged the removal of McClellan from command, Lincoln feared a further decline in the morale of the Army of the Potomac, given McClellan's continued popularity, so begrudgingly gave him the task of pursuing Lee's army. Lee's invasion was fraught with peril though; his force was vastly inferior to McClellan's, he could be cut off from Virginia and his line of retreat blocked, and the citizens of Maryland, a state that remained loyal to the Union, did not greet his army warmly. His forces were dangerously spread out, especially since Stonewall Jackson's corps had been given the task of capturing the Union garrison at Harpers Ferry, Virginia, to eliminate the threat to Lee's rear. On September 13,

Union soldiers discovered a copy of Lee's Special Orders 191, wrapped in three cigars, that revealed Lee's battle plan and the deployment of his forces. This intelligence was brought to McClellan's attention, who boasted that he would "whip" Lee, though did not order his troops into action until the following morning. McClellan had an unparalleled opportunity to divide Lee's forces and attack his army piecemeal, but the delay in taking action gave Lee an opportunity to consolidate his forces. As with the Gettysburg campaign the following summer, Lee's army moved northward behind the long ridge of South Mountain, protecting and screening his flank. On the morning of September 14, the Union VI Corps was ordered to drive rebel forces off South Mountain, who defended a pass through the ridgeline known as Crampton's Gap. The Second and Fourth Vermont regiments were deployed at the front of the Vermont brigade, with the Sixth in support, so although close to the main action, Mason was not in the thick of it. He told Harriet, "As we were in the valley & they on the steep side of a very high range of hills their bullets most of them passed harmlessly over our heads while ours made sad havoc in their ranks," but Mason spilled most of his ink in defending himself against a charge from Harriet.

Camp near Burk[itt]sville, MD

Sep[tember] 16th 1862

Dear Harriet

I received your letter of the 3d a few days since while on the march & it is with pleasure that I embrace the first opportunity which presents itself to answer the welcome visitor. Since I last wrote you we have been moving about so much that I have not had time to write much & if I had as we go in light marching order without knapsacks only a rubber blanket & half tent & the necessary amount of provision I cannot carry paper & envelopes, so you will see that I cannot always write when I should be glad to & you need not think strange if you do not hear from me very often, though I will write as often as possible & wish you to do the same or at least answer my letters promptly as you always have. . . . Judging from your last letter you think me a very poor hand to keep a secret. You almost accuse me of letting my fellow soldiers read your letters. I hoped you had a better oppinion of me than that. In reply to that accusation I will simply say that I never did it. I always was very car[e]ful to keep them out of sight & as I am likely to lose them out of my pockets or Portfolio when moving about so much I burn them with the rest of my letters though I should be very glad to keep them. You intimate that I have done something as bad as to do the above mentioned crime. Which gives me some unpleasant feelings for I cant imagine myself as a sincere lover should keeping all secrets. I think some tatling mischief maker has been trying to kick up a row. Please give me some light on the subject in your next. I must now close hoping that your next will make all plain

yours with much love
Dan

Three days after the Battle of South Mountain, the Army of Northern Virginia and the Army of the Potomac clashed in the bloodiest single day in American history at the Battle of Antietam. Though the Vermont Brigade was exposed to artillery fire during the afternoon, for much of the day it was held in reserve. In his letter to Harriet after the battle, he described seeing the carnage at some of the most infamous locations on the battlefield: the Dunkard Church, "the Cornfield," and "Bloody Lane."

Camp near Hagerstown Maryland Oct[ober] 2d 1862

Dear Harriet

It is (as you well know) against my principles to write oftener than I receive letters, but circumstances alter cases, & I will for once write you two letters in succession without receiving any from you. For some unknown cause we have not had a mail for nearly 2 weeks. . . . Since I last wrote you at or near Burkettsville (where we drove the rebs [off] the mountain) we have fought a great battle near Sharpsburg called the Battle of Antietam it was fought the Wednesday after the Sunday which the above mentioned battle was fought—We were aroused from our slumbers early Wed[nesday] morn by heavy cannonading in the direction of Sharpsburg 5 or 6 miles distant—We ate our breakfasts packed up & started. We arrived at the Battlefield about 10 A.M. I should judge.

The battle was raging very fiercely. We met men coming from the field wounded some in one arm some in both, some had both hands shot—yet they did not seem to mind their wounds. They seemed to think of nothing but beating the rebs. They cheered us on as we passed telling us to give it to them. Such roar of cannon such volleys of musketry I never heard before & I hope never to hear again under like circumstances. Yet it was grand, awful, terrible, sublime. We were kept as reserve & moved along at the rear of our line of battle ready to act where we were most needed. In moving along we had a good view of the battlefield though dense clouds of smoke prevented our seeing every movement. It was an open field fight, some times raging fiercely in a large cornfield then in an orchard then in the front yard of some fine dwelling house. Many houses were pierced with balls & shells. The inmates of course fled much frightened to some place of safety. We drove the rebs & held the battle field with their killed & wounded but we had not men enough to rout them completely. About one P.M. we moved up into a Cornfield under a shower of shell which burst all around us wounding several of our Reg[iment] yet we moved on & formed just behind the front line of battle in a little valley being just rising enough in front to hide us from the enemys view thus we laid until Friday about 10 A.M. when we followed up the rebs which left the night before we followed them to the river. Found they had crossed. The first night we laid & slept with the dead & wounded lying around us some of the dead rebs within a few feet of us. While we lay thus several were wounded [by] fragments of shell & balls from the rebel sharpshooters. Fri[day] morn before leaving I went over the field. What a sight—I should say there was 2 dead rebs to one of our men in an old road in particular they lay in heaps for a long distance in the Cornfield just beyond the ground was thickly dotted with them but enough of this such looking faces such a stench as arose. The heart sickens to tell. I must now close by tendering to you my best wishes & much love.

Direct as usual

I expect the recruits will be here in a few days they are at Washington now

Dan

{4}

"I Don't Know What the Next Flop Will Be" (Fall 1862)

The Sixth Regiment was augmented by the arrival of seventy-seven new recruits after Antietam who surely felt the intense pressure from their communities to enlist, following Lincoln's calls for additional troops after McClellan's defeat on the peninsula. McClellan had failed to pursue Lee after Antietam, allowing the Army of Northern Virginia to escape back across the Potomac to safety. A furious Lincoln finally removed McClellan from command. The Vermont Brigade spent the next month at Hagerstown, Maryland, with no imminent threat from the enemy. During this time Mason's attention turned primarily to a quarrel with Harriet that took several exchanges of letters to resolve. Harriet had accused him of sharing her letters with his fellow troops, an accusation that Mason vehemently denied, although he did admit to showing Harriet's "miniature" to his comrades, as well as that of his sister Emily. Even this seemed controversial by the standards of Victorian-era decorum.

Camp near Hagerstown, MD
Oct[ober] 22d 1862

Dear Harriet

I received your letter (bearing date Oct[ober] 8th) yesterday. I had been anxiously expecting it for several days but our mail still continues irregular we get a good amount of mail matter when it does arrive. We average about one mail in a week. About a week ago I received a letter from you answering the one which I wrote at Crawford Gap near Burkettsville after the fight (or more properly South Mountain Pass). In the above letter I was gratified to learn the crime that I was guilty of which had caused you to place such an extremely low estimate of my secretive faculties, so much so as to intimate that your lover was silly enough to allow his tent-mates to read the warm frank outbursts of affection which would naturally flow from the pen of a true loving woman when writing to her lover hundreds of miles away. I acknowledge that one day while at Montpelier several of the Glover boys were sitting in the tent showing the Miniatures of their friends. Some I knew & some I did not. As usual at such times there was some joking & hinting in regard to these strange ladies being their sweethearts &c. Some one asked me to show my pictures. I gave them to understand that I was not ashamed to show any that I had & finally took out yours & Emilys Miniatures the only ones that I had. They looked at them & pronounced them good pictures. There was no low vulgar expressions or comments made nothing of the kind. I cant see the harm in ones showing a lovers picture under such circumstances. Every one present knows that we were on quite intimate terms. For my part I am not ashamed of the original & why should I be of the picture. No, far from this I feel proud of it. I have carried it on my person in the heat of Battle through all the different engagements which I have participated in & have it now. Perhaps I am short sighted & display a weakness in regard to this but really I can't see it so. But enough of this please give me your views in regard to this in your next. . . . I must now close hoping the time is not far distant when this wicked unholy Rebellion shall be blotted out. Oh what a happy time it will be when we can meet face to face after such an absence. It gives me great pleasure to gaze on your Miniature but Oh how much greater satisfaction it would give to grasp your loving hand & plant on your rosey lips (that which I have been so long deprived of) A kiss

yours with much love
Dan

Harriet, apparently not satisfied with Mason's initial response, implied that his display of her "miniature" was indiscreet. Again he defended his decision to showcase it:

Camp near White Plain Station on the branch of the Mannassas Rail Road leading from M[anassas] Junction to Mount Jackson Va
Nov[ember] 8th 1862

Dear Harriet

Yours of the 29th came to hand in due season & was read with the usual degree of interest—I was happy to learn of your good health also to learn that you had resolved not to borrow any more trouble about me. I see there is no use in trying to reckoncile you in regard to showing your Miniature. You say in your last letter that showing your Miniature was virtual[l]y saying to those present that we were engaged. Well for the sake of arguement we will admit it to be so. I was not ashamed to have them think so Every one present knew or at least I have no doubt but what they knew that I was keeping company with you. . . . I say I was not ashamed to have them think so if having your Miniature in my possession caused them to think so. I have given my views in regard to this. Your greatest objection to my showing your likeness was that it was the same as telling them that we were engaged. I will now ask you if you are ashamed to have people know that you are keeping company or engaged to Dan Mason if you are not I cant see as there was any harm done. If you are you have carried things to[o] far. You was to blame for giving me any encouragement or at least for going so far as to pledge heart & hand to me. But I think when you come to consider the matter candidly you will see the point of my argument & think differently in regard to it. I frankly confess that I admire your frank plain manner of expressing your opinion in regard to the subject of discussion. Hereafter if you hear any stories about me or any thing disrespectful I want you to let me know dont be bashful about letting me know all about it. Perhaps you may think that I am questioning you rather closely but this is the way I view the matter. I shall expect an answer in your next. The Glover Boys are now all well. . . . I am well & enjoying myself very well. I must now close by asking you to excuse all my faults & failings for I know that I have many

receive from Dan

The Army of the Potomac, now under the command of General Ambrose Burnside, began to move south toward Richmond after a long delay in Maryland. The news of McClellan's replacement was not exactly welcomed among many of the troops. Fred Kimball wrote, "When we went up the peninsula the rallying cry was 'On to Richmond,' but we failed to reach it, and blame was heaped upon Gen. McClellan, but he did in no way merit it.—A better general never commanded an army, and all the troops under his command have the greatest confidence in him."[1] Oliver Stiles added, "Our army, as a general thing, feel very much dissatisfied with the change that the War Department has seen fit to make in regard to our commanding General. Many troops would have been glad to [have] thrown down their arms and gone home. They would do for him what they never will do for any other general. He had their entire confidence."[2] Among the explanations for why McClellan commanded such loyalty *was* his caution in committing troops to battle. The men felt as if he had their best interests in mind and did everything he could to spare them from unnecessary sacrifice. Many soldiers were frustrated with civilians at home who balked at McClellan's lack of aggressiveness. Fred Kimball complained that "the North is prone to murmur at 'Little M[a]c,' that he does not accomplish more. . . . Let those who grumble come into the field and they will think differently; and after twelve months service as rough as this army has seen, their fighting spirit will be somewhat tamed."[3] McClellan was indeed less popular at home. The editor of the *Standard* proclaimed, "The army of the Potomac has a new commander. Gen. McClellan is removed, and with his removal we hope and pray that the spell which bound so many hearts to the great imbecile, to his 'masterly strategy,' and his 'bagging' propensities, is broken. The long period of sloth and inactivity that has had such a crushing, deadening effect upon the patriotism of the country, let us believe, is over. Burnside is in command. How much better he will prove than McClellan remains to be seen. He cannot prove worse."[4] Burnside, unfortunately, proved no better. On Thanksgiving Day Mason wrote to Harriet and described, among other things, some of the small amusements of camp life.

Camp on Aquia Run

Nov[ember] 27th 1862

Dear Harriet

I take this opportunity to inform you of my whereabouts. I wrote you a letter when at White Plain Station about 3 weeks since & have received no answer. . . . I suppose you are enjoying good sleighing now I should like to spend Thanksgiving with you firstrate I understand Dec[ember] 4th is the day appointed in Vt. Today is Thanksgiving in many of the States. Our Reg[iment] is on Picket today it is a pleasant day & our Co[mpany] is having a good time it so happens that I remain on the reserve with the Capt[ain] & Lieut[enant]s of our Co[mpany]. Fred & Elbert are also with us. Fred is very busily engaged making a bone slide for a Gents handkerchief. He has made several very nice pipes to send home to his Father & friends. Elijah Stone has made a cane top out of Laurel root—also some rings to send to his F[ather] & sisters. S[tephen] Baxter has made several. I have made a number of bone rings. I enclose this one for you not because I think it anything very nice but to give you some idea how we pass the time in Camp. I fear it will be to[o] small for you. I made it from a solid piece of beef bone it was [a] rather slow tedious process but perseverance conquers all things. I expect the next mail will bring the letter due from you. I must now close hoping this will find you enjoying good health.

receive from your sincere lover

Dan

Burnside led the Army of the Potomac to another disastrous defeat at the Battle of Fredericksburg on December 13, 1862. The VI Corps, under the command of William B. Franklin, occupied a position toward the center-left of the Union line and, although exposed to enemy fire for days, never participated in the suicidal frontal assault that occurred against Marye's Heights to the right. Franklin was subjected to severe criticism following the battle for failing to advance his corps. The Vermont Brigade exchanged fire with the rebels along a skirmish line, where it suffered a number of casualties, although the Sixth Vermont only lost one man killed and two wounded. After the debacle at Fredericksburg, which Mason referred to as a "flop," the Army of the Potomac once again retreated and went into winter quarters at White Oak Church, Virginia.

Camp near White Oak Church
Stafford County Va Dec[ember] 21st 1862

Dear Harriet

Your letter of the 9th arrived safely last eve which was a very welcome visitor. I was highly grattified to learn of your good health & judging from the tone of your letter I should think you were in good spirits which was also highly pleasing to me. I am well & enjoy a contented mind most of the time. The letter due when I last wrote you came to hand a short time after. Since I last wrote you the Army of the Potomac has advanced & fell back to its old camp ground. Thursday morn Dec[ember] 11th we were roused from our slumbers about 4 oclock & ordered to pack up ready to march as soon as possible. We started before daylight—we had not gone far before our ears were greeted with heavy cannonading in front in the direction of Fredericksburg. After marching about 5 miles we came near the Rappahannock River about 2 miles below the City of Fredericksburg. We stacked our guns & remained quiet the remainder of the day our men kept up a heavy cannonading the rest of the day while the Engineer Corps were throwing a Pontoon Bridge across the River near sun set. Newtons Divis[ion] crossed meeting with no opposition except a few shots fired by the Reb Pickets who fled but were taken prisoners by our Cavalry. Friday morn our Divis[ion] crossed the 6th Vt Reg[imen]t were ordered to the front & thrown out as skirmishers. . . . As our Reg[iment] advanced across the plain it was greeted by the whistling of bullets which is not the best of music to step to. After advancing about 40 rods under a brisk fire we were ordered to halt & lay low & watch the enemy, while our men crossed the remainder of the day. We were relieved by the Vt 4th. We then marched back near the River & stretched ourselves on the cold damp ground with no shelter but our blankets. Sat[urday] morn they commenced fighting on our left in good earnest. . . . The 3rd 4th 5th & 2d Vt Reg[iment]s lost quite a number killed & wounded our Reg[iment] was very lucky we lost 1 man killed & 2 wounded. Mon[day] eve we recrossed the River & encamped in the woods about a mile this side of the River. The 19th we marched back near our old Camp ground where we still remain. I dont know what the next flop will be. I hope peace will be restored on fair & honorable terms (the Glover boys are all well)

receive with much love from
Dan

{5}

"Disgusted with the Manner the Machine Is Handled" (Winter 1862–63)

On January 1, 1863, Lincoln's Emancipation Proclamation, which he had issued five days after the Union's victory at Antietam, took effect. It transformed the meaning of the war and reflected a shift in Northern public opinion toward a total war policy of striking at the very heart of the Confederacy's strength. It was opposed by conservative Democrats as going too far, and many radical Republicans thought it didn't go far enough, as it allowed slavery to continue in the border states, but there was no doubt that the stakes of the war had been raised much higher. While the Vermont press leaned strongly Republican, notable exceptions existed, such as the *Burlington Weekly Sentinel* and Montpelier *Argus and Patriot*. The *Burlington Weekly Sentinel* blasted the new policy, condemning Lincoln for "giving in to the more energetic and over-bearing radicals, and his issue of the proclamation of negro-slave emancipation as a war measure. . . . With the utter failure of that measure to bring the rebellion any nearer its close, which every sensible man sees and feels will be the case, and with our armies everywhere baffled in the field, what will remain to Mr. Lincoln but to perceive and realize the mistakes of his administration."[1]

Such Democratic voices, though loud, were in the minority in Vermont. While Democrats made gains in the midterm Congressional elections in several states, the Republican candidate for governor in Vermont won 87 percent of the vote. Of Vermont's thirty state senators in 1860, only one was a Democrat. The Emancipation Proclamation was hardly universally accepted throughout the North, though, and its fate rested on Union military success, which had been sorely lacking in the eastern theater. The sentiment in the Sixth Vermont seemed to be strongly in favor of emancipation. Fred Kimball began his diary for 1863 by announcing that "a new era has dawned upon the world. This year will tell greatly upon the destiny of the country. . . . This new *epoch* will tell *greatly* upon the destiny of mankind through all coming time, not only of our own country but of every nation. May it demonstrate that a free people can govern themselves & that *American Slavery* will be *no* longer. *Slaves no longer slaves* & *Rebels* no longer *rebels*."[2] The Army of the Potomac had been chastened by numerous defeats, but its resolve had not been broken. Mason explained the condition of his quarters in his first letter of the new year.

CAMP NEAR BELL PLAIN LANDING
OR WHITE OAK CHURCH VA
Jan[uary] 5th 1863

Dear Harriet

I received your letter yesterday morning. Was highly gratified to learn of your good health. I am enjoying the same great blessing. The rest of the Glover Boys ditto—except E[lijah] Stone & Geo[rge] Telfer. Elijah is rather slim though he is performing Guard duty today Geo[rge] is excused from all duty by the Surgeon. He ought to be discharged this is no place for him he ought to have known better than to enlist. Since I last wrote you our Reg[iment] has moved Camp about 100 rods we have constructed quite comfortable quarters. Perhaps a short discrtiption of my house or hovel would be interesting to you. Elbert Nye Oliver T Stiles H[obart] Bliss & I tent together. We first cut & split Oak & Pine slabs about 12 feet in length for the sides & 7 in length for the ends. These slabs are notched & fitted at the corners similar to log houses in Vt—after laying the slabs 4 in height we place our shelter tents (2 in number) on the top for a roof then plaster the crevices with mud we then have 2 extra pieces of tent to hang up at the ends. We then dug down about 2 ½ feet—throwing the dirt outside for banking. We then dug a small fire place in the side of the bank, then dug a small passage from the fire place outside of the tent, then build a chimney of pieces of wood 1 ½ feet in length laid up cob house fashion plastering the inside wall with mud to prevent its taking fire. The soil is so clayey that it soon burns very hard so that it dont cave in. Our bed is made of pine poles elevated about 2 feet from ground & covered with cedar brush, then spread rubber blankets & Woolen Blankets & overcoats over us using Knapsacks for Pillows, which makes a very good bed for a soldier. Never slept sweeter on feather bed. We have 2 short shelves in one corner where we keep our plates knives & forks tin cups can of sugar salt pepper &c (this we call our butt[e]ry). Just at the right we have a small table made of a cheese box cover which we use to write on. We have a 2 q[uar]t & 1 q[uar]t pail which we make Coffee in 2 frying pans to fry our meat & crackers in so you see we are quite well provided for. I hope we shant leave here at present. We have 2 drills each day Co[mpany] drill from 9 to 10 A.M. Battalion from 2 to 3 P.M. Dress Parade at 4. We are having very fine weather no snow. Nights seldom cold enough to freeze ground we have not had any snow since the first of last month, then had about 2 inches but it soon left us. The weather is quite warm today makes the Boys sweat to drill. I must now close hoping to live to see an honorable settlement of this war. Give my regards to your Mother & all inquiring friends

receive from your sincere lover
Dan

General Burnside, eager to redeem himself after his ignominious defeat at Fredericksburg, planned another winter offensive that he hoped would catch the Army of Northern Virginia by surprise. On January 20, Union forces began a march up the Rappahannock River on frozen roads, with the intent to cross the Rappahannock upstream of Fredericksburg (as would occur again in the spring during the Chancellorsville campaign) and attack Lee from the north and west. That night it began to rain, turning the roads into a quagmire of mud. The infamous "Mud March" thus marked the end of Burnside's command of the Army of the Potomac. Fred Kimball vividly described the misery of the Mud March in his diary entry for January 21:

> Last night it rained & the mud is *abundant*. It is the ruin of this expedition. Trains, artillery, wagons, pontoons & everything *stuck* in the mud. Our Brigade is ordered out to help a pontoon train. March through mud two miles & then stacked arms, unslung knapsacks & went to the relief of trains, *mules* & *men*. Fasten ropes to the wagons & a company would take hold & with the help of mules draw the pontoons through the mud. . . .

It rained *all the* time & we did not get back to camp until long after dark *hungry & tired* fellows & all covered with *mud* from *head to foot*. Clothes wet through. Patriotism was at a low ebb, the men were hard up.

When the Sixth Vermont was back in its winter quarters, Kimball again lamented, "I never saw patriotism run so low as when we got back to this camp. We were all jaded out and *nothing* was gained. This looks discouraging at times. We are willing to endure hardships & privations if it does any good but to see rebellion no nearer crushed is enough to make one at times almost discouraged."[3] Mason similarly expressed rare disillusionment and wrote to Harriet that he was "much disgusted with the manner the machine is handled." In his diary he simply stated, "Had a very hard march, mud very deep."

Camp near Bell Plains Va

Jan[uary] 29th 1863

Dear Harriet

Since I last wrote you the Army of the Potomac has made another grand raid got stuck in the mud & after a good deal of floundering whipping & tall scolding attended with quite a loss of mule flesh we have wallowed back to our old encampment much disgusted with the manner the machine is handled. Tuesday morning Jan[uary] 20th we marched with 3 days rations. We encamped near night in a piece of Pine woods having marched about 14 miles up the Rappahannock River we were about 2 miles from the River. We were much fatigued. We were ordered not to build large fires nor make any unnecessary noise. Wednesday we remained in Camp until about 2 oclock P.M. We were ordered to pack up ready to march (perhaps it would be well enough to say that it rained the night before all night consequently it was very muddy) we marched about a mile & half & then stacked arms & unslung knapsacks & then ordered to help Pontoon train through the mud which was awful deep the horses & mules were all jaded out & discouraged. We attached long ropes to them & then 30 or 40 men got hold & drew them about ¾ ths of a mile wheels axle deep in mire. We worked in this manner until dark.

We then slung knapsacks & marched back where we left a few hours before it had stormed occasionally all day so we were wet & completely daubed with mud. 12 & 14 horses were seen struggling to move a 6 lb cannon & after many unsuccessful efforts were unhitched & the gun left stuck in the mud. Horses & mules were left to die struggling in the mire broken waggons were very plenty. Thursday we were ordered to march but the order was countermanded & we did not—Friday morning early we started for the old Camp we arrived about 2 oclock much exhausted. We went into our old palace (as you term it) we found Alex Davis anxiously awaiting our arrival (he now tents with us). Yesterday & last night was very stormy much of the snow melted as fast as it fell yesterday but last night it increased so that this morning it was 8 inches deep. The Glover Boys are all well. I hope Josie wont get enamored after an old married man I guess the girls are getting hard up in Vt. I guess this war makes the young men scarce, but when the soldier boys get home the old married men will have to stand one side. I will now close hoping to meet you before many months

Dan

For the rest of the winter, the Vermont Brigade remained encamped outside of Fredericksburg. Almost daily Mason concluded his diary entries with "All quiet along the Rappahannock." Aside from drill, dress parades, picket and guard duty, and arms inspections, the men occupied themselves by writing letters, reading, smoking, playing backgammon and checkers, playing "football," singing, making "bone rings," and having snowball fights. It snowed frequently enough in Virginia that soldiers often noted engaging in this form of combat in their diary entries. Martin Warner Davis, for example, described such an incident on February 25: "Snowballed after supper and Sergt. Nye threw one that hit me in the eye which soon became purple."[4]

Boredom—and the coping mechanisms that accompanied it—were also a fact of camp life. On February 6 Mason wrote in his diary, "Nothing to do. Coffee and hard bread for supper, also butter and cheese. Dress parade as usual." He mentioned that he was surrounded by "vices" and "temptations," but told Harriet that just the thought of her kept him from succumbing to the "vices & evils which human flesh is heir to." Martin Warner Davis also prided himself in his avoidance of vice. On February 5 he noted, "Nothing new. Spent my time reading and the best I could, rather lonely time with nothing to do. Snowed in the AM, turned to rain in the PM. Looks like a heavy storm. I am sometimes tempted to play cards but I hope I shall resist even appearance of evil and not indulge in low language."[5] On February 20 Hobart Bliss, one of Mason's tentmates, wrote in his diary, "No drill. Went on fatigue. . . . Co. D all Drunk."[6] On March 8 Fred Kimball's diary entry indicated, "Some of our officers are having a *drink*. I don't delight in such times, yet they try to have me join—I spurn it." On March 29 Kimball again noted, "Drunkenness in camp. O deliver me from this baneful vice."[7]

CAMP NEAR BELL PLAINS VA
Feb[ruary] 19th 1863

Dear Harriet

Your letter bearing date Feb[ruary] 6th mailed the 10th came to hand this morning. It was due the last of last week consequently I had been anxiously awaiting its arrival. I learned from your letter that you were well which was highly gratifying. I began fear[ing] that you were sick the reason of your not writing. Consequently your letter was read with more eagerness if possible than usual. I am well & enjoying myself very well in the same old palace heretofore spoken of. . . . I am glad that I am single. It seems to me that a married man who has been blessed with little ones at least most of folks consider them a blessing I suppose we may as well look at them in that light, but, but, yes, we were all little squalling bits of humanity once. But what I was going to say was a married man must have a great many sad reflections concerning the dear ones at home. Perhaps you will think that I should have just as sad thought of home & near friends as a married man but I fail to see it—I am free & independent no one leaning on me for support. Yet I hope to live & see the day when a certain young Miss will look to me for support & protection. May our thoughts & actions cooperate in all that we undertake thereby insuring to us a life of happiness. I am now a soldier surrounded by all the vices & evils which human flesh is heir to. Yet I hope to retain my virtues (though they are small) so that I may be worthy of your love. I feel thankful that I have something to prompt me to do right when so many temptations are thrown around me. . . . I dont see much prospect of a move at present on account of the mud. I must now close. Please remember me to all friends

yours in haste
Dan

On March 2 Mason noted in his diary, "Very pleasant, no drill. Reg[imen]t have a game [of] foot ball. . . . Pitched quoits, dress parade as usual. Coffee & hard bread for supper—all quiet along line." The next day: "Brigade reviewed by Gen. Howe at 1 o'clock & 30 minutes dress parade as usual. Reg[imen]t plays football & quoits, drew soft bread." And the next: "Pleasant, cold & windy. Cleaned gun & equipment. Brigade drill from 2–4 pm. Dress parade as usual. Company drew soft bread, pitched quoits." An activity noted almost daily in Mason's diary, "pitching quoits" involved throwing a metal ring—often a horseshoe—at an iron stake.

While Mason pitched quoits on March 3, Congress authorized the first wartime draft in U.S. history. The draft allowed a conscript to avoid service by paying a $300 commutation fee or hiring a substitute. More than ever, class conflict threatened to destabilize the war effort. The veterans of the Sixth Vermont had no stomach for anyone who expressed any criticism of the draft or attempted to avoid it in any way. Resistance to the draft in whatever form was equated with disloyalty and treason. The officers of the Sixth Vermont wrote a series of resolutions and sent them to the Vermont press condemning "Copperheads," the faction of the Democratic Party that was most critical of the draft:

> *Resolved*,—That we regard the men who have announced by resolution their intention of refusing to furnish men or means for the prosecution of the war, as traitors to their country, deserving the execration of all patriotic citizens in the present, and worthy [of] a monument for shame for coming generations.
>
> *Resolved*,—That we have every confidence in the honesty, integrity, and patriotism of the President of the United States, and are in favor of

> any and every measure that in his opinion, under the constitution, may tend in the remotest degree to the suppression of this rebellion, including the celebrated proclamation of Jan. 1, 1863.
>
> *Resolved*,—That we are in favor of a vigorous prosecution of the war until our flag floats free; North, East, South, and West; and for this purpose we pledge to each other as our fathers of old "our lives, our fortunes, and our sacred honor;" determined to sacrifice everything rather than live to behold the broken and dishonored fragments of a once glorious union.[8]

Mason clearly showed all of these same sentiments, as he penned a lengthy letter to the editor on March 9 rebuking "traitors" in very strong terms. He began by chronicling all of the engagements that had thinned the ranks of the Vermont Brigade, in addition to losses from disease, then continued,

> I imagine there will be some chafing and foaming; also some right smart attempts to skedaddle. Some doubtless will talk of showing resistance, but I guess I wouldn't tamper with Uncle Samuel's authority very much—no, if I was in your place I would come—well, yes, indeed I'd come. . . .
>
> In regard to the change of army commanders I have but little to say. Time will tell whether Gen. Hooker is more capable of running the machine than the two that preceded him or not. I wish him good success; But I consider Gen. Geo. B. McClellan the smartest and the most capable of handling so large an army. I know he is accused of being a traitor and acting in disobedience to orders; But I shall not believe it until it is proved and substantiated. I speak the minds of nine-tenths of the soldiers that come within the extent of my knowledge in regard to Gen. McClellan. As for Gen. Burnside, his career was short and unsuccessful, and needs no comment.
>
> One word to Mr. Conscript and I will close. Allow me as a friend who feels a deep interest in your future welfare, to give you a little wholesome advice.—Pray, don't show any resistance to Uncle Samuel when he bids you come. Don't play any of your jackass games by settling into the breaching and refusing to come, for you have played these games long enough; It will only make a bad matter worse. . . . March boldly to the

field of battle and make yourself conspicuous with your shooting-iron.— Show yourself valiant and courageous, and in the course of time you will in a great measure wipe out the shame and disgrace that you have so needlessly brought down upon your own head.

Perhaps some of your readers may think I am rash and do not take a candid view of the matter. Doubtless some, yes, many flatter themselves that they have good reason for not enlisting; But in nine cases out of ten the excuse rendered will not bear investigation. I will admit that there are cases where it seems very hard—yes, almost inhuman for a man to lay his life upon the altar of his country. Perhaps an aged mother leans upon an only son for support, where a family of little ones look to him for daily bread. But Uncle Sam pays good wages and the working class can earn more here than at home. Perhaps some will not relish my sayings in regard to traitors in Vermont. In reply to any who endeavor to justify themselves in regard to this matter I will use brevity—if the shoe fits anyone let him wear it—if not, all right. I remain your ob't serv't.

Dan Mason[9]

{ 6 }

"You Cannot Imagine the Thrill of Joy" (Spring 1863)

On March 26 Mason noted in his diary, "Received paper from A. A. Earle," the editor of the *Orleans Independent Standard*, perhaps in appreciation of Mason's recent letter to the paper. While Mason and the men of the Sixth Vermont railed against "copperheads," the Democratic Party argued that it was the one remaining national party that was the *real* unionist party. Democrats accused the "Abolitionist Republicans" of seeking disunion through "unconstitutional" policies such as conscription. The Republican press engaged in a hotly contested war of words with the Democratic press throughout the war, including in Vermont, but especially during the early months of 1863. In response to the Conscription Act, the Democratic *Burlington Weekly Sentinel* opined,

> We need not say that the people will indignantly repel all such attempts at destroying their most cherished rights. For ourselves we have but to say that if to render fealty to the constitution before the administration, if to condemn the illegal and tyrannical acts of public officers, if to prefer white men to negroes, to yearn for and to esteem the restoration of the old "Union as it was and the Constitution as it is" as of more importance than the perpetuity of the republican party—if to so think, say and act, entitle us to be stigmatized as copperheads and traitors, then do we cordially accept the epithet. It carries with it honor, not ignominy.[1]

In this context Mason further elaborated on his disdain for "traitors" in his next letter to Harriet, even saying that he found Confederate rebels to be more "honorable" than "Northern traitors." He also continued to strongly defend McClellan, months after his removal from command. In addition, Mason was distraught that he hadn't received a letter from Harriet in response to his last one and said, "Have anxiously looked in vain for an answer." A delayed response from a loved one back home was often agonizing and could portend trouble, including illness or even a loss of romantic interest. Soldiers often assumed the worst. Fred Kimball was similarly anguished over not having heard from his sweetheart in weeks. A sampling of diary entries reveals his state of mind:

> March 15. Write Sue. Four long weeks have passed since the date of her last to me. Why don't I hear from my darling girl? Is she sick or what can be the trouble? In my anxiety I fancy every evil. I must hear from her soon.
>
> March 16. Ah! No letter from Sue this mail. What shall I do?
>
> March 17. No letter this mail.
>
> March 20. No mail to get today. Remain on the reserve. Oh my darling Sue. Is there still not time?
>
> March 21. Thank heaven I get a letter from *Sue*.[2]

Mason broke his usual policy of waiting for a reply from Harriet before penning another letter.

CAMP NEAR BELL PLAINS VA
March 25th, 1863

Dear Harriet

I take this opportunity to write you a few lines to inform you of my whereabouts health &c. . . . I dont see much prospect of moving from here at present. We have had good deal more snow here this winter than last. We have had several batches of 6 or 8 inches stopping with us several days & then disappearing leaving slathers of mud to use an army phrase. . . . Doubtless before you receive this you will be somewhat surprised to see a letter in the Standard with my signature attached. I guess you will think I am down on Conscripts. Well I confess that I am ugly enough to hector them as much as possible especially those traitors that have laid back & breathed forth their poison treason thereby making themselves our worst enemies. I honor & respect a traitor in the rebel lines because I believe in most cases they are sincere yet blinded by their leaders, but cursed be the Northern traitors. I dont wish to be understood that I am at all friendly to Southern traitors, no, I say whip them until they will return to their allegiance, but of the two I consider them the most honorable men. I must now close hoping to hear from you soon give my regards to your Mother & all inquiring friends.

Yours with much love
Dan

Still in winter quarters, Mason focused much of his next letter commenting on courtships back home, poking fun at a man for growing "homely" as a result of marriage and suggesting that he would try to return home to attend other weddings with Harriet. He explained that he hadn't been to a wedding in a long time because there were none to attend in Virginia: "White girls are very scarce the colored ladies are quite plenty but I dont real[l]y fancy the color."

Camp near Bell Plain Va
April 5th 1863

Dear Harriet

Yours of the 28th came to hand this morning & was a very welcome visitor it was read with an unusual degree of interest. . . . I hope there will not be another as long period elapse without hearing from you during my term of service. . . . Capt[ain] Dwinell arrived from Vt last Sunday. Lieut[enant] Kimball comes over to see us quite often. . . . I think you are getting quite fleshy you used to laugh at me last winter when I wrote you my weight so it is no more than fair that I should do the same if you keep on you will be as fleshy as Jane Emerson or Aunt Mary Strong but you must not be offended at what I dont say. I dont see why Jack Bean should grow hom[e]ly so fast after getting married. I did not think it had that effect but I am not posted in regard to such things. . . . I have not attended a wedding for a long time we dont have any in Va. White girls are very scarce the colored ladies are quite plenty but I dont real[l]y fancy the color. I dont think we shall move very soon yet we are liable to leave on short notice. I guess you will think the letters are coming thicker & faster but we must make up lost time. I shall expect an answer for every one that I write. I hope this will find you enjoying yourself & growing fleshy. Remember me to all the friends

yours with love
Dan

Three weeks later Mason wrote to Harriet on his twenty-fourth birthday and commented on the "thrill of joy" that he felt upon receiving her letters. Fred Kimball's thoughts were also occupied by home. On April 12 he wrote, "I love to dwell on thoughts of my native land and its happy scenes. Thoughts of *my devoted Sue* are foremost in my mind. I grasp my pen & write her. May God spare us to meet again & live happy in each others *love*. For this my darling girl I pray."[3] The Army of the Potomac was about to leave its winter quarters to open its spring campaign. Mason admitted that "I dont see the prospect of peace being restored in a few months as favorable as one year ago," though he reassured himself that victory would ultimately come.

Camp near Bell Plain Va
Apr[il] 26th 1863

Dear Harriet

Yours of the 15th came to hand this eve & I need not tell you it was read & reread with much pleasure indeed it was a very welcome visitor. I dont think it is possible for you & the rest of the friends to realize how welcome a letter from a dear one at home is to a soldier far from his dearest one you cannot imagine the thrill of joy that courses through my veins when I receive a letter mailed at West Glover. It seems yes I almost imagine that I am in your presence conversing with you, but alas I soon awake from my visions of fancy & find myself in the army trying to blot out a wicked rebellion. I dont see the prospect of peace being restored in a few months as favorable as one year ago, yet I am not discouraged we shall conquer in the end it will take some time but we have so much greater resources & right on our side we must be victorious. Some doubtless are discouraged & think we have not accomplished anything but we have gained a great many points of importance in the west & south & western Virginia. I have about made up my mind to serve my term of enlistment in the army. I am glad that I enlisted when I did for I should hate to come as a conscript. I am going to content myself looking on the sunny side knowing that I am contending for the right. I admire your patriotism & the cheerful tone of your letters. Your words give me courage & make me valiant & determined. I know life is uncertain & that war is dangerous business (to use a common term) but I have faith to believe that I shall be preserved & live to meet you & grasp you by the hand & call you mine what a happy time it will be when peace shall be reenshrined & we shall be bound in the sweet ties of matrimony 2 in one. I hope you dont give yourself any unnecessary trouble about me for trouble comes fast enough without borrowing it. . . . Our Corps was reviewed by President Lincoln Gen[eral]s Hooker & Sedgwick the 8th of Apr[il] near Falmouth. We are now under marching orders & have been for near 10 days. I dont see any more signs of moving now than a week ago but we are liable to go most any time. . . . The boys have all gone to bed & I must seek rest on my cedar brush wrapped in my blanket

I remain your sincere lover

Dan

(Monday morning Apr[il] 27th 1863 I am 24 y[ear]s old today. Write soon & all news)

Mason described being reviewed by President Lincoln and the Union high command on April 8. Lincoln was close enough that Martin Warner Davis wrote on April 8, "Saw the President Lincoln, Genl Howe, etc. Very interesting time. The President looked careworn."[4]

On April 23 Mason recorded in his diary that he had "Potatoes for breakfast, Beans for dinner. Played back gammon with Lieut. Kimball & Sergt. Stiles. . . . All quiet along lines, rainy night." Oliver Stiles, Mason's tentmate, reported:

We have had balloon reconnaissance almost daily now for some time period it has made two ascensions to-day, and we expect to start tomorrow morning. All sorts of rumors are afloat to-day concerning the course we are to take. Some say we are going to cross the Rappahannock below, and some say we are going to cross above, and others say we are going to Charleston, S.C., but another class, of which I am a member, say that we do not know anything about where we are going. One thing we do know, and that is this, Gen. Hooker knows where we are going, or at least where we are to start to go, and I believe that this army has enough confidence in him so they are all willing to follow him in his first attempt.[5]

Fred Kimball was more guarded in his assessment of Hooker: "We look forward with high hopes to the time when Gen. Hooker will do something decisive for our cause; Yet I am not in favor of applauding him to the skies before he has achieved the glory. This is too much the case with the American nation. They will cover a man with glory as soon as he has gained a high position, before he has distinguished himself, or won a name; and then if he makes a misstep or a failure, he is trampled to the lowest depths."[6]

Finally, on April 28, the spring campaign began. The Vermont Brigade moved out of camp with eight days' rations: three in their haversacks and five in their knapsacks, a heavy, cumbersome load for an individual soldier to carry. Mason wrote in his diary that day, "Fell in stacked arms. . . . Marched about 7 miles encamped near Falmouth. Ordered to have no fires our 8 days rations hung down heavy." Martin Warner Davis expressed the anxiety about the coming campaign in his diary entry for April 28: "No jokes allowed. We are all in good spirits. There Is a dread to enter the conflict yet we are ready and with God I believe we shall be victorious."[7]

Hooker took the main body of the Army of the Potomac on a long march up the Rappahannock River and crossed twenty-seven miles above Fredericksburg. Meanwhile, the VI Corps, now commanded by General John Sedgewick, remained at Fredericksburg, with the intention of crossing the Rappahannock there as a diversionary force. While Hooker and Lee clashed at the Battle of Chancellorsville, which resulted in yet another humiliating defeat, Sedgewick sent his corps across the Rappahannock on the same night that Stonewell Jackson was mortally wounded by friendly fire. The following morning the VI Corps assaulted Marye's Heights with far greater success than Union forces did the previous December. The VI

Corps pursued the fleeing rebels toward Salem Church but, owing to a lack of support from Hooker, had to retreat across the Rappahannock, the Vermont Brigade covering the corps' crossing at Banks's Ford, four miles above Fredericksburg.

Mason and the other men of the Sixth Vermont were hotly engaged in this fighting. Mason's descriptions of combat were often detailed and at times graphic, but one wonders if his letters—or any letters by any soldiers, for that matter—could possibly describe the physical and psychological effects of participating in a battle: the deafening noise, fear, rage, adrenaline, bloodlust, uncertainty about whether one would survive, demoralization that accompanied defeat, exhilaration that accompanied victory, or the myriad other emotions and experiences that are probably impossible to understand for those who have never been in combat. Mason did say that when the opportunity to open fire on the rebel ranks came at Banks's Ford, his regiment "poured into them then charged on them yelling hideously." Combat-induced hysteria has been well documented by Civil War historians. The historian James McPherson noted, "This physiological response to emotional trauma vastly increases the body's capacity for 'flight or fight.' The more extreme the stress the greater the amount of adrenalin and norepinephrine secreted by the adrenal glands, giving an individual almost superhuman strength and agility. The most stressful situation imaginable is combat. . . . Another term for this state of super-adrenalized fury is 'combat narcosis,' because its effect 'acts almost like a hallucinogenic drug.'"[8] When Mason and the men of the Sixth Vermont charged the enemy, "yelling hideously," all one can do is imagine the fury of that particular moment. It would be difficult, if not impossible, for any Civil War soldier to fully capture that experience in words to a loved one back home, nor would any soldier necessarily want to even try. Fred Kimball wrote, "The greatest anxiety I know must prevail at home, to hear of the fearful ordeal through which we have passed, and I feel it will be vain for me to attempt to portray in any degree the fearful struggle; it beggars language to tell. . . . I can scarce believe my own senses."[9] Captain M. W. Davis of the Sixth Vermont tried to capture the scene as best he could in the present tense: "The rebels are now within 4 rods of us; we can see their heads and their filthy rag; our bayonets are fixed; *Now Sixth Vermont is your time!* the order, 'Arise, fire, and charge!' They fly! They fly! We have saved the field! The Louisiana Tigers that were never driven before are flying before the Vermont Brigade." Despite his dramatic literary retelling of the scene at Banks's Ford, even Davis admitted, "No one can describe it as it is, or have but little idea of what a battle is until he is engaged."[10]

CAMP IN FIELD 2 MILES ABOVE FALMOUTH VA
May 7th 1863

Dear Harriet

As the 6th Vt Reg[imen]t has done some right smart fighting within a few days for which we receive much praise & thinking you might feel anxious to hear from me I seat myself in my little shelter tent for the purpose of giving you a few particulars in regard to the Battle. April 28th we marched toward Falmouth with 8 days rations in Haversack & Knapsack which with blankets under clothing guns & acoutriments &c made a heavy load we encamped about a mile from the Rappahannock just below F[redericks]burg. We were ordered to build no fires. During the night the Pontoon Bridges were carried down to the river by hand so as to not give the enemy notice of our approach. About daylight one Brigade was carried across in the Pontoon Boats & charged on the rebel Pickets taking 150 prisoners 1 Major 1 Lieut[enant] it was a perfect surprise. The Engineer Corps then proceeded to lay across the Pontoon Bridges the same place that we crossed last Dec[ember]. . . . Gen[eral] Hooker took the rest of the army several miles up the river leaving only the 6th Corps & 3d Divis[ion] of the 2d Corps (we are in the 6th Corps) at this crossing. We did not cross until Saturday night. Sunday morning we were rounded up & fell in expecting to charge on the heights under cover of darkness we did not move until daylight—we then marched up toward F[redericks]burg when within half mile of the city we halted in the road & laid until about noon our cannon was constantly playing shell on to their earth works the enemy returned the compliments with much spirit. About noon we were suddenly called into line & ordered to unsling Knapsacks & pile them up. We then charged on the earth works back of the city. We had to march about a mile across an open field the enemies cannon rained a shower of shell on us they burst all around us wounding 8 men & killing Lt Col Hales horse under him (our former Capt[ain]) the reason of our loss being so small was we kept closed up & in good line many other Reg[imen]ts suffered much more because they scattered so thereby covering much more space. Still we pressed on not a man faltered the 6th Reg[imen]t was the 2d one to place its colors on the breast work we took 5 cannon at this place & on our left they took 10 more it was a brilliant affair the boys felt well. As I have not time nor space to give many particulars, our co[mpany] had but 2 slightly wounded Geo[rge] Partridge & W[illia]m Mitchell the one that used to work for your father. Mon[day] near night the rebs having been reinforced made a desperate attack in front of our Brig[ade]. Our reg[imen]t was placed on the left of a Battery to support it—we laid behind a swell of ground hid from the rebs view several reg[imen]ts were in front of us & fought bravely for a while but the rebs came on in such force that they were obliged to give way. Some however broke & disgraced themselves more scart than hurt—the 26th New Jersey in particular 9 mo[nth]s men who were connected with our Brigade at Hagerstown. They broke & run like sheep over our reg[imen]t. On came the masses of Gray backs sure of victory they intended to take the Battery which we were supporting. We were ordered to lay low until they were close on to us then rise fire a volley & charge bayonet. Just as they came over the brow of the hill waving their Battle flag triumphantly when they got within about 4 rods we rose & poured into them then charged on them yelling hideously they broke & run for dear life we pursued them about 100 rods loading & firing into them fast as we could. After charging until the enemy was fairly broken we took 200 prisoners among which was 21 officers 1 Brig[adier] Gen[eral] 3 Col[onel]s 1 Maj[or]. This was just what the 6th did. The other Vt Reg[iment]s took some prisoners. Our Co[mpany] lost 1-2 wounded none killed Hobart Bliss was severely wounded in left shoulder. Soon as it was dark our whole force fell back to the river. Our Pioneers brought Hobart far as they could & left him as the reb skirmishers were close on to them. I fear he is mortally wounded but hope he will turn up all right some time. It seemed hard to leave him in the hands of the enemy but—such is war. Our Corps crossed the river safely during the night. Our Reg[imen]t has the praise of saving the whole Corps if our reg[imen]t had broke the whole of us would have been driven to the river & captured I must now close. I should be glad to write more

from your lover Dan

The reason of our army falling back was that the rebs had heavy reinforcements. Today we marched back to old Camp near Bell Plain Hookers whole army fell back next day after we did. Write soon

Although the Chancellorsville campaign as a whole was an utter defeat for the Army of the Potomac, the Vermont Brigade, including the Sixth Vermont, was singled out for praise for its actions in averting an even worse disaster. After Hooker's defeat at Chancellorsville, Lee saw an opportunity to crush the Union VI Corps and dispatched two divisions for this purpose. The Vermont Brigade was positioned on the left of the Union line at Banks's Ford. General Albion Howe, commanding the division to which the Vermont Brigade was attached, said, "The enemy, apparently thinking our left was giving way, rallied and confidently advanced until they brought their flank opposite the woods in which was placed those sterling soldiers of the Vermont Brigade. At the favorable moment, this brigade opened its fire upon the flank of the enemy's columns. . . . The effect of this flank and direct fire upon the enemy was most marked."[11] After the initial attacks on the other regiments of the Vermont Brigade failed, Lewis Grant, who commanded the Vermont Brigade, reported,

> At this time the enemy had a large force in front of our entire line, attempting with desperate vigor to force or turn it; but the Vermont regiments remained firm and unbroken, closely hugging the crest and literally presenting a wall of fire. Baffled in his efforts to break our line, and perceiving that the battery on our right had changed its position, the enemy rallied, and made an attempt to turn our right, but the Sixth Vermont was there. The enemy rushed desperately forward, and nearly gained the crest immediately in front of the Sixth Vermont, when that regiment suddenly rose and gave him a terrible volley, and immediately charged upon him down the slope through the ravine and onto the crest which had previously been held by the Third Brigade. . . . The enemy was utterly routed. The masses (there seemed to be no distinction of

the enemy's lines at this time) gave way in great confusion, and many of them were taken prisoners. The ground in front of the Second and Third Vermont, and the ravine through which the Sixth Vermont and Twenty-sixth New Jersey charged, were literally covered with the rebel dead and wounded.[12]

Colonel Elisha Barney, who commanded the Sixth Vermont, said that the "intrepidity and gallantry of both officers and men" at the Battle of Second Fredericksburg and the Battle of Banks's Ford "are deserving of the highest praise."[13] Hobart Bliss, Mason's tentmate, was left wounded on the battlefield. Mason said, "I fear he is mortally wounded but hope he will turn up all right some time. It seemed hard to leave him in the hands of the enemy but—such is war." Describing a series of events that nearly defies belief, Bliss recorded the following entries in his diary:

May 4. Pleasant. Firing along the lines. No rebs in sight. Formed a line behind the first MD Battery. Fight at sunset. Drove rebs. Wounded & layed on the field all night.

May 5. Layed on the field all day. Some Georgia boys fixed a shelter for me. Rained at night wet & cold & about played out all for the Union.

May 6. Cold & rainy. Laid all day. The Hospital Steward of the 26th Jersey came to see us. Suffered enough to put down this rebellion.

May 7. Rainy laid all night & then carried to a farm cold & uncomfortable.

May 8. Cold. A Sergeon from the 5th was here. He and a Reb serg[eon] cut off some limbs.

May 9. Pleasant but cold. Crawled out doors. Our Serg[eon]s came over & dressed our w[oun]ds felt better did not rest well.

May 10. Warm & pleasant. More help came from over the River also rations. Rebs come from over thick as bees.

May 11. Hot & sultry. Arm pained me some. Took morphine.

May 12. Pleasant got some soft bread. Stretcher came over for us. Went over the river slept in the ambulance.

May 13. Warm. Got ready & started. Went 10 miles to Potomac Creek. Tired but glad to get on a bed.

May 14. Rainy & windy. Band played. The 3d [regiment] Chaplain here. . . . Got a letter from Arabel with the news of Father's death!

May 15. Pleasant. Went over to the station. Tired slept well.

May 16. Warm. Wound pained me some. Walked a piece.

May 17. Very lonesome.[14]

The first page of Bliss's diary stated, "If it should be my fate to fall on the battlefield or die in a Hospital any one finding this would oblige me by sending it Mr. Stephen G. Bliss, Glover, VT." As it turned out though, Stephen Bliss died on May 2 at forty-six years old, two days before Hobart was wounded at Banks's Ford. His obituary stated that "the deceased was widely known as a teacher of sacred music, and was greatly beloved for his amiable qualities as a teacher, and correct deportment as a Christian and citizen of the town."[15] Five days after the Battle of Banks's Ford, Captain M. W. Davis wrote, "Poor Bliss I fear will not survive his wound, however I hope he will; he fell into the hands of the rebels, so we know nothing how he is. I heard yesterday that his father was dead; what an afflicted family!"[16] Bliss was paroled on May 16, then over a month later, on June 22, he boarded a train and started for home, where he spent three months convalescing in hospitals in Brattleboro, then Burlington. While at Burlington he made excursions to Plattsburgh, New York, to see the circus, fished on Shelburne Pond, and went boating on Lake Champlain. Finally, on September 21, Bliss arrived home in Glover. Two days later he noted that there was "a hard frost last night—did not sleep very well."[17]

The defeat at Chancellorsville was perhaps the bleakest one yet for the Union. Captain Martin Warner Davis immediately recognized that the situation was not bright. As the VI Corps retreated across the Rappahannock River after such hard fighting, he wondered in his diary, "Two nights in succession we did not sleep any. . . . What this is going to amount to I cannot tell. Not favorable I fear." The next day he added, "Hooker is falling back across the river. Looks rather discouraging yet I hope for the best."[18] When Lincoln heard the news of Hooker's defeat, he lamented, "My God! My God! What will the country say?" The *Orleans Independent Standard* praised the actions of the Vermont troops but offered a withering critique of the overall Union war effort:

> Well, the army is back again, safe and sound, and now—what next? When shall the army of the Potomac take its next whipping? And where shall it take it? There is no need to ask, how shall it take it? For reasoning from the past sad history of that army we should say that it has to go but a little ways into Virginia, meet the half starved and ragged rebels anywhere, and it will get it speedily. Such has been its fate since it was organized, from the first Bull Run battle to the second battle of Fredericksburg and Chancellorsville. Its commanders—no matter what were their laurels, nor in how high esteem they were held before their commands were given them, have all met with much the same fate, been repeatedly drubbed, defeated, retreated, and removed. McDowell of Bull Run fame, copperhead McClellan, the digger of ditches, brave braggart Pope, unfortunate Burnside, have all been shorn of their strength: and last, and greatest of all, we now have Hooker who is smarting under his first reverse. The army of which he is chief is two years old, and it has had five generals, all of whom have been defeated, while not one of them has gained a substantial victory.[19]

For the next month after Chancellorsville, both armies licked their wounds and awaited each other's next move. Fred Kimball was among the wounded, though he was spared a more grievous wound by a stroke of luck: "I was hit by a rifle ball upon my belt plate & had it not been for that I should be in eternity. I can but thank my heavenly father for sparing me in that fearful charge. God kept me safe and I will praise Him. O Father of heaven I thank thee. . . . Our army had to fall back over the river for want of reinforcements. The day they charged upon us we lost many a brave & noble soldier. . . . I want to avenge their death, the wrong we suffer for by traitors." Mason told Harriet that "Fred [Kimball] was hit in the last fight on the brass clasp of his sword belt which dented it glancing off & hitting his arm not breaking the skin but making a soreness." When it became apparent that the Army of the Potomac was once again in retreat, Kimball sighed, "May God save our country. I am not at all discouraged yet, still it looks dark if this movement has to be given up. Corp. Bliss . . . was hit in the shoulder. . . . Our country-May God save it."[20] Another account of Kimball's wounding provides a harrowing account of the fight at Banks's Ford:

> His belt plate turned a minie ball and saved his life, but the glancing ball wounded him slightly in the arm. The regiment captured over four hundred prisoners in this charge. One Confederate captain, who had been shot through the face, surrendered his sword to Captain Kimball, together with the remnant of his company, who then threw down their muskets, and being placed in the charge of two or three privates, were ordered to the rear. Captain Kimball had only turned to go forward, when a rebel, who had surrendered, picked up a gun which was lying on the ground, and was in the very act of shooting him, when the movement was seen by Sergeant Cleveland of his company, who, with the quickness of thought, drew his gun upon the rebel and shot him dead. Thus was Captain Kimball's life twice almost miraculously saved during that one engagement.[21]

On June 1 Mason wrote to Harriet without much news to report, but he offered a sharp rebuke of a fellow soldier in Company D, Stephen Baxter, whom he often singled out for criticism, although he warned Harriet, "You must not tell this to any one for if it should get to his folks they would be awful mad at me." On June 5 the Vermont Brigade crossed the Rappahannock River for a third time. Lee had begun marching north again on June 3, though his intentions were not yet known to Hooker, so the brigade's movement across the Rappahannock was part of a broader effort to determine the enemy's whereabouts and strength. What followed was a sharp skirmish along the banks of the Rappahannock, but nothing as serious as the two previous Union attempts to occupy Fredericksburg. Mason described the simultaneous hostility and fraternization that often occurred between pickets and skirmishers. He also mentioned Hobart Bliss's parole and visitations to the Sixth Vermont.

Camp in the field near Falmouth Va
June 9th 1863

Dear Harriet

Yours of the 1st came to hand last night was perused with much satisfaction &c &c. Since I last wrote you our Division has crossed the Rappahannock took a position & are now throwing up fortifications. . . . Saturday morning our Reg[imen]t went on to the skirmish line. The rebs were very plenty a short way off soon after we got the line established the rebs advanced on us & we poured into them which made them lay low. After some sharp firing both sides seemed willing to stop firing & there was not much firing in front of us the remainder of the day. On our left they were more hostile & kept popping. In the Afternoon our Boys would stand up & salute the reb skirmishers by waving the hand or swinging cap the rebs would return the compliment. . . . Our boys would take up Canteens & drink the rebs would do the same making motions that they were drinking each others health. Such is war 1 hour we are fighting striving to kill each other the next hour perhaps making friendly salutes at a distance many of the reb prisoners when taken will extend the hand of friendship & crack jokes with our men, who but a short time before were engaged in deadly strife. Our Reg[imen]t lost 4 killed & 13 wounded our Co[mpany] lost 2 wounded Hazen Wood & Dana Cook. Cook is [a] Glover boy. A spent ball hit him in the shoulder bruising & dislocating it not entering the flesh. The rest of the G[lover] boys are all right. Hobart Bliss was up to our old Camp twice to see us he was doing finely he was paroled & our Ambulances were allowed to cross the river & get the wounded a few days after the fight. Sat[urday] night we were relieved on the skirmish line Sun[day] night our Brigade was relieved & we recrossed the river our men throw up breastworks every night & I judge the intention is to keep a fast hold on the other side so to keep the rebs from drawing away troops to reinforce at Vicksburg. I must now close. I dont know if my looks have changed much since I left you I am certain that my love has not & I am quite certain that you remain the same loving Harriet, true blue

Dan

On June 12 Mason "Bathed in the Rappahannock River." The next day at 9 p.m., the brigade left Fredericksburg and marched until 2 a.m. When it became clear that Lee's intention was to attempt a second invasion of the North, the Vermont Brigade left its position on the Rappahannock River and began a march northward, along with the Army of the Potomac, which shadowed the Army of Northern Virginia and kept itself between Lee and Washington. Mason wrote that he was marching to some "unknown point," while enduring long marches in hot, dusty conditions. The next several weeks brought little relief. On June 14 Mason wrote in his diary, "Marched about 9 in eve. Marched all night. Very tiresome march." The next morning: "Warm & pleasant, crossed Aquia River this morning. March to Dumfries extremely warm. Great many fell out nearly dead with heat. Very dusty. Regt. very small when we got into camp." Martin Warner Davis was also exhausted and dispirited. He noted on June 15, "Had the hardest march we ever experienced. It was a shame the way they marched us. A great many fell out. . . . Very very hot."[22]

Camp most anywhere, Bradley Va
June 24th, 1863

Dear Harriet

Since I last wrote you the army of the Potomac has changed base or in other words fell back in the vicinity of Manassas Fairfax &c. After holding & fortifying our position on the south side of the Rappahannock for about a week, we evacuated in the night & marched in the direction of Washington after several days hard dusty marching we reached Wolf Run shoals on the Occoquan River where we saw the 14th Vt Reg[imen]t. . . . We passed over the outskirts of the Old Bull Run Battle field yesterday morning our Reg[imen]t left Camp at Bristoe with 3 days rations in haversack for some unknown point. . . . We are having a fine time the weather is pleasant & the tame Cherries which grow spontaneously by the road side & are now ripe suffer exceedingly. We buy some warm biscuit[s] Milk hoe cakes &c of the citizens. I dont patronize them near as much as some but occasionally get a few eatables for a rarity. I bought a Canteen of Milk for 20 c[en]ts this morning. I have known the boys to pay 25 c[en]ts. A canteen holds 3 pints. I dare-say your father would be glad to sell all of his Milk at that rate. Warm biscuits not very large 10 for 25 c[en]ts. I had a good breakfast of crackers & Milk & Cherry Sauce. I guess you will think it was a queer breakfast—we dont usually eat plum sauce with bread & milk at home but I got my sauce stewed before I knew that I could get the milk so I thought I must eat them & make sure of them. I guess you would laugh to see us cook & see us seated around on knapsacks boxes &c in the shade of some tree partaking of our choice viands consisting of fried Hard Bread Pork & Coffee which are dainties for an epicure. I am well the rest of the Glover Boys ditto. I rẹceived your letter of the 15th a few days since. I think the prospect is quite good for us to stay our term of enlistment & I console myself with the thought that as each day expires I have one the less to serve. When at home I used to have some sad thoughts in regard to the flight of time, but here I can fully coincide with the Psalmest—"Fly swifter round ye wheels of time & bring the welcome day" when I shall return to my dear friends and home

from your lover Dan

{ 7 }

"It Begins to Look Like Putting Down Rebellion" (Summer 1863)

The marching that the Vermont Brigade did since leaving Fredericksburg was trivial compared to the marching that was to come. On June 27 Mason wrote, "Crossed the Potomac at Edward's Ferry on Pontoon Bridges. Near noon encamped near river. Bathed in Canal." In the days leading up to the Battle of Gettysburg, the Vermont Brigade was pushed at a relentless pace, averaging over twenty miles a day. On June 29 Martin Warner Davis wrote, "Marched 30 miles, the hardest march we ever saw. A negro came to us." The next day he wrote, "We have done some very hard marching, and it has been shamefully conducted, not [stopping] long enough to make coffee until 2 P.M. Men march very well. Pass through a beautiful country." Two days later, on July 2, the brigade made its most famous march to arrive on the battlefield late on the second day of the fight. Davis wrote, "Was on the march at daylight, stoped at Union Mills to get breakfast, had hardly time to drink our coffee before we had to march. It is now 6 P.M. We have marched nearly 30 miles since midnight, no sleep. We are near Geyettsburg. They are firing rapidly. I do not want to go in tonight nevertheless I am ready to if necessary. We are very tired, but got quiet, moved on to the line, got ready to lie down at 10 P.M."[1]

Mason's diary entries during that week attest to the rigors of the march toward Gettysburg. Marches often began during the middle of the night and continued throughout the following day:

> June 28. Cloudy marched at 5 o'clock, reveille at 3 marched through Barnsville. People just going to church. Stopped & took dinner half a mile beyond village. Marched by way of Hyattstown. Encamped 2 miles beyond. Hooker reported resigned.

June 29. Cloudy. Reveille at 3 ¼ o'clock am. Marched . . . through New Market, Ridgeville, Mount Airy . . . distance 27 miles.

June 30. Cloudy & showery. . . . Encamped near Manchester. Had hard days march. . . . Great times eating cherries.

July 1. Cloudy went out & bought 2 cherry pies 25¢ each. Marched near midnight.

July 2. Cloudy marched on turnpike leading to Gettysburg. Arrived there near night. Hard fighting going our Brig. as Reserve. Saw many wounded our men drove the rebs & held the ground taking many prisoners.

July 3. Cloudy fell in under arms at daylight. Terrible cannonading near noon. Our men broke the enemies center. Took 5000 prisoners.

July 4. Pleasant quite warm, thunder showers last night. All quiet along line as yet. Heavy shower near night. No fighting today except occasional shot from either side.

July 5. Rainy had a very wet night. Marched about 8 o'clock. The rebs left last night. Engaged rear guard 2 or 3 times during day. Rebs left all their wounded & many tents. We passed 12 Hospitals full.

In the end the Vermont Brigade was not engaged at Gettysburg, although its arrival on the field along with the rest of the VI Corps at the close of the second day bolstered the Union left, which had come close to breaking earlier that day on the crest of Little Round Top. On July 3 the men of the Vermont Brigade, like Mason, noted the sensational artillery fire that accompanied Pickett's Charge. Martin Warner Davis, for instance, wrote, "1:20 P.M. the heaviest cannonading I ever heard, terrific. 5 P.M. the firing was subsided, for the 1st time since daylight. We have had verious reports. It is said that we have taken on the right 5,000 prisoners and that we have Genl Longstreet's body. O if we can only be successful here it will do much toward ending the rebellion."[2]

Lee's demoralized and battered army slipped away on July 4, the same day that Confederate forces surrendered at Vicksburg. The *Orleans Independent Standard* proclaimed, "The army of the Potomac has been victorious at last. After enduring defeats and disasters without number for the last two years, without a substantial victory to cheer its despondency, it has at last won a victory that amply compensates it for all its long and patient waiting. . . . The army [of Northern Virginia] is fleeing in such a demoralized condition as to warrant the assertion that they can make no successful stand this side of Richmond if they should have the good luck to escape utter annihilation."[3] George Meade, the new commander of the Army of Potomac, was pressed by Lincoln to pursue Lee aggressively and ensure that he did not escape back to Virginia. Meade has suffered much criticism ever since for his failure to do so, though his army had also suffered enormously, and he was urged by his corps commanders not to pursue Lee directly, but rather indirectly by maintaining the "inside track" between Lee and Washington. Meade wrote two days after the battle, "I knew he was in a strong position, awaiting my attack, which I declined to make, in consequence of the bad example he had set me in ruining himself attacking a strong position."[4] Not knowing where exactly Lee was moving, Meade was cautious, but only to a point. Many units of the Army of the Potomac did aggressively pursue Lee, including the VI Corps. Fred Kimball wrote that on July 5, "At 10AM we move—pass over a portion of the battlefield—the sight was awful. In many places the ground is literally covered with dead rebs. Many a miserable wretch bit the dust. They have left thousands of their wounded. Every building for miles around is full of them. Their loss is immense. Our victory was at every point."[5] As was the case before the battle, Mason's diary entries in the days following Gettysburg capture the incredibly trying ordeal of numerous consecutive days of forced marches with little food, rest, or protection from the elements:

> July 7. Cloudy & Misty marched toward Frederick City. Crossed the Mountain at Highland Gap commenced to ascend near dark, very steep rough road. Terrible rainy many fell out exhausted. Encamped in the top of Mount near midnight—wet weary.
>
> July 8. Rainy marched at an early hour. Blankets & clothing very wet started without breakfast no supper last night dreary time.

Fred Kimball wrote on July 7, "I never passed a more miserable night. O how it rained."[6] Martin Warner Davis said that crossing Catoctin Mountain in Maryland amounted to "the hardest time we ever saw. It was like climbing Mt. Pisgah," the prominent peak that looms over Lake Willoughby in Westmore, Vermont.[7] Understandably, Mason's letter to Harriet the next day was very brief. He had little time to write, as the brigade was in pursuit of the fleeing rebels.

Camp near Boonsboro, Md.
July 9th 1863

Dear Harriet

As there is a chance to send a letter to Frederick City tonight I will write a few lines just to let you know that I am well I received yours of the 22d today the first mail we have had for 9 days. I am well the rest of the G[lover] Boys ditto. . . . We had a terrible fight with the rebels at Gettysburg the 1st 2d & 3d of this month & beat them badly. They have now fell back near the Potomac I dont know whether they intend to make another stand or not our Cavalry have a fight with theirs every day. Our Brigade was not engaged we were up to the front but our portion of the line was not attacked. I must make haste & close for the man is waiting

receive from your sincere lover,
Dan

Meade was also stymied by Confederate cavalry under the command of J. E. B. Stuart, who did an excellent job screening Lee's retreat. In the week following the Confederate withdrawal from Gettysburg, Union cavalry occasionally clashed with Stuart's troopers, as they did at Funkstown, Maryland, on July 10. Though not remembered as a significant clash in the larger context of the Gettysburg campaign, the Vermont Brigade was involved in a sharp fight in support of the Union cavalry. The Confederate rear guard that engaged the Vermont Brigade at Funkstown allowed Lee to cross the Potomac River to safety in Virginia.

Camp in the field near Berlin Md
July 17th, 1863

Dear Harriet

I take this favorable opportunity to answer your last which came to hand in due season was perused with much pleasure &c &c. Quite probably you have heard about the fight our Brigade had with the rebs on the 10th. I will endeavor to give you a few particulars concerning it. That morning we marched from Boonsboro. We had not gone far when the Cavalry which our Brig[ade] was supporting run on to rebs & skirmishing commenced. The rebs continued to fall back until within about 1 mile of the village of Funkstown, when the rebs made a stand supported by Infantry which had come up. The Cavalry dismounted leaving their horses behind. They held their position until near noon when their ammunition being nearly exhausted, Our Reg[imen]t was ordered to the front to relieve them. We had not been there long before they opened a Battery on our line (rebs) a shower of shell & grape & cannister was hurled among our line. We had a good position on a rising piece of ground in a piece of Oak woods near the edge fronting an open field. After shelling us smartly a column of Gray backs were seen moving down the road we directed our fire in that direction soon after they advanced across the field in line of Battle colors flying. As we were nothing but a skirmish line with no support near it looked possible for us to be overpowered, but all the time we kept loading & firing as fast as we could. When they got within 30 rods of us they broke & run. We hooted at them & they rallied & advanced to within 20 rods of us we poured a deadly fire into them & they broke & ran. Our ammunition was nearly exhausted when the 4th Reg[imen]t came up & relieved us. The rebs loss was very severe many lay among the Corn dead & wounded. Our Co[mpany] suffered quite severely Serg[ean]t Moses Abbott of Troy was shot through the head killing him instantly. Geo[rge] Partridge was also shot dead the ball passing through his head Henry McGuire of Albany was wounded in the arm & Alonzo Priest of Coventry was knocked down with a piece of spent shell. Our Reg[imen]t lost 3 killed

& 2 wounded (some have since died). The rebs crossed Monday night. The next morning Our Cavalry pursued to the river taking 1500 prisoners, 2 cannon some Caissons. I was in hopes we should damage the rebs more than we have but we have punished him severely I dont think he will invade our soil again. We have cheering news from the Mississippi such as the fall of Vicksburg Port Hudson Morris Island near Charleston &c. It begins to look like putting down rebellion. But I am sorry to hear of riots in New York occasioned by the draft—I should like to fight them chaps & clean them out—I have not so good opinion of them as of rebs in the South I would shoot one quicker

I must close give my regards to your Mother & all the friends

Dan

The day after the battle, Mason wrote that "Geo[rge] Partridge buried in woods near F[unks]town Battlefield." Fred Kimball, now a lieutenant in Company G of the Sixth, was wounded at Funkstown. He had suffered a previous wound at Banks's Ford. Kimball's diary entries for the next several days speak to an experience that was similar to Hobart Bliss's ordeal after Banks's Ford; a long, slow, painful recovery coupled with feelings of loneliness, bearing witness to the suffering of others, and being "lost" away from the Sixth Vermont.

July 11. Our regts that were engaged suffered a good deal loss. Our regt. had about 25 killed & wounded. Geo Partridge & Moses Abbott were killed, poor fellows. They were good soldiers. George is the first of our Glover boys killed. . . . I was stung this time & I am thankful tis no worse. Was hit in the thigh with a rifle ball. Last night I was taken to the Hospital established in an old barn, where I am today the 11th as comfortable as I can be with my painful limb. Two of the wounded died last night. Two have had limbs amputated.

July 12. This day all the wounded were taken from the hospital near Boonsboro to Frederick Md, a distance of 20 miles. O wasn't I glad when we got there after being jolted far in an ambulance. Still I look upon what I suffered as slight compared with many poor fellows with much worse wounds than mine. I am thankful that I am able to get up & can hobble around a little. . . . I can but thank God for his wonderful preservation in the hours of danger. He has kept me through many a bloody scene.

July 13. I am now in a U.S. Gen. Hospital at Frederick Md suffering from my wounded limb. The Surgeon in charge has examined it. I think the ball must be in my leg, yet I hope to be able soon to return to my regt. I have been unable to write in my diary for three days & will now go back & fill up. It rains today.

July 14. In hospital in Frederick Md. Tis lonesome & I am tired of lying here. Wish I might get home & see my friends. Now that I am off duty I shall try to get a leave of absence, though twould be hard for me to ride now. Wound is very painful.

July 15. I feel lost away from the regt.[8]

Kimball returned home on a leave of absence. The wound he received at Funkstown pained him daily. A sampling of diary entries after his return home indicates the range of emotions and experiences he had, culminating with a "beautiful day" on September 27:

July 21. Ride today from Springfield, Mass to Barton. Get very tired. . . . Rained most all day.

July 22. Arrived home at last. Came in last night. Have suffered a great deal with my wound in my way. My limb is lame & painful. I cannot find words to tell my joy of seeing my parents. Everyone in to see me & inquire after myself & friends in the army. I shall have to go back to fill up my diary for 6 days.

July 23. Have visitors all the time. Glad to see my friends once more—How glad. Have not been out any for I am so lame. My wound pains me a good deal, though it is doing as well as I can expect. Happy to meet my friends once more. Sue I long to see.

July 24. Dr. Bugbee examines my wound & by probing it he gets out a piece of a ball. It must have been an explosive bullet.

July 29. The days wear away in time. Tis lonesome in Glover now.

July 30. All day lonesome indeed it is.

Aug 8. This morning I start for a visit to Cabot & Peacham. I reach my darling Sue at 11AM. Can it be I have been at home so long & not seen her, the girl I love so well, but my wounded limb prevented me from enjoying thy society so long.

Aug 9. Sue, thou art dearer to me than all the world beside. Crowd as much enjoyment into the space of one visit as possible. We attend Church in the PM. Form new acquaintances & pleasant ones. My own darling Sue.

Aug 22. Go to Peacham & from there to Cabot. My heart is happy only with my darling Sue. I find true happiness in the society of Sue & Sue alone. Sue thou art all to me.

Aug 26. At 11AM . . . start at Glover & take tea with my folks. Start from there & arrive at Newport at 9PM. Have a pleasant ride. Day more than pleasant.

Aug 27. At 7AM we take passage upon the *Mountain Maid*. Have a delightful ride upon the beautiful lake and disembark at the Mountain House where we pass the day in a most happy manner. All but Sue & I go onto Owls Head. We remained because I am lame. Take the boat at 7PM for Newport.

Sept 27. The clouds break away. The sky becomes bright—after the darkness that has overcast it. Tis a beautiful day. This day at 7PM Sue & I were made one for life. I was given the partner of my choice. I am a married man. Long shall I remember this day—so beautiful. The bright moon in its full, succeeds in splendor the setting sun.

Sept 28. Today we with Enoch & Abbie go to Montpelier. I am on my way to the army & Sue is going as far as New York. We shall stop there about a week when Sue will return home & I go on to Washington.[9]

Meanwhile, after Funkstown, when Lee had reached safety on the south side of the Potomac, Lincoln fumed at Meade in a letter that he never sent:

My dear general, I do not believe you appreciate the magnitude of the misfortune involved in Lee's escape. He was within your easy grasp, and to have closed upon him would, in connection with our other late successes, have ended the war. As it is, the war will be prolonged indefinitely. If you could not safely attack Lee last monday, how can you possibly do so South of the river, when you can take with you very few more than two thirds of the force you then had in hand? It would be unreasonable to expect, and I do not expect you can now effect much. Your golden opportunity is gone, and I am distressed immeasureably because of it.[10]

Mason's remark from his July 17 letter that "I was in hopes we should damage the rebs more than we have but we have punished him severely" was fairly mild by comparison. Oliver Stiles, like Mason, expressed a disappointment with Lee's escape, but took a measured view of the matter that was tempered by two years of fighting in the Army of the Potomac:

While in Maryland and in pursuit of old Lee the boys were willing to do anything, fight or march day and night if necessary, only drive the rebels from our soil. This we succeeded in doing, but many were disappointed on learning that Lee had escaped with his army into Virginia, as they had made up their minds that his army was going to be bagged, but after being in the army two years and hearing about bagging so many times and never seeing it done, I have made up my mind that this bagging an army as large as ours or Lee's is entirely out of the question. Our Captain—[M. W.] Davis—is now in Vermont after drafted men.[11]

Captain Martin Warner Davis was on his way to Orleans County to round up conscripts. Never before had the federal government directly drafted men into military service, but in the summer of 1863, 420 men from Orleans County, including 20 from Glover, were drafted, and they did augment the depleted ranks of the Vermont Brigade.[12] As great a stigma as conscription carried, Oliver Stiles looked forward to the arrival of the draftees. He admitted, "We are now in camp near Warrenton, Virginia . . . and report says we are to stay here until our recruits come and get them drilled, but we cannot tell much about these camp reports, so we do not put much stock in it—hope however that it is so, for many of the boys are about played out."[13] Mason was as hostile to draft resistance as ever and wanted to "clean out" rioters in New York City, whom he would "shoot quicker" than rebels in the South. However, he needn't have feared any sort of Democratic tide in Vermont. In late August Republican candidates won handily in the statewide elections and fared even better in local elections. In Irasburg the Republican candidate won by a margin of 166–12 votes. In Derby the race was closer. The Republican candidate edged out his Democratic rival by a vote of 167–23. The editor of the *Orleans Independent Standard* boasted sarcastically, "We are surprised to see so large a copperhead vote cast as there appears to be upon examining all the returns. . . . We hope to see another year that those who voted for these reptiles have repented of their iniquity; and we shall not probably hear a hiss, for the rebellion will be crushed, when the rebels will have no further need of their services—hitherto more valuable to them than their armies in the field. But for them the rebellion would have ended long ago."[14]

Back in Virginia the Army of the Potomac had recrossed its namesake river but would not fight any major actions against the Army of Northern Virginia until the following spring. Mason told Harriet that "since I last wrote you we have not had any fighting but some very hard marching the weather has been very warm much of the time." He also noted that blackberries were in season and asked Harriet, "I should like to go Blackberrying with you tonight after supper will you accompany me?"

After languishing in Virginia for several weeks, the Vermont Brigade was given orders to travel to New York City to help restore order to the streets in the wake of the draft riots. That summer, shortly after the fighting at Gettysburg ended, Manhattan was engulfed by four days of rioting. The riots were the result of racial, ethnic, and class tensions that had reached a fever pitch as the draft began in New York City on July 11. The Enrollment Act, passed by Congress in March, had allowed a draftee to avoid service by hiring a substitute or paying a $300 commutation fee. Democratic partisans seized on the classist undertones of this provision, though some historians have argued that Democratic claims of a "rich man's war and a poor man's fight" were exaggerated. James McPherson, for instance, points out that while 30 percent of the eligible male population in the Union states was foreign born, immigrants constituted 25 percent of the ranks of the Union armed forces.[15] Regardless, working-class whites, especially Irish Catholic immigrants in urban areas, feared competition for jobs with emancipated slaves. In the New York City draft riots in July 1863, over one hundred people were killed. Blacks, abolitionists, and Republicans were targeted, though in the end, the largest number of victims were rioters themselves. It took the arrival of Union troops fresh from Gettysburg to quell the violence. The Democratic *Argus and Patriot* of Montpelier supported the recruitment of an all-volunteer force but lamented, "For some reason . . . the conscription bill was passed, and its terms are odious to the people, and its provisions, in the honest judgment of many, entirely unconstitutional. To them the arbitrary will of the President seems to have taken the place of the Constitution of the United States, and the sovereignty of each individual state has become a thing of the past. Resistance to the draft, and riots, have been the result." However, the editor added, "if the laws are wrong the courts will rectify them in that respect; but mobs, or riots, can never remedy any evil, real or imaginary, and all high-handed outrages, such as have been committed in New York, and Boston, cannot but recoil upon the perpetrators, and instigators, of them with double force." To save face, the editor suggested that Republicans were guilty of a double standard by condemning the draft riots while also having supported John Brown's Raid and the violation of the Fugitive Slave Act before the war.[16]

In late August the draft resumed, this time under the supervision of twenty thousand troops. Despite the opposition of some Democratic newspapers like the *Argus and Patriot* to the draft, there was little sympathy for draft resistance in Vermont. The Yankee population of Vermont—composed primarily of literate, native-born, Protestant, small-scale independent farmers of modest means—was exactly the demographic that leaned strongly Republican. Unfortunately, as the Vermont Brigade was being transported to Manhattan, two soldiers fell overboard and drowned: Hollis Sanborn of Derby and Truman Blood of Essex. Mason also wrote in his diary on August 19, "Sea very rolling. Boys sea sick—a great deal of spewing." Once in New York, the Sixth Vermont enjoyed a tranquil stay in Manhattan, the draft riots having subsided by the time of their arrival. Oliver Stiles wrote that "we had a very pleasant time in New York, and especially in Kingston.—It certainly seemed like getting home again instead of all citizens being enemies as has been the case with us for the last two years. We found friends and those who were willing to do any thing for the good and comfort of the soldiers."[17] Mason toured the city, including Broadway, which he described as "a great business thoroughfare." It would not become known as a performing arts thoroughfare until later in the nineteenth century.

Camp New York City Aug[ust] 27th, [18]63

Dear Harriet

We are now encamped on Tompkins Square or 7th St Park in the Eastern portion of the City. We arrived here last Friday noon we embarked at Alexandria [Virginia] Tuesday morning. Tuesday night when near the entrance of Potomac river into Chesapeake Bay Our Boat which was the Ocean Steamer *Illinois* ran into a schooner damaging the Schooner so that it came near sinking & damaging one of our wheels so that we had to cast anchor & repair damages. The ship Carpenters repaired it enough during the night so that we proceeded on our way soon after sunrise. The Capt[ain] of [the] Boat said it would cost five thousand doll[ar]s to make as good as before. We (the 6th Reg[imen]t) lost 2 men overboard 1 named Hollis L Sanborn from our Co[mpany] & Truman Blood Co[mpany] I. Neither have been seen or heard from since as it was dark the night very warm many slept on the Wheel house & upper deck rather than in the berths down in the Cabin & when the Boat struck it gave all a shock or tendancy forward & set the Steamer to rocking & doubtless they were asleep & slid off & found a watery grave. The commander of the schooner was deceived by our lights & thought he was running clear of us when he was running in front of us. I am well the rest of the G[lover] Boys ditto. We have not seen any trouble as yet here dont think we shall. . . . We have to obtain passes to get outside the Guard signed by Col[onel] Grant commanding Brigade. I have been out several times. Henry Bickford (he plays in the Band) & Edwin Gray & I went down Broadway 2 or 3 miles a few days since it is a great business thoroughfare I assure you. We passed Barnums Museum the *Tribune* office, *Times* Office, Astor House visited Trinity Church &c we went inside it is the most splendid Church I ever saw by a great deal. The people here are very good to soldiers sending provisions hot Coffee ice water &c by their little Boys pedlers are very plenty but are not allowed to take exhorbitant prices of the soldiers. The policemen march them off the Park in a hurry if they do. If we stay here several weeks I think they will grant short furloughs if so I shall go home I have spoken so if any go I shall. But dont make up your mind to[o] strong for you know furloughs are doubtful documents I must close hoping to meet you before many months

Dan

After spending fifteen days in New York City, an order came for "the Fifth and Sixth Vermont Volunteers to proceed this afternoon, or early this evening, to the village of Kingston, Ulster County, N.Y., where the draft for the Thirteenth Congressional District takes place on Monday, the 7th instant."[18] At Kingston Mason was paid a visit by his father, whom he had not seen in two years. He "visited right smart" with his father, but after a stay of only one day, Moses Hazen returned to Vermont. He also assured Harriet that "you need not entertain any fears of my reenlisting or falling in love with any of the City flirts." Avoiding the temptations of the "city flirts" may have been one thing, but avoiding reenlistment was something quite different.

Camp at Kingston N[ew] York
Sep[tember] 11th 1863

Dear Harriet

I take this opportunity to acknowledge the receipt of 2 letters one in NY City & one here this morn. . . . Father Geo[rge] Jenness & wife Mr Nye & wife & Olin Gray arrived here day before yesterday in the P.M. they left this morn for Vt. I visited right smart yesterday all day. Night before last I went down to the Kingston Hotel & stayed with Father all night. He made rather a short stop but he thought he would start so as to get home Saturday night & I took a rational view of the matter & was thankful for a short visit. I got a furlough started a week ago today I was in hopes it would get around properly signed so that I could return with father but it did not. It is for ten days I am afraid it will not be approved yet I have some hope that it will yet come it is a hard matter to get a furlough unless it is a case of sickness or death. . . . I shall go home if my furlough is granted father is just as anxious to have me come home as before he came out. I think quite probably we shall be back in Va before a week or down south somewhere. Still we may stop around NY for sometime. We have not been called upon to quell any riots except the 3d Vt which went to Newark N[ew] Jers[e]y the day we came here. . . . You need not entertain any fears of my reenlisting or falling in love with any of the City flirts—my affections are set upon one & nothing but death or some unaccountable treachery on her part can change me or to express myself in different words as long as you remain true I shall also. I place all confidence in you

I must close

accept with much love from Dan

SIXTH REGIMENT INFANTRY.

TO those desirous of joining a company for the SIXTH REGIMENT Vermont Volunteers, notice is hereby given that by order of the Governor, a Recruiting Office for Orleans County has been opened at BARTON, and as the Regiment must be full by the first of October, it is of the utmost importance that the requisite number be enlisted at the earliest possible day. Each recruit receives Twenty Dollars per month and rations. Also $100 bounty, at the expiration of the service, (and undoubtedly a Quarter Section of Land,) from the date of his enlistment until he is discharged from service.

ELISHA WHITE,
Recruiting Officer.

Barton, September 21, 1861.

1. Sixth Regiment Infantry recruitment. *Orleans Independent Standard*, September 27, 1861.

2. Camp of the Sixth Vermont at Camp Griffin, Virginia, 1861. George Houghton Civil War Photographs, Vermont Historical Society.

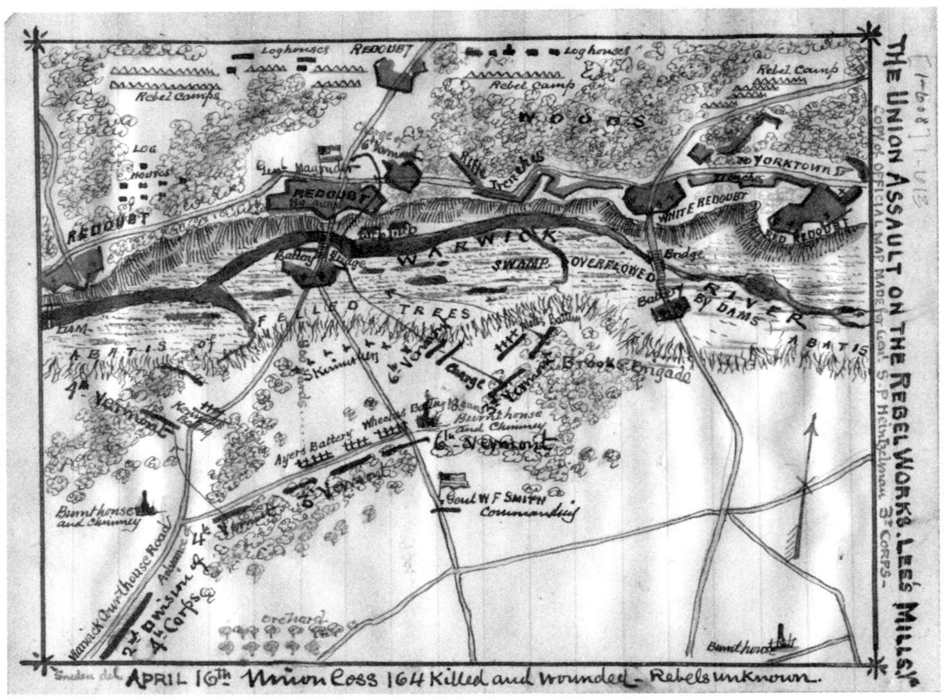

3. Robert Knox Snedden, "The Union Assault on the Rebel Works at Lee's Mills, VA." Note: The Charge of the Sixth Vermont is shown on a dotted line at the center of the map. Library of Congress, Civil War Maps, https://www.loc.gov/item/gvhs01.vhs00075/.

4. Julian Scott, *The Rear Guard at White Oak Swamp*, 1869. Mason simply said of the fighting at Savage's Station and White Oak Swamp, "We had a pretty rough time." Vermont State Curator's Office.

BULLY ORLEANS!

Recruiting Office

NOW OPEN IN

IRASBURGH!!

A COMPANY OF VOLUNTEERS FOR ONE of the regiments now being raised in this State is expected of Orleans County in 15 days. Shall we disappoint that expectation? The honor of the county is at stake.

REMEMBER LEE'S MILLS!!

Our brave old flag has been driven from Western Virginia by those vile traitors of the South, who seek the disruption of the Union, and devastation of our land. Our country calls----that country which has been baptized in the blood of the revolution, and sanctified by the memory of Washington, ----that country which protects us, our property and our homes. History will tell of these days. Stand among the heroes. Shame not posterity by refusing to place your name on the glorious roll of patriots. Seek not to excuse yourself. It is OUR country that is in danger, and no one can say, "It concerns not me----let others go down to the battle." Disgrace not the memory of ETHAN ALLEN and the GREEN MOUNTAIN BOYS of '76. Rally round the flag. Let Orleans be first in the field.

Pay.

$20 per month and rations, to commence at date of enlistment, and

$100 BOUNTY

5. After the Union's failures during the Peninsula campaign, the Lincoln administration called for additional recruits using the threat of conscription as an inducement to encourage volunteer enlistments. *Orleans Independent Standard*, June 20, 1862.

6. Fred Kimball, Glover, Vermont, wounded at Banks's Ford and Funkstown. Orleans County Historical Society.

7. Alexander W. Davis, Glover, Vermont, wounded at Savage's Station and taken prisoner. Davis and Mason received officers' commissions in the USCT at the same time, Mason in the Nineteenth USCT and Davis in the Thirty-Ninth USCT. Their paths would cross several times throughout the war, most notably on July 30, 1864, at the Battle of the Crater. Borland Family Collection.

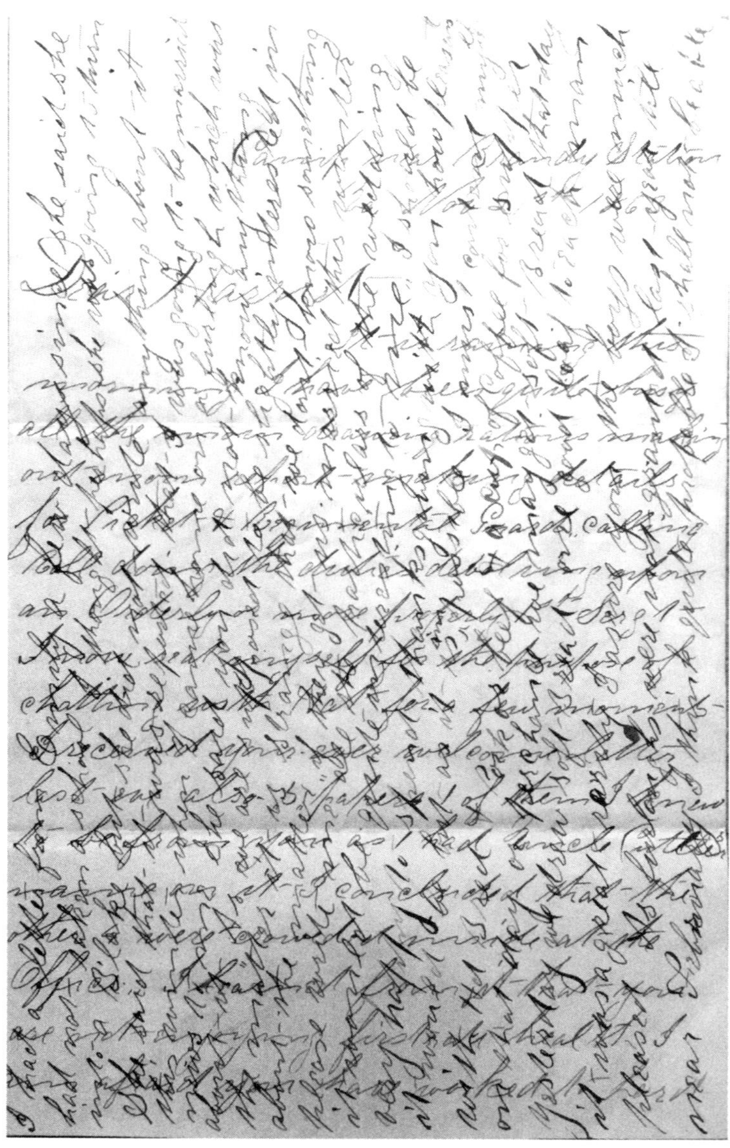

8. Mason's cross-written letter of November 21, 1863. Two days after Lincoln delivered his Gettysburg Address, Mason described his purpose for fighting as "knocking out the rotten treacherous walls of slavery on which our government has tattered & reeled . . . and substituting in place of the granite walls of freedom." Vermont Historical Society.

9. Carte-de-visite of Dan Mason, C. L. Howe, photographer, Brattleboro, Vermont. Mason wrote to Harriet on January 3, 1864, "I went down to the village yesterday & got my Photograph taken they will not be completed until next Thursday. I will forward you 1 by mail." Mason was still a sergeant in Company D of the Sixth Vermont. Glover Historical Society.

Whereas my slave Samuel Adams enlisted as William S. Adams in the service of the United States: now in consideration thereof. I Grafton Burgee of Frederick County State of Maryland, do hereby in consideration of said enlistment, manumit, set free, and release the above named Samuel Adams from all service due me: his freedom to commence from the date of his enlistment as aforesaid in the 19th Regiment of Colored Troops in the service of the United States. Witness my hand and Seal this 19th day of July 1864.

Witness

Grafton Burgee (Seal)

J. G. Wood

J. P. Todd

J. M. Harding

Frederick County State of Maryland July 19th 1864

Before me appeared this day Grafton Burgee and acknowledged the above Deed of Manumission and Release of Service to be his free act and deed.

J. M. Harding

10. ABOVE: Deed of manumission for Samuel Adams, an enslaved man from Maryland who enlisted in the Nineteenth USCT. His owner received $300 in compensation for proving his "loyalty" to the Union. National Archives.

11. Casualties at the Wilderness, Company D, Sixth Vermont. The deadliest day in Vermont's history. *Orleans Independent Standard*, June 17, 1864.

Killed.—Sergt. Wm. S. Livingston, Albany, Privates, Wm. A. Cook, Brome, C. E., Samual Forsyth, Sheffield, John LaMarsh, North Troy, Henry Filden, Potton, C. E.

Wounded.—First Sergt. Oliver T. Stiles, shoulder, severely, Sergt. W. I. Chesmore, thigh, slightly, Corps. Wm. L. Snell, arm, severely, E. J. Williams, thigh, severely, since died. Privates, Luther J. Adams, neck, severely, Wm. Brunning, thigh, severely, Stephen W. Baxter, hand, slightly, Augustus P. Folsom, neck, severely, Edwin S. Gray, thumb, slightly, Ira A. Hadlock, arm, slightly, Geo. Jenness, side, severely, Ezekiel Miles, knee, severely, Horace S. Rollins, thigh, severely, Horace Sargent, back, severely, John Upton, knee, severely, Chester C. Wheeler, arm, slightly, Henry G. West, chin, slightly, Stephen S. Huntly, arm, severely. *Missing.*—Levi C. Allen, supposed killed, Louis LaBounty, supposed killed.

12. LEFT: Carte-de-visite of Dan Mason, Nineteenth USCT, photographed in Baltimore, Maryland. Borland Family Collection.

13. "The Siege of Petersburg—Burying the dead before Cemetery Hill under a flag of truce after the repulse of the Ninth Army Corps." *Frank Leslie's Illustrated Newspaper*, September 3, 1864.

I certify, on honor, that John H Addison a Corpl of Captain Dan Mason's Company (H) of the 19th Regiment of U S Colored VOLUNTEERS, ~~of the State of~~ ...., born in Prince George Co, State of Maryland, aged 37 years; 5 feet 6½ inches high; Black complexion, Black eyes Black hair, and by occupation a Farmer, having joined the company on its original organization at ...., and enrolled in it at the muster into the service of the United States at ...., on the .... day of ...., 186 , (or was mustered in service as a recruit, by Gen Wm Birney ...., at Charles Co Md, on the 13th day of January, 1864, or was drafted and mustered into the service of the United States from the .... Enrollment District of the State of ...., at ...., on the .... day of ...., 186 ,) to serve in the Regiment, for the term of Three years: and having served HONESTLY and FAITHFULLY with his Company in the field to the present date, is now entitled to a DISCHARGE by reason of Death caused by ~~action~~ wounds received in action Near Petersburg Va July 30th 1864 (without effects)

The said Corpl John H. Addison was last paid by Paymaster Maj Hooper to include the 29th day of February, 1864, and has pay due him from that time to the present date; he is entitled to pay and subsistence for TRAVELING to place of enrollment, and whatever other allowances are authorized to volunteer soldiers, drafted men, or militia, so discharged. He has received from the United States CLOTHING amounting to $ 42, 96/100 dollars, since the 13th day of January, 1864, when his clothing account was last settled. He has received from the United States .... 100 dollars advanced BOUNTY.

There is to be stopped from him, on account of the State of ...., or other authorities, for CLOTHING, &c., received on entering service, ... 100 dollars; and for other stoppages, viz: ....

.... 100 dollars.

He has been furnished with TRANSPORTATION in kind from the place of his discharge to ....; and he has been SUBSISTED for TRAVELING to his place of enrollment, up to the ...., 186 .

He is indebted to ...., SUTLER, ... 100 dollars.

He is indebted to ...., LAUNDRESS, ... 100 dollars.

Given in Duplicate, at Camp Near Petersburg Va, this 27th day of August, 1864

Dan Mason
Capt
Commanding Company.

[A. G. O. No. 95—First.]

14. Casualty report of John Addison, a formerly enslaved man of Company H, Nineteenth USCT, signed by Captain Dan Mason. Addison was wounded at the Battle of the Crater and died the following day, leaving a pregnant wife and son behind. National Archives.

THE SUN.

FROM THE ARMY OF THE POTOMAC.

THE ASSAULT ON PETERSBURG.

The Causes of Its Failure.

The Colored Troops Give Way.

Extraordinary Efforts to Rally Them.

The Rebels Refuse a Flag of Truce to Remove the Wounded on the Battle-Field---Unwillingness to Exchange Newspapers.

15. The Democratic press was quick to blame the catastrophe at the Crater on the Black regiments that suffered enormously there. Instead of a lack of courage and conviction, they were the victims of poor leadership, racial politics, and military calculations. Mason vehemently defended the conduct of his troops against such attacks. *Baltimore Sun*, August 3, 1864.

16. Thomas Nast, "Compromise with the South—Dedicated to the Chicago Convention." Mason sent this image home to Harriet, writing, "The soldier on his crutches The Goddess of Liberty weeping over the graves of heroes sacrificed in a useless war. . . . All combined makes me disgusted with the peace policy. That defiant rebel with his whip in hand with the enslaved around him disgusts me. I say fight them." *Harper's Weekly*, September 3, 1864.

Orleans County Vote.

The following is the vote of Orleans county for president, as compared with the vote for senator in September last. Both sides gain, but the republican gain is by far the largest:

	Lincoln	McClellan	Senators. Union	Dem.
Albany,	176	43	134	44
Barton,	236	44	168	47
Brownington,	135	14	94	12
Charleston,	210	22	130	18
Coventry,	158	21	95	18
Craftsbury,	197	34	137	46
Derby,	211	45	203	27
Glover,	165	60	113	51
Greensboro,	122	54	90	51
Holland,	48	57	61	57
Irasburgh,	189	9	145	12
Jay,	39	11	47	18
Lowell,	100	22	74	41
Morgan,	76	13	65	10
Newport,	272	70	61	57
Salem,	27	00	41	1
Troy,	170	58	169	55
Westfield,	130	37	79	19
Westmore,	35	12	32	00
	2,696	636		

17. As of 1860 Orleans County gave a staggering 81 percent of its popular vote to Abraham Lincoln. *Orleans Independent Standard*, November 18, 1864.

18. "The Effect of the Rebellion on the Homes of Virginia." Mason sent this home to Harriet and wrote, "The pictures showing the effects of war on Va homes looks very much like houses that I have been in. The one where the young Mother sits watching her Infant is very good representation. The old Clock the Coffee mill with the spiders web woven over it showing that it has not been used for a long time for want of the material, the old ladies &c &c." *Harper's Weekly*, December 24, 1864.

RICHMOND

OURS!

After nearly four years of terrible fighting for the possession of this focus of treason, we this week have the pleasure of announcing to a certainty that the rebel capital is ours. Gen. Weitzel with his negro troops entered the city at 8 o'clock on Monday morning, and was received with every demonstration of joy by the people. Richmond was evacuated by Lee who is now beating a hasty retreat, closely followed by Sheridan and his invincible cavalry. With what success it is now too early to know. Petersburg is also evacuated. The war is virtually over. Now " Glory to God in the highest, and on earth peace and good will to men."

19. OPPOSITE TOP: Lemuel Dobbs, Mason's first lieutenant, who was captured at the Battle of the Crater and later escaped a Confederate prison by tunneling. While many captured white officers in Black units did not reveal what unit they belonged to for fear of being summarily executed, Dobbs indignantly replied upon capture, "Lemuel D. Dobbs, Nineteenth N———rs." His captors spared his life, but his lengthy absence hurt Mason's chances of having his resignation approved in 1865. Borland Collection.

20. OPPOSITE BOTTOM: Frank Holsinger, a Pennsylvania soldier thrice wounded at Bermuda Hundred. While stationed on the Rio Grande, Holsinger said, "The native Mexican is the laziest creature I ever saw." Borland Family Collection.

21. ABOVE: Which exact unit entered Richmond first remains a subject of historical debate, though the XXV Corps and the Nineteenth USCT were among the first troops to enter the city. *Orleans Independent Standard*, April 17, 1865.

22. ABOVE: “The First Bridge That Ever Spanned the Rio Grande. Laid on Sunday Nov. 27, 1866, by William Welsh Lieut. Col. 19th USCTroops.” Borland Family Collection.

23. Corporal Jacob Johns, Nineteenth USCT. Johns was a formerly enslaved man from Talbot County, Maryland, who, like Mason, was hospitalized in the post hospital in Brownsville, Texas, in November 1865. Unlike Mason he survived and was mustered out in 1867. Collection of the Smithsonian National Museum of African American History and Culture, Gift from the Liljenquist Family Collection.

24. ABOVE: A young Harriet Clark Mason, date unknown. Borland Family Collection.

25. An older Harriet Clark Mason Borland, date unknown. Borland Family Collection.

{8}

"The Rotten Treacherous Walls of Slavery" (Fall 1863)

Mason's hopes of making a quick trip home from New York were dashed when the Vermont Brigade was sent back to the front in Virginia. Martin Warner Davis, who did have an opportunity to go home and see his wife and children, was also dispirited upon returning to the front. He wrote on October 3, "We pass the day as best we can. I am indeed very lonely. O I would gladly return to my much loved family and may that time soon come. I am tired, tired of this war, the Separation from those I love." Three days later Davis added, "I am rather tired of the service, my family being so discontented."[1] Mason also desperately wanted to go home and told Harriet he was "sick of courting at a distance . . . I am mad sometimes at myself to think I left you to come out here & be deprived of your society for 3 long long years."

Camp about 4 miles South west of Culpepper
Va Sept[ember] 24th, [18]63

Dear Harriet

I take this opportunity to write you a few lines & inform you of my health &c. You will notice by the heading that we have got back into old Virginia. We came to South Amboy New Jersey from Kingston, then took cars for Philadelphia arrived there about 9 oclock in eve the Brigade ate a good supper furnished by the patriotic citizens of that City. Every Reg[imen]t that passes through there to or from the seat of war is the recipient of their bountiful refreshments. We arrived in Washington Tuesday eve slept in the Soldiers Home took supper at Soldiers retreat & breakfast. I visited the Capital the Senate Hall & House of Representatives Hall. . . . My furlough never got around I have given up visiting

Vt for the present but if furloughs are granted next winter I shall come if it is possible. . . . Harriet I like to read your long interesting letters but I cant say that I like to write long ones. You dont doubt it do you? I hope that the time will come when we can enjoy each others presence & be as one flesh I am sick of courting at a distance aint you? I am mad sometimes at myself to think I left you to come out here & be deprived of your society for 3 long long years, what an age, how many have already paid the great debt of Nature by shuffling of[f] the mortal coil both in civil & military life.[2] The King of Terrors is ever active in hurling his darts. But then I console myself with the thought that it dont make much difference where we are if we are doing our duty & making ourselves useful. I dont have these gloomy thoughts very often, Thank God. I have a faculty of looking on the sunny side most of the time. I must now close by tendering to you my best wishes. Give my respects to all the Glover people that inquire after my welfare.

Good bye
Dan

The ranks of the Vermont Brigade had been thinned significantly since the beginning of the war. By October 1863 only 322 of the original 1,000 members of the Sixth Vermont remained.[3] Oliver Stiles expressed some relief that

> our brigade has been partially filled by drafted men. . . . Guess they will learn to be soldiers after awhile. I learn that most of them are substitutes, but all the same, all that is wanted is the men; no matter whether they are volunteers, conscripts, or substitutes, a soldier is a soldier wherever you meet him. Some blow the idea of being a conscript, but there should be no distinction between a volunteer and a drafted man.—Perhaps duty has detained him at home and it has been his luck to be drafted.—Now it seems that he is entitled to the same respect as a volunteer, but he does not get it, at least by some.[4]

Stiles's magnanimity didn't last long. After he spoke generously of conscripts, he read a letter to the editor from a conscript, John B. Webster, who was serving in the Fourth Vermont. Webster was actually a substitute for a Barton man and had already volunteered for a stint in the nine months' Fifteenth Vermont. Nevertheless, Webster complained,

> people at home have no idea of the treatment of the poor soldiers; if there is anyone on God's footstool deserving of the prayers and sympathies of those left at home it is the poor, mean, contemptible soldier; in fact this is the light a man is looked upon by his superior officers, no matter whether he is a drafted man, a substitute, or even a volunteer. . . . Our living is not of the first class, neither of the second, or third; it is so confounded mean you would have to knock a cypher into a ten thousand pieces to find a number mean enough to express it. The principal part of our food consists of poor coffee and bread; this we have for breakfast and supper.[5]

Stiles was enraged and fired off an angry response to set the record straight as he saw it:

Even if he spoke the truth, as he strongly asserts that he did, it would have been more becoming in him as a soldier of the United States not to have spoken it, and much more to have written such agreeable news to his wife at home who will think that her poor unfortunate husband, as he is pleased to term himself, is being made a martyr of, and so abused by his superior officers. It shows very plainly that he is a man that has hung back until forced into it. . . . Among other bickerings of his he sees fit to complain most bitterly of his rations, such as bread, soup and meat, or as he terms it, salt horse. . . . Mr. J. B. Webster should have been in McClellan's retreat before Richmond, and been unfortunate enough to have been taken prisoner and live with Jeff. [Davis] six weeks as I and some others did and then see if he would complain of Uncle Sam's rations. While we were there we lived on half rations of bread, no meat, only every other day we got a small piece of fresh meat boiled up without salt and very poor beef at that. . . . Hoping that no one will take any offense at what I have written, I subscribe myself as ever, your humble servant,

O. T. Stiles[6]

Stiles, who had been taken prisoner at Savage's Station along with Alex Davis and spent months in Richmond's Libby Prison before being paroled, had no patience for the tone of Webster's letter. Webster eventually deserted his regiment in February 1864.[7] Where he went thereafter is a mystery. Stiles, like many soldiers, believed that letters written for publication should refrain from self-pity. Indeed, private letters often expressed a greater degree of vulnerability than letters written for a broader audience, as was the case with Mason himself. At least there were opportunities to relieve stress; on October 4 Mason recorded in his diary, "Capt. [Martin Warner] Davis, Sergt. OT Stiles & I were invited to Col. Barneys tent for to sing. Had a good sing." On many an evening in camp, Mason and his friends enjoyed "a good sing" with one another.

In addition to conscription, the army incentivized veterans to reenlist. G. G. Benedict noted, "During the month of October, the subject of re-enlisting for the war was much discussed by officers and men."[8] Cases of fraternization with the enemy were also common at this time, as Mason explained to Harriet. Benedict wrote that "the service on the line—though requiring especial vigilance, was amicable as between the opposing pickets, and daily exchanges of newspapers, instead of bullets, took place between them."[9] Mason also noticed in the "Irasburg Paper" that Fred Kimball had married his sweetheart Susanna Hoyt when he was home on leave of absence after being wounded at Funkstown, then saw Kimball himself when he rejoined the regiment in early October. In terms that might offend modern sensibilities, or may have even offended Harriet, Mason joked that Kimball had committed "Susanside." Mason, tormented by the question of reenlistment, suggested that if he were to come home and "stick my head into the matrimonial noose & enlist for during life instead of the war," it would be "about the same as enlisting after all." Choices had to be made. Harriet was likely not impressed.

Camp near Rapidan Station Va

Oct[ober] 9th 1863

Dear Harriet

As I have not much to do this afternoon & am alone I will write a few lines to my dear Hattie. Serg[ean]t OT Stiles of Albany & Alex W Davis (my tentmates) & 11 Privates have just gone on Picket from our Co[mpany] for 2 days. . . . It is a very pleasant day quite warm in the middle of the day but we have very chilly nights. We came here last Monday & relieved the 2d Corps. . . . After marching near 2 miles we came on to the line & relieved the 7th Virginia Reg[imen]t (Union) from Western Va there is a 7th Va in the Rebel army & at the Battle of Antietam they were engaged in deadly conflict each Reg[imen]t taking prisoners from the other. It seems sad to have citizens of the same State warring against each other perhaps brother against brother or father against son but we have many such cases in this Cruel unnatural war. But to return, we saw plenty of Gray or But[t]ernut backs about half a mile across the open field doing picket duty same as we. The boys we relieved said they had exchanged News Papers with the rebs. So our boys were anxious to get a rebel paper. Alonzo Priest a dare devel in our Co[mpany] got an *American Messenger* and stepped out in front of our line & began to flourish it—one of the rebs soon answered the signal & Priest advanced the reb did the same (both without arms or equipments) the rebs were a little cautious & sent 2 men but as Priest was a match for 2 common men he went alone. They met about half way between the 2 lines & saluted each other as old friends exchanged Papers & each party returned to his Reg[imen]t. The rebs belonged to the 4th Georgia (Ewells Corps) during the day more than a doz[en] papers were exchanged. Elijah Stone went down once & shook hands with one & exchanged papers. They had to do it on the sly the Officers did not allow it. As I did not have charge of any Picket I liked to see the fun go on I simply went because the Co[mpany] went & I wanted to be with them the other Serg[ean]ts had to tend to the relieving of Guards. It seems inhuman for men to come up to each other shake hands perfectly friendly & perhaps in an hours time be engaged in deadly conflict—but such is war. I am well the rest of G[lover] boys ditto. I see by the last Irasburg Paper that Fred Kimball is married I learn that he is on his way to the Reg[imen]t between Alex[andria] & here. Just this morning I looked up & saw him coming riding he is some lame but looks quite fleshy & tough for a young man so lately married. I should suppose he would look more haggard after committing Susanside no I would say suicide but enough. I mean to get a commission & go home & well yes, what is it—enlist no? Stick my head into the matrimonial noose & enlist for during life instead of the war? So it is about the same as enlisting after all.

receive from your true lover
Dan

Kimball returned to the regiment prematurely. His wound was still quite painful, and in only a matter of days, he was hospitalized again. His diary entries in October reveal why he returned to his regiment, but ultimately why he was transferred, like Hobart Bliss, to the Invalid Corps (later called the Veteran Reserve Corps):

> Oct. 13. I cant see why I came back so lame as I am. Shall be obliged to go to a hospital & I dread it the hardest kind. O could I be with my darling wife. Why did I leave when I was so unable for duty when I could remain with her so well, but I felt anxious to get to my regiment.
>
> Oct 16. Last night Dr. Ducachet Surgeon in Charge called for me & after examining my case tells me I must be discharged. That I will not be fit for duty with my Regt. for a year. I feel bad. It seems as though I could not have it so. But if I must go. I must. Shall try & get into the Invalid Corp.
>
> Oct 18. Tis lonely enough. For the first time in my life I have a feeling of homesickness. Am in such suspence. Hope to get into the Invalid Corps. Three weeks ago this day was my wedding day. Happy day. Oh I am blessed with a lovely wife, so good, so true, so noble.
>
> Oct 24. My discharge is presented me this morning so I am but a humble citizen of Vt & not a U.S. Officer. I shall get in the Invalid Corps if possible. My discharge is honorable on account of wounds received in battle. After much "red tape" through the different war Depts I get my pay in full with mileage in all $441.65.
>
> Oct 25. This morning I write Father, smoke a segar & now I think of attending Church. Attend the Methodist Church. A good meeting & interesting.[10]

Mason's thoughts turned toward the possibility of a furlough home, one of the great inducements for veterans to reenlist. He asked Harriet, "Who would not be a soldier & after upward of 2 years active campaigning in an enemies country battling for the right—return to his dear friends to enjoy the sweets of civil life for a few days? After such an absence one learns how to prize the privileges & comforts of a home among his native hills surrounded by dear friends." But before that could happen, he and the Vermont Brigade were busy chasing Lee's Army through northern Virginia, though no serious fighting occurred in the fall of 1863.

By early November the Army of the Potomac had settled in for its third winter in Virginia at Brandy Station. On November 19 Lincoln spoke at the dedication of a new national cemetery at Gettysburg and made it clear that the nation was in the midst of a terrible struggle to redefine itself with a "new birth of freedom." Two days later Mason wrote one of his most eloquent and remarkable letters of the war to Harriet, echoing many of Lincoln's sentiments in the Gettysburg Address. Was Mason aware of Lincoln's address or was his timing a complete coincidence? Either way Mason acknowledged that "the eyes of all civilized nations are looking on speculating whether a Republican government can sustain itself or not." In other words, the war was testing whether "that nation, or any nation so conceived and so dedicated, can long endure." It was also perhaps the strongest abolitionist message in all of his letters, but it was cross-written, so Harriet would have had quite a challenge to read it.

Camp Near Brandy Station

November 21, 1863

Dear Harriet,

I now seat myself for the purpose of chatting with Hat for a few moments—I received your ever welcome letter last eve, also 5 papers. . . . I learned from it that you are not enjoying first rate health. I am afraid that you have worked to[o] hard the past season. You must be careful about your health for one cannot enjoy true happiness with poor health, therefore we should be very careful & not transgress Nature's law in any manner. You must bear in mind that you are mortal & cannot endure everything. Perhaps you will think I am giving you quite a lecture but you must take it as a little good advice from one who feels a deep interest [in] your welfare. Since I last wrote you we moved about 2 miles to the right—which brought us into the midst of a large rebel encampment where they had fixed up quite comfortable quarters doubtless intending to stop here through the winter but the Yanks came on to them so suddenly they thought best to leave in great haste. We have been here nearly 2 weeks. The men have erected quite comfortable houses with chimnies & arches attached by tearing down the rebs cabins and taking the timber. Some reg[iments] moved on to the same ground & occupy the same tents or rather spread their shelter tents over the wood work. I tent with Capt[ain] Davis now and have good quarters. I am very healthy at this time. Am getting my usual amount of fall flesh on so to speak. If I could only get at my father's bin of apples occasionally. Would not I enjoy the treat. What? Perhaps you don't think I like apples, but—well I would like to see the man that dare offer me a 2 qt. dish full just for a taste. Last Tuesday the Division was called out to see a couple of deserters branded, 1 from the 2nd Vt.—1 from the 49th N.Y. The victims were brought onto the ground followed by a forge drawn on wheels (every battery has one), their sentences read which were to serve as many months in the service after their reg[iments] were discharged as they were absent from them. To forfeit all pay due now from Government & be branded with the letter D, 1 on the right hip, 1 on the left shoulder which was done in our presence. It looked rather cruel to see a red hot iron stamped on the bare flesh. It made them squirm I tell you. There has been several shot in the Army of the Potomac for desertion. Next Friday (27th) there is to be a man shot for the same in this Divis[ion] belonging to the 7th Maine. The whole corps will doubtless be called out to see it so as to warn any (there may be who harbor such thoughts) what their fate will be. Yesterday this corps was reviewed by Gen[eral] Sedgwick, the commander. It was a grand military display. The long lines of infantry marching with colors flying headed by splendid bands of music with guns & bayonets glistening in the sun. The great display of batteries of artillery scoured to a dazzling brightness all united made a grand display, one that I would have freely given $500 to witness 3 years ago, since which I have seen many such, some of which were very telling in their results. I mean when these masses of bristling steel & thundering artillery are engaged in deadly conflict, it is terrible. Yet when one feels he is battling for the right when he thinks of the principles he is supporting, when he thinks that he is knocking out the rotten treacherous walls of slavery on which our government has tattered & reeled threatening to engulf us from the commencement and substituting in place of the granite walls of freedom, when he thinks that his government is passing through the fiery ordeal, when he thinks that the eyes of all civilized nations are looking on speculating whether a Republican government can sustain itself or not—then it is that the soldier's heart swells with emotions of pride & patriotism & trusting in the God of battles, he nerves himself to the conflict. Under such feelings the roar of cannon & the rattle of musketry & the din of war become grand & sublime. . . . I should be very happy to spend Thanksgiving with you how pleasant it would be but as it is impossible I must content myself with the bread & pork or beef & a cup of coffee for supper on that day or perchance we may get soft bread on that day. Yesterday we drew soft bread one good loaf to each man. It was a great rarity. I assure you the boys were much pleased. [Our] furloughs were not granted last year till near February & think quite probable I shall not be able to visit you before the above named month. The Glover boys are all well except Carlos Drew. He is sick with a fever though not considered dangerously. Remember me to all the friends write soon.

Receive from your Lover
Dan

{9}

"There Is Something Wild and Exciting That Makes It Bewitching" (Winter 1863–64)

G. G. Benedict wrote that "in December, the question of whether to re-enlist or not to re-enlist was presented by the government's offer of bounties and furloughs to re-enlisting veterans, and formed a steady subject of discussion among the men. The result was that one thousand and thirty men of the brigade, who had served two years or more, re-enlisted for three years more or for the war."[1] In the Sixth Regiment, of the 322 original volunteers who remained in the regiment, 191 men (59 percent of the veterans) decided to reenlist.[2]

Martin Warner Davis wrote almost daily in his diary in December that the reenlistment question was *the* prevailing topic of conversation in camp. On December 16 he wrote, "Some interest about reenlisting." A day later he added, "The subject of reenlistment is the most that occurs of interest." Three days later, again: "There is more interest about reenlisting than anything else."[3] Mason waited until March to reenlist, but on November 24, he started for Vermont with the purpose of recruiting volunteers and filling Glover's quota. He also was given the task of sending home the body of Carlos Drew, a Glover man who died of disease that same day. Three days earlier Mason had written: "He is sick with a fever though not considered dangerously." On November 25, while at Washington, Mason wrote that he "obtained coffin for Drew" and sent him "through to Barton" for $135. Mason then made a long trip by train to New York City, then to Burlington, Vermont, where he remained for four days on account of bureaucratic red tape. Mason griped, "Hope to get our papers so to start for home tomorrow morn. Time drags heavily here." Finally, on December 3, he took a train from Burlington to White River Junction, then another to Barton. On December 5 he at last saw Harriet again after more than a two-year absence. He also noted that the "town voted $215 Bounty to volunteers."

On December 7 he "went to Barton reported to Col. W. W. Grout was assigned to Glover to cooperate with the selectmen to encourage volunteering as much as possible." He remained home throughout the month of December, and while he was successful in encouraging a number of men to enlist, his diary entries also offer a glimpse of daily life during a Vermont winter. Far from being dull and isolating, his calendar was packed full of social activities and work. He seemed to "visit" just about everyone in town:

> December 8. Cold & pleasant. Helped father kill his hog. Also helped Rob kill his pig. Visited Mrs. Mccloude & Deans in the eve. Had a good time.
>
> December 9. Cold & squally. All the forenoon went up to Mr. Drews & carried some trinkets that belonged to Carlos. Mr. Drew paid me $43 to defray expenses of sending home Carlos. Elbert Luther [and] I. Adams enlisted for Co. D. 6th.
>
> December 10. Emily & I visited Mr. Frenchs in the eve. Had a good time popping corn cracking butternuts etc.
>
> December 13. Brooks very high. . . . Had a good sing in eve. River very high men had to loosen ice & flood wood to prevent bridges from being carried off.
>
> December 14. Cloudy & foggy some in forenoon. Father & I went hunting game very scarce.
>
> December 16. Cold & pleasant. Sugared off at Mr. C's.[4]
>
> December 17. Cold & cloudy. Quite snowy some portions of the day. . . . Glover's quota full.
>
> December 19. Bought some velvet ribbon to put on pants. Cracked some butternuts. Went to band school in the eve.
>
> December 23. Cold & very pleasant. Went over to West Glover & got HBC brought her over to Fathers. Done Father's chores. Trees very frosty.
>
> December 24. Had the old mare to draw wood.

December 25. Very pleasant, quite cold. Done chores & visited. Had a good time slide on the ice by moonlight with the fair ones.

December 26. Very pleasant, HBC & I went and visited Mr. Barbers. Bell Cutler was there. Carried H. Home near sunset. Emily & I visited at Mr. Hebbards in the eve.

December 27. Went to church to hear Mr. Perkins. . . . Willie Phillips played the violin had rather poor singing. Missed many faces that are in the army.

December 28. Emily & I went to Mr. Harts singing school in eve.

December 31. Started for Irasburg early to see Col. Grant to obtain transportation papers from Barton to Brattleborough. . . . Arrive Mr. C's near sunset. . . . Expect to start for Brattleborough tomorrow morning.

Mason's first letter to Harriet in 1864 offers some insight into the experience of departing back for the front: a late night out with Harriet until 1:30 a.m., a short night's rest, and then a departure from Barton the next morning. His sister Emily bade him a tearful goodbye, although Harriet apparently held back her tears until Mason was gone. He then captured something of the simultaneous joy and agony of his final night with Harriet: "What a night that was I believe I never enjoyed myself so well before yet it was a sad time." There was no doubt that leaving Harriet weighed heavily on him, and he said that his time with her "has cured me of the reenlist fever. I cant bear the thought now."

Camp Brattleboro, VT, *Jan[uary] 3d, [18]64*

Dear Harriet

As it [is] Sunday & I have not much to do I will pass a few moments very pleasantly chatting with you at a distance. I am now in charge of No. 11 Barracks containing 55 recruits from all parts of the State all strangers to me. Perhaps a short sketch of my experience journey &c since leaving you would be interesting to you. I got home about half past 1 oclock that night crept softly up the back way to my chamber & was soon lost in the land of pleasant dreams. Slept about 2 hours got up &

made arrangements for leaving. Father carried me out to Barton. I had a worse time leaving Emily than you. These womens tears are terrible affecting I was so glad you held out bravely to the last—daresay you had a good cry as you tell about after I left & doubtless a sleepless night but I hope not—what a night that was I believe I never enjoyed myself so well before yet it was a sad time. But enough of this. . . . I went down to the village yesterday & got my Photograph taken they will not be completed until next Thursday. I will forward you 1 by mail. I bought 2 Albums for you & Emily as I could not send them by mail less than 6 cts per ounce I sent them by Express directed to Father so you will get it in course of time. I bought 2 coppies of sheet music, 1 Bingen on the Rhine & Who will care for Mother now. You must learn them both. Harriet—you shant laugh at me but I believe I am homesick lovesick or something else I never have felt so discontented since I have been in the service as now. You dont know how I long to see you I dont know but it has cured me of the reenlist fever. I cant bear the thought now. A commission would not tempt me feeling as I do today but perhaps when I get back to the army I shall think differently. Harriet—your image will rise before me at all hours in the day but I must be reconciled to my lot.

"Good by Hattie"

Receive from your sincere lover
Dan

Despite Mason's claim that his visit home had "cured" him of the "reenlist fever," as he predicted then, once he was back at the front, he waffled on the issue. It seems clear that Harriet urged him not to reenlist. Mason acknowledged, "I learned from your letter that you were not reconciled to my reinlisting & spoke of my extorting an unwilling consent from you," but then proceeded to offer some sarcastic remarks about how she should support his correct view on the matter. Why more than half of Union veterans reenlisted in the winter of 1863–64 can be explained by numerous factors: ideological conviction, the promise of furloughs and bounties, or what military historians term "small unit cohesion," which meant, among other things, that one could not disappoint his fellow troops. In Mason's case all of these factors could have influenced his decision, but as he explained to Harriet, "I tell you Hattie there is something about a military life that civil life cannot give. There is something wild & exciting that makes it bewitching."

Camp near Brandy Station Va
Feb[ruary] 16th 1864

Dear Harriet

I seat myself pen in hand to acknowledge the reception of your worthy letter of the 3d which was as ever a welcome message & read with no small degree of satisfaction. . . . I am well & enjoying camp life firstrate. I tell you Hattie there is something about a military life that civil life cannot give. There is something wild & exciting that makes it bewitching. I dont think I should be contended in Vt to settle down as long as we have war in the land. To be sure Glover has some very strong attractions your own dear self being the most prominent one. Perhaps you will say to yourself if he loves me as well as he pretends if he did he would be contented with me. Harriet you can do all that woman can to make me contended there & if peace was restored to our country I think I would as live in Glover as anywhere with my darling Hattie. I learned from your letter that you were not reconciled to my reinlisting & spoke of my extorting an unwilling consent from you. I am sorry you have not strength of mind & will to resist your lover. I was not aware that I had such command of your mind. Pardon me for such an unhuman act as that. But I can see why you could not say no. It was because your own good sense told you it was the best thing under the circumstances to reinlist. I have not reinlisted yet—think I shall the last of the month or the 1st of next. I would like to be married while home on my 35 days furlough if you were able you of course know best about that & I shall of course leave it to you to decide. I am not very anxious to be married now yet—for some reasons I think perhaps it would be best for us to unite our destinies if I should be wounded or sick & sent away to the Hospital it would seem very pleasant to have you come & take care of me again if I knew I was to be taken away I would rather you would have what effects I might leave than any other person. But perhaps on the whole it is better to wait until another winter, as you know the state & condition of your health best. I leave it entirely for you to decide. Lieut[enant] Nye Cap[tain] Dwinell Alex & Oliver got back a few days since. I tent with Oliver & Alex. Glover boys are all well. You must now excuse me, accepting best wishes. Give my regards to all your folks. Write a long letter on receiving this. Be a good girl & mind your Mother

Receive from your lover, Dan

Mason had made up his mind to reenlist and went to Washington to seek a commission as an officer in the newly organized U.S. Colored Troops (USCT). He told Harriet, "You may think it strange of my asking to command a Co[mpany] of colored soldiers, but a commission is a commission with all the pay & emoluments." Colonel Elisha Barney of the Sixth Vermont (who was later killed at the Battle of the Wilderness) recommended Mason for the position, describing him as "a young man of strict moral habits" who had "proved himself to be a brave soldier, and efficient as a Serg[ean]t. I can heartily recommend him to the board of Examiners for Comm[ission] in Col[ore]d Regi[ment]s and believe he will make a brave & accomplished officer."[5] Much has been written about the motives behind white officers volunteering to lead Black troops. Mason's motives were not entirely altruistic, as he admitted to Harriet, but he added, "I believe in making soldiers of them," which was hardly a sentiment shared by the white population as a whole. James Rickard, a soldier in the Eighteenth Connecticut who would end up serving with Mason in the Nineteenth USCT, was similarly enchanted by the prospect of receiving a commission as an officer. In January 1864 he told his sister, "I can't make up my mind about trying for a commission." Although he expected to be promoted to sergeant in the Eighteenth, "that is not much in comparison with a Capt[ain]s commission which I think I should get."[6] A week later he wrote to his brother and said,

> I want to be sure of a Captaincy & I am self-conceited enough to think that I am capable of that. . . . I should get $120.00 per month & I could not do as well as that anywhere else. . . . In regard to the dangers I look at it in this light—most probably this Reg[imen]t will do some fighting in the spring if not before & it don't matter where a man fights he is in as

much danger in the ranks of the 18th [Connecticut] as . . . a Reg[imen]t of Colored Troops.[7]

Getting a commission dominated Rickard's thoughts all winter. In February he told his brother, "If I get a commission the people of Abington might present me with a sword."[8]

After Mason reenlisted he told Harriet that he would be home soon on a thirty-five-day furlough, where he hoped to get "warm sugar."

Camp near Brandy Station Va

Mar[ch] 13th, [18]64

Dear Harriet

I dare say you are expecting me every night in accordance with my last letter. When I last wrote I expected to be on my way before now. I reinlisted Feb[ruary] 26th was mustered in to the service the 27th just before we started on that raid the mustering officer did not register my muster & consequently I was not good for the month of Feb. I got my 35 days furlough approved & it has remained in the Adj[utant]s office since. Oliver Stiles & I have since been ordered before Maj[or] Gen[eral] Caseys board of examination at Washington to ascertain if qualified for a commission in the Regular Army (to command colored troops). We started last Wedns[-day] morn on 3 days abscence. We passed the Board Gen[eral] Casey presiding (he made the military tactics we use). I was recommended for a Captain & Oliver for a Lieut[enant]—the recommend[ation]s were sent to the Secretary of War. We have returned to our Reg[imen]t to await orders the commissions which will be given by President Lincoln will not get around for several weeks I think. Yesterday I reinlisted again so as to get a town Bounty & I intend to start for Vt next Tuesday morn on 35 days furlough. You may think it strange of my asking to command a Co[mpany] of colored soldiers, but a commission is a commission with all the pay & emoluments. I believe in making soldiers of them Besides a Captains commission in the Regular US Army is considered a grand position by all officers. My pay will amount to $128 per month $1536 a year. Besides I can resign any time when sick of it. Alex Davis is now posting himself for an examination at Gen[eral] Caseys Board. I hope he will get a recommend[ation] & we shall try & all get into one Co[mpany]. I am well & enjoying myself well. I hope you are getting along well perhaps we may conclude to be married when I get home. I am betting upon getting warm sugar what gay times we will have.

Yours with much love
Dan

{ 10 }

"I Was Really Proud of My Command" (Spring 1864)

The recruitment of Black troops was sanctioned by the Emancipation Proclamation, which had been issued on January 1, 1863. Blacks had served in previous American wars, but only in local or state units, not in the regular army. At the beginning of the Civil War, the army did not allow the arming of Black troops. For multiple reasons the Lincoln administration did not support such a move. Much of Lincoln's political calculus early in the war centered on keeping the border states of Missouri, Kentucky, and Maryland in the Union, which meant that he moved cautiously on all questions of race, including allowing Blacks to take up arms for the Union. In August 1862 a delegation of "western gentlemen" met with the president and offered to organize two regiments of Black troops, but Lincoln indicated "that he was not prepared to go the length of enlisting negroes as soldiers. He would employ all colored men offered as laborers, but would not promise to make soldiers of them. . . . The President argued that the nation could not afford to lose Kentucky at this crisis, and gave it as his opinion that to arm the negroes would turn 50,000 bayonets from the loyal Border States against us that were for us."[1]

As a result of pressure from Radical Republicans in Congress, abolitionists, and Blacks themselves who argued that arming Black troops would give the Union a political, military, and moral advantage, and because Union military setbacks prior to Antietam had prompted a reevaluation of war aims and a new willingness to adopt a total war strategy, by late 1862 and early 1863 public opinion on this issue had shifted significantly. The Emancipation Proclamation, the draft, and the arming of Black troops all meant that the war would be conducted more aggressively. Even though enslaved and free Blacks could now conceivably shoulder a musket, the intent was to use them in limited roles to free up additional white troops for frontline combat, a pattern that would not be unknown in later American wars, where Blacks continued to fight in segregated units.[2] Black troops were eager to fight the rebels and to prove their worth not just as support troops, but as combat forces. It would take the shedding of much blood to win over Northern skeptics.

Northern white troops harbored a great deal of racism toward Black troops, even in Vermont. Private Wilbur Fisk of the Second Vermont noted in May 1862 that "Negro prejudice is as strong here as anywhere and most of the boys would think it a humiliating compromise to the dignity of their work to have it declared that the object of their services was to free the repulsive creatures from slavery, and raise the negro to an equality with themselves."[3] Even after Black troops had proved themselves in combat at places like Fort Wagner, South Carolina, and Milliken's Bend, Louisiana, a white officer penned a letter to the *Burlington Weekly Sentinel* in February 1864; while allowing that Black troops had their uses because "their peculiar constitution enables them to resist the attacks of disease . . . when the white man would perish," he continued to blast their qualities as soldiers:

> Unfortunately they are very badly officered, the Col. for instance, of the colored regiment here would be refused a second Lieutenancy in a well organized white volunteer regiment from Vermont. This is the more to be deplored, as the negro, to be kept in wholesome discipline, requires officers, who from their education and character, can command the respect of the soldier. The negro freed from slavery is almost utterly helpless, and is dependant upon the advice and instructions of others. . . . While the negro is obedient and respectful, two good qualities in a soldier, he is improvident and *un*-self-reliant. I am suspicious too as to their fighting qualities for various reasons.
>
> 1st. My experience with the Black as an individual, is that they are inferior in mere physical brute courage to the white.
>
> 2d. They of course are almost deficient of that higher order of courage, based upon a sense of duty and honor, and strengthened by that feeling of responsibility.
>
> 3d. A people who have been so entirely kept under, so thoroughly under the sway and upon the support, advice and assistance of the whites, must

have their manhood degenerated. Like a dog or a child who has always been harshly ruled and punished, loses spirit and courage.

For these reasons, I have not much confidence in the negro as an active soldier, though behind breastworks and urged on by others, he might make a fair resistance and something of a fight.[4]

Southern responses to Black soldiers—and their white officers—were often hysterical. The nightmare scenario of armed Blacks instigated to "insurrection" by white radicals prompted Southern calls for violent retribution against Black prisoners of war and the white officers who led them into battle. The most notorious example of the mistreatment of Black troops by Confederates was at the Fort Pillow Massacre on April 12, 1864, where rebel troops under the command of Nathan Bedford Forrest murdered over three hundred Black troops after they surrendered. Indeed, the entire process of prisoner exchange began to break down in the summer of 1863 as Confederate officials refused to exchange captured Black troops, who were viewed as stolen "property," not as prisoners of war. This led to devastating consequences, as thousands of Union soldiers who may otherwise have been exchanged ended up dying in Confederate prisons, most infamously at Andersonville, Georgia. To join the Union army as a free Black or formerly enslaved person carried enormous risks. And while many white officers volunteered to lead Black units to satisfy their personal ambition, the risks of doing so were hardly insignificant.

The Emancipation Proclamation had authorized the freeing of slaves in areas that were in rebellion against the United States, but it allowed slaveowners in border states who had remained loyal to the Union to retain their "property." If a slaveowner could prove their loyalty, they could seek compensation for any enslaved persons who joined the Union forces. The War Department issued general orders on October 3, 1863, which stated that slaves in the loyal states could not be recruited without the "written consent" of their owners, with the caveat, "If within thirty days from the date of opening enlistments, notice thereof and of the recruiting stations being published, a sufficient number of the description of persons aforesaid to meet the exigencies of the service should not be enlisted, then enlistments may be made of slaves without requiring consent of their owners; but they may receive compensation as herein provided for owners offering their slaves for enlistment." Slaveowners could claim compensation to the amount of $300 "upon filing a valid deed of manumission and of release and making satisfactory proof of title."[5]

Recruitment for the Nineteenth USCT began in late 1863 and continued into 1864. The regiment was organized in Maryland, and although it included some free Blacks and hired substitutes, most of its rank and file consisted of enslaved men from the Eastern Shore of Maryland, including from Talbot County, where Frederick Douglass was born. Captain James Rickard of the Nineteenth USCT remarked that the regiment was "composed entirely of slaves."[6] Colonel William Birney, a Southern-born officer and strong abolitionist, oversaw the recruitment of Black troops in Maryland. Union troops fanned out through the countryside to directly recruit enslaved men from plantations under the noses of their owners. By October 1863 Birney reported to Lincoln that he had recruited between 1,250 and 1,300 enslaved men in Maryland. Numerous enslaved individuals altered their names when they enlisted to avoid detection by their owners. This commonality created complications for slaveowners who sought compensation. For example, Samuel Adams, a twenty-two-year-old "mulatto" man from Frederick County, Maryland, belonging to a Grafton Burgee, enlisted as William S. Adams. When his owner filed a claim for compensation, he attested, "The slave in question, has always gone by the name of Samuel Adams—but recently has added the name of William, so that the 'William S. Adams' on the muster roll is the 'Samuel Adams' claimed in my application." In order to receive compensation, Mr. Burgee filed a deed of manumission in the local courts and was eventually awarded $300 by the Board of Claims.[7]

The War Department's order that "enlistments may be made of slaves without requiring consent of their owners" after a thirty-day period caused an uproar. Democratic Maryland governor Augustus Bradford sent a telegram to the War Department protesting these actions:

> A novel experiment of the kind will have various prejudices to encounter, and must necessarily be a subject of discussion and deliberation before it is definitely adopted. Thirty days will be entirely too short a period

> to furnish a fair trial. Let me beg, therefore, that you will make the time sixty days at least.
>
> I cannot forbear again attempting to impress upon you my views of passing no order at this time commanding a resort at any specified period to enlistments without the owner's consent. . . . Not only does the exhausted condition of the productive labor of our State, as I urged upon you to-day, require, but the good will of our people toward the Government would be vastly promoted and the success of state constitutional emancipation secured, by suspending the compulsory enlistment until after we have made the experiment of enlisting with the owner's consent.[8]

In short Governor Bradford urged a more gradual approach to the recruitment of Black troops. Maryland was a slave state that had remained loyal to the Union, although its population included a large number of individuals who sympathized with—and fought for—the Confederacy. Colonel Birney acknowledged the difficulties of recruiting in such an environment. He reported that one well-known Confederate sympathizer had "become a virulent enemy of the Government and associate with well-known secessionists; that he proposed to two secessionists to raise a mob at Chestertown and burn the small Government steamer employed for the transportation of recruits for the U.S. Colored Troops; and that he was busy and officious in advising masters of slaves to offer armed resistance to the recruiting officers." Undaunted, Birney then added, "They are, I am happy to say, not sustained by the mass of the population, which earnestly desires the enlistment of the negro, especially the slaves. My officers went unarmed and alone through nearly every county in the central part of the Eastern Shore, and everywhere received aid and sympathy from the people, except the rebel sympathizers among the slaveowners and except a few politicians."[9] The dangers of recruiting slaves directly off plantations were real. Benjamin Brown, for instance, a private in Company D of the Nineteenth USCT, a twenty-two-year-old "Griff" (a racial classification of the time between "negro" and "mulatto"), was shot while on recruiting service at Greensboro, Mayland.[10] Birney was even reported to have released prisoners from a "negro jail" in Baltimore. Upon releasing the inmates, "they all appeared to be much delighted, and on the men being asked the question, 'whether they would enlist or not' . . . they all replied 'yes.'"[11] The *Baltimore Sun* reported on October 22 that "planters on the Patuxent River having found yesterday that a large armed negro force had been suddenly stationed along its borders, for the purpose of enlisting negro slaves, they applied to their late member in Congress (Mr. Calvert) on the subject, and through him obtained an interview to-day with the President." Lincoln was sensitive to such concerns. In reply to the Maryland slaveowners, "the President asserted, first, that he did not know by what authority the force in question had been sent there. . . . He thought that negroes might be recruited in Maryland by consent of masters, as they had been in the Army of the Cumberland, but he did not wish to effect the object in any rude or ungentlemanly manner. . . . He thought he would order the withdrawal of the negro troops now upon the Patuxent."[12]

Lincoln then wired General Robert Schenck, who was in command of the Union VIII Corps in Baltimore: "A delegation is here saying that our armed colored troops are at many if not all the landings on the Patuxent river, and by their presence, with arms in their hands, are frightening quiet people, and producing great confusion. Have they been sent there by any order? and if so, for what reason?" Schenck responded later that evening:

> The delegation from St. Mary's County have grossly misrepresented matters. Col. [William] Birney went under my orders to look for the site of a camp of instruction and rendezvous for colored troops. . . . They are under special instructions, good discipline and have harmed no one. . . . The only disorder or violence has been that two secessionists . . . have killed second Lieut. White . . . at Benedict, but we hope to arrest the murderers. The officer was a white man. The only danger of confusion must be from the citizens, not the soldiers—but Col. Birney himself visited all the landings, talked with the citizens, and the only apprehension they expressed was that their slaves might leave them. It is a neighborhood of rabid secessionists. I beg that the President will not intervene and thus embolden them.

Lincoln, not satisfied with Schenck's response, wired back: "Please come over here. The fact of one of our officers being killed on the Patuxent, is a specimen of what I would avoid. It seems to me we could send white men to recruit better than to send negroes, and thus inaugurate homicides. . . . Please come over."[13] The officer, Lieutenant Eben White of the Seventh USCT, while on a recruiting mission, was accosted by two slaveowners, a father and son: "The father called White a 'Damned N———r-stealing son of a bitch,' and the son spat in his face; each fired at him, the father with a shotgun, the son with a revolver. Another shotgun blast took off the hat of Pvt. John W. Bantum, who accompanied White, and lodged a few bird-shot pellets in his scalp. Bantum ran for his life and took news of White's death to his captain."[14] Despite Lincoln's promise that no additional slaves would be forcibly removed from their owners, the *Baltimore Sun* added, "the members of the deputation obtained nothing that looked to them like an assurance that negroes would not ultimately be enlisted in Maryland."[15] The issue was hardly resolved. In January 1864 the Maryland legislature debated a joint resolution that stated:

> Whereas the Senate of Maryland has this day received information from a member of the House of Delegates, and from other reliable sources, that Gen. Birney, who is in command of the "negro encampment at Benedict," has sent out about one hundred and fifty negro soldiers in the counties of Charles and St. Mary's, with orders to seize upon and carry into the encampment at Benedict all negro men found upon plantations and otherwise, for the purpose of forcing into the military service of the United States all such as are capable of bearing arms, and of setting at liberty all who are not fit for such service.
>
> And whereas, in the opinion of the Senate, this outrage upon the rights, property, and security of her citizens has been perpetrated by said Birney without the authority, knowledge, consent or approval of the President; therefore
>
> *Resolved*, that a joint committee of not less than three on the part of the Senate, and not more than five on the part of the House of Delegates, be, and hereby are, appointed to repair to Washington to confer with the President, and ask such redress and protection for her citizens as the necessitee of their condition claim, and demand protection at the hands

of the government, and at their earliest possible convenience report to their respective bodies.

Illustrating the precarious political balance in Maryland, the resolution failed to pass by one vote; the ayes were twenty-six, and the nays were twenty-seven.[16]

It was in this context that Mason became an officer in the Nineteenth USCT. After he reenlisted Mason left for Vermont on March 16. His visit home wasn't long; shortly after arriving he received word from the War Department that he had received a commission. On March 23 he wrote to the War Department and said, "I have the honor to acknowledge the reception of my appointment to Captain in the 19th U.S. Colored Troops. . . . I am now on a thirty five days furlough having reenlisted as a veteran volunteer previous to my examination before Gen[eral] Casey's Board. Under the circumstances I shall be obliged to cut short my furlough several days at least."[17] He headed back south on March 28, so he was only home for just over a week. Mason was now a captain of Company H of the Nineteenth USCT. His close friend Alex Davis was also now a captain in the Thirty-Ninth USCT. Mason reported to Camp Birney outside Baltimore, then shortly thereafter went to Harpers Ferry (now in West Virginia) on a recruiting mission. Captain James Rickard of the Nineteenth USCT said that he had been given orders to "recruit vigorously."[18] Mason described his first experience as an officer in the Nineteenth USCT in a letter to the *Orleans Independent Standard* on April 8, 1864:

I was assigned to the command of Co. H. Thursday forenoon we were ordered to be ready to march at 5 o'clock P.M., with three days rations to go on a recruiting expedition, the detail to number 280 men, exclusive of officers. At the above specified time we took the cars for Harpers Ferry, arriving there at 12 o'clock, Friday, soon after which we marched in the direction of Charleston, Va., arriving there near dark, the afternoon being rainy we were a little moist, having marched 8 miles. You will recollect the above place is where Old John Brown was tried and executed. As we entered the town the soldiers struck up the tune of

Old John Brown, which made the citizens look very sour especially the ladies, if I may be allowed to use the term; some of them shook their fists and showed considerable of the Old Serpent. As the men were wet it was necessary to burn some rails. I went to a house nearby to get supper, I was met at the door by a thing in crinoline, who was full of anger, she wished to know if those devils were going to be allowed to burn rails. I told her the men were wet and cold and must have fuel. I concluded it was not a very good boarding place and looked further and found good accommodations.

Saturday morning it snowed very fast, we marched to Berryville, a distance of 10 miles where we found a few union people and many secesh. Sunday we marched to Winchester a distance of 10 miles, stopped there long enough to make coffee, then resumed our March to Bunker Hill, where we encamped for the night having marched 22 miles, the men having their knapsacks some of them as large as small bureaus, had to forge several streams, and March with wet feet, yet they stood up bravely. I think they will endure far more than white men. I find they have a much better understanding of matters pertaining to our government than many suppose. I have no doubt that they will fight desperately.

Yours truly,
Dan Mason[19]

After leaving Harpers Ferry, the Nineteenth USCT moved back to Baltimore by rail, then to Annapolis by water, and then overland by foot to Washington DC. As the regiment marched through Baltimore, the *American and Commercial Advertiser* recorded the scene:

> The three regiments of colored troops recruited in this city and State, nearly three thousand men, under the auspices of Colonel Bowman, made a dress parade through our streets this morning previous to their departure for the scene of—it is to be hoped—active operations. No man desiring the speedy overthrow of the rebellion, and its proper termination, could have looked upon the spectacle with other than feelings of satisfaction. Only one of the regiments was armed (the Nineteeth), the other two were fully equipped except arms. A splendid brass band was

on the right of the line, and a full drum corps accompanied each regiment. The men all marched proudly and soldierly, and nothing could have been more perfect than their movement, evidencing a great deal of care in their management and drill.

Magnificent working and fighting material was in that column. Sturdy, stalwart, able-bodied and healthy men, well disciplined by careful training, proud of their new and novel position, they looked every inch the soldier. A few years ago the man who would have said that the negro would have marched through the streets of Baltimore in military equipments and unarmed without being assaulted, would have been considered a fit candidate for a lunatic asylum. But such is the case, and during their march this morning it was pleasant to see . . . that they were lustily cheered. In many places along the route of march, flags were waved from the stateliest or from the humblest dwellings. Several of the men were accompanied to the point of embarkation, the foot of Long Dock, by their wives and sisters, and many were the leave-takings there witnessed.

Some of the more rabid of the rebels in our midst gave vent to their spleen in silent murmurs and "curses not loud but deep." One female, who was standing at the Institute as the procession turned down the market space, thought it had come to a pretty pass when she had to stand to allow "n——rs" to pass, and that they were a nice crowd to send to fight white men. But notwithstanding the grievances of the fair secesh, the troops passed quietly by, amid the congratulations of those who think the United States government can rightly use the colored man for a soldier or a laborer, as well as the rebel oligarchy at Richmond. May we have many more such regiments to credit to the quota of Maryland, as those that passed the *American* office this morning.[20]

Alex Davis remembered that earlier in the war, "there were the following in Co. D. 6th Vt who usually slept and messed together. Kimball. Mason. Nye. Bliss. Stiles and Davis." Between the loss of Hobart Bliss and Fred Kimball to wounds, and now Mason and Davis to new assignments in the USCT, the only members of Mason's original cohort in Company D that remained were Elbert Nye and Oliver Stiles. As Mason indicated in his next letter to Harriet, Nye was "lonely" after he and Davis left. Oliver Stiles had applied for a commission in the USCT but did not receive it, so he also remained with the Sixth Vermont. Davis said that "on April 9th I bid Co. D. 6th Vt. Good Bye—and slipped away to Baltimore Md. Leaving Oliver alone—As I dreaded to be—my commission having come as 1st Lieu[tenant] of Co. E. 39th USCTroops, Col[onel] Ozora P. Stearns commanding."[21]

Dan Mason and Harriet Clark were engaged on Mason's recent furlough. He referred to Harriet as "the lady of my choice" and told her that "though I have had bad influences thrown around me of a carnal kind I have resisted all such temptations." Mason reassured her that his actions had always been chaste, but especially now that he was engaged, she should have no concern whatsoever of his succumbing to any temptations of a "carnal kind" while at the front. With that said he mentioned that he had bought a new suit of clothes, and that "I should like to go courting in them to christen them I think a little pressing would do them good."

Upon its arrival in Washington, the Nineteenth USCT marched through the city and was reviewed by, among other dignitaries, President Lincoln and General Burnside, who watched the procession from the steps of Willard's Hotel, the same hotel where Julia Ward Howe penned the "Battle Hymn of the Republic" and where Dr. King would stay the night before the March on Washington ninety-nine years later. The crowd, according to Mason, did some "right smart cheering." He added, "I was really proud of my command." The *American and Commercial Advertiser* of Baltimore wrote, "Major General Burnside's Corps this afternoon passed down Fourteenth street, in the presence of President Lincoln and General Burnside. Thousands of persons congregated about Willard's Hotel and on the street, and the troops were enthusiastically received. As the colored brigade passed, their fine marching and orderly bearing elicited the highest praise, and they were loudly cheered. The troops all presented a magnificent appearance and were in good health and spirits. Business was quite suspended for the time, and citizens generally crowded the sidewalks to view the spectacle. Much enthusiasm was manifested—men cheering, and ladies waving their handkerchiefs."[22] The *Annapolis Republican* said that "the negroes were loudly cheered and told to 'Remember Fort Pillow.'"[23] Both houses of Congress adjourned to see the parade. Thaddeus Stevens, a Radical Republican member of the House, said that he "wished the Opposition to have an opportunity of seeing a specimen of his 'ghosts,' alluding to the colored troops."[24] Walt Whitman, a nurse in army hospitals in Washington DC, also was present in the crowd. In addition to his description of the scene to Harriet, Mason wrote a letter to the editor of the *Orleans Independent Standard* where he said, "We marched through Washington in columns by platoon; the men seemed to take pride in doing their best; the sidewalks were crowded by people waving their handkerchiefs, swinging their hats and cheering the colored volunteer. Uncle Abe and several other government officials reviewed us as we passed and seemed highly pleased with the military display of the Ethiopians."[25] The *Constitutional Union* of Washington was less impressed: "As the column of colored soldiers passed down Fourteenth street, last evening, the office holders, from the Treasury and other places, whose number are legion, and who lined the streets, set up a shout of exultation, at the picture before them. They had no shout for the white soldiers—no, none. Their hurras are for miscegenation and the new order of affairs."[26]

The Nineteenth USCT entered Virginia after its march through the capital, where, Mason noted, "we relieved some Penn[sylvania] troops who did not fancy the idea of going to the front & being relieved by Colored Troops." He also mentioned having a "Colored servant." A regimental order from December 1863 stipulated that "all officers are provided with servants. The servants of an officer not mounted should be an able-bodied man capable of carrying on a march his own knapsack and that of his employer."[27] Mason paid his servant from an allowance he received.

Camp Ferrerow Manassas Junction
Va Apr[il] 30th [18]64

Dear Hattie

I once more seat myself to write you a few lines on the sacred soil of Va. I received your very welcome letter of the 14th inst[ant] a few days since & have not had time to answer until now. Since I last wrote you we have done some quite smart marching. A day or 2 after I wrote we that were left at Bal[timore] took the Steamer *Baltim[ore]* for Annapolis arrived there about noon found the whole 9th Corps on the move we pulled ahead & overtook them about 2 oclock in the PM. We continued our march to Washington marched through the City the soldiers marched splendidly. President Lincoln & a large crowd on either side reviewed us & done some right smart cheering I was really proud of my command. . . . All of the old troops are being sent to the front. We relieved some Penn[sylvania] troops who did not fancy the idea of going to the front & being relieved by Colored Troops. We expect to stop here sometime perhaps all summer & drill & do guard duty which is not like field service. I am not very well just now have had a sort of dysentery for several days. Think I shall be all right in a few days. I have an A tent by myself (so called from its resemblance to that letter). I have had it raised up on boards nailed together in the shape of a pen & set the tent on for a roof. I have a board bed stead with hay for bedding, a table with an oil cloth spread on it (which was a blanket) a floor to my tent & all cozy. I have a Colored servant who sleeps in one of the cabins vacated by the reg[imen]t we relieved which has a large stone fireplace table &c. My cooking utensils consist of Coffee pot, spider, bake pan, &c. I had some baked beans yesterday. It is an iron pan with a heavy cover made dishing so that you can put coals on top. I am going to get some flour & have biscuits baked & flapjacks fried. I think I shall have some pies baked. My servant is quite a good cook. I wish you could be here & eat some of his cooking dont you? . . . I have not much to write this time. I see Alex nearly every day. In regard to my not bidding your mother good bye I must beg her pardon. I thought I would not get out that night as it would create some unpleasant feelings I thought the less ceremony the better. Give my respects to Miss Sweeney & all the folks

accept from Dan

The Nineteenth USCT marched into Virgina as part of Grant's overland campaign to Richmond. Grant, who had enjoyed numerous successes in the western theater, was brought east by Lincoln in the spring of 1864 to directly engage Robert E. Lee. The first showdown between Grant and Lee occurred at the Battle of the Wilderness on May 5–6, 1864. The Nineteenth USCT was not engaged, but Mason's old unit, the Sixth Vermont, suffered enormously. The Vermont Brigade lost over 1,200 men killed, wounded, or missing after the horrific two-day battle, which proved to be the deadliest day in Vermont's history. Both armies hammered away at each other inconclusively in dense undergrowth at close range, with many of the wounded being burned alive in the night due to brush fires that had been set by sparks from rifle fire. Captain Martin Warner Davis of Company D described something of the horror of the Wilderness:

> At 3 P.M. we were ordered to advance upon the enemy, the order was soon obeyed and long lines of brave soldiers pressed their way through an almost impenetrable growth of scrub oak; We were soon made to realize that we were upon the foe, as we received a heavy volley of musketry which brought many a brave boy to the ground to rise no more; The conflict had already begun, and for three hours we remained almost stationary, receiving and returning an incessant fire of musketry. At one time we were ordered to fix bayonets and charge upon the enemy through the dense thicket—the order was obeyed, but it was to no purpose. It was impossible to penetrate the natural abbatis under such terrific fire.
>
> At dark the fighting of the first day closed by our holding the same line where we had first met the enemy. We went into the fight with 46 muskets, and when we came out 25 of the men that bore them in were killed, or more or less wounded. . . .
>
> During these three days fighting our loss was very heavy and I have no reason to suppose the enemy suffered less. I think the slaughter of human beings was much greater than at Gettysburg or any other battle of the war. . . .
>
> We the surviving members of company D, deeply mourn the loss of our brave comrades that fought so bravely at their posts, and have fallen a sacrifice for their country and deeply sympathize with the friends that are called to mourn for the loss of our brave boys. They are gone—yet their names will live as men that were willing to give their life in so noble a cause.

Typical of the messages that Captain Davis had to send after the battle was one he sent to the parents of William S. Livingston of Albany, Vermont, a sergeant in Company D:

> Your son was killed in the first day's fight in the Wilderness. No one saw him fall as we made a charge through a thicket of oaks, but were obliged to fall back a short distance, leaving our dead between our lines and the enemy's. We did not know whether your son was killed or wounded until the 7th, when I went on to the ground and found him dead and it was with sorrow that I found your noble son; He was hit in the breast, probably died instantly. When I found him everything had been taken from his pocket and knapsack by the enemy. He was soon buried with the rest of our dead on the battlefield. Thus fell a brave and faithful soldier. We all deeply sympathize with you and your bereavement.—William was one of the best of soldiers, always ready to do his duty without complaining, and we have the consolation of knowing that he fell at his post nobly fighting for his country.[28]

The Wilderness was not as deadly as Gettysburg, though Captain Davis's belief that it was speaks to the scale of carnage and intensity of fighting in this engagement. Captain Davis later wrote that when the Vermont Brigade reached the North Anna River,

> we received an order from General Meade that the 6th Corps would have that day for rest, unless we were needed in case of an engagement.—We were very glad of the privilege; for twenty days we have not seen a quiet day, and no opportunity for a change of clothing; the day has been well improved, a great part of the time the river has been alive with human beings, many of the men washing their clothes and putting them on, not having change of clothes. . . . I shall only say that everything looks favorable to our being very near Richmond within a week.[29]

Though not a tactical victory for either side, Grant, unlike previous commanders who led the Army of the Potomac, continued to move south after the fight. Another bloody, violent clash occurred a few days later at Spotsylvania Court House. The extreme losses of the Vermont Brigade were clearly on Mason's mind.

Camp near Chancellorsville Va May 13, [18]64

Dear Harriet

I seat myself to inform you that I am well. We have not been engaged in any fighting. We have been used to guard the waggon trains back to the rear. . . . Our army has fought some terrible battles since I wrote you. We left Mannassas Junct[ion] a day our two after I wrote you. We are now about 5 miles from Fredericksburg. I have seen the remains of my old Reg[imen]t since coming here. The old Vt Brigade has suffered terribly since crossing the river. Co[mpany] D of the 6th Numbered 39 officers & men when it went in to the fight. It came out with 14 all told. Capt[ain] Davis & Elbert were not hurt at last acc[oun]ts. Oliver Stiles was I fear mortally wounded in the shoulder. S[tephen] Baxter was shot through the left hand. 7 were killed & 18 wounded in D Co[mpany] other Co[mpanie]s lost heavily. Since the above the 6th Corps has been engaged Gen[eral] Sedgwick the Commander killed. I have not heard from my old Reg[imen]t for several days. The fighting was desperate yesterday. Our army took many prisoners & pieces of Artillery. The rebs fell back last night so reported. Yours with much love

Dan

PS. Excuse scarcity of paper & write soon good Bye Hat

Mason's friend and former tentmate Oliver Stiles was wounded badly at the Wilderness. Stephen Baxter, who Mason had often critiqued as a poor soldier, was wounded as well. Both, like Hobart Bliss and Fred Kimball before them, would eventually be discharged from the service on account of their wounds. Elijah Stone, a Glover man and private in Company D, wrote home to his brother after Spotsylvania and succinctly explained the suffering that Company D had endured:

> I take this opportunity to let you know that I am still alive. We have not got any mail since we left camp. It is 12 days since we left camp and we have been under fire every day since but 2. We left camp with fifty men this morning, we have 10 left—there is 3 missing, we expect them up. It is a hard fight but we are getting the best of it. Yesterday morning we

took 4 thousand prisoners. Co. D and A skirmished yesterday and the rest of the brigade [fought] behind a breastworks, the rebs on one side and our men on the other side about 10 feet apart. Stephen Baxter was wounded the first day's fight in the hand. I am well and have come out all right—so far. Our loss is very heavy all through the brigade.[30]

Mason and Alex Davis, though in different units, saw each other almost daily. The two friends went to visit their wounded comrades in the Vermont Brigade the day after the Wilderness. As Davis recalled,

On the 7th Dan, in company with myself, visited a field hospital and found Sheperd, Folsom, and several others of Co. D. who were wounded on the 5th—and learned of the killed.

In conversation we concluded that had we remained with the boys, we should one or both shared their fate.

On Monday the 16th of May, I went to the door of a shanty. We were passing and saw a soldier laying on the floor. I stepped in to see if I could do something for him—and it was Oliver, the same who took examination for the Colored Troops when Dan did—had his examination proved 1st instead of 2nd class, he would have escaped a Minnie ball through his right shoulder.

I felt that I must do something for him. . . . I made quick time to the 19th—told my story to Dan, and we went to the Col[onel]—told our story . . . and in less than two hours, Dan and I had helped Oliver into an ambulance, and he started for Fredericksburg. Oliver lived until October 10, 1875, when he died from his wound in Topeka, Kansas as a cashier in a bank.[31]

Of the original tentmates of Company D—Dan Mason, Alex Davis, Hobart Bliss, Oliver Stiles, Fred Kimball, and Elbert Nye—only Nye remained in Company D fit for active service. Mason described his encounter with Stiles in his next letter to Harriet. He also spoke ill of his lieutenants, "fast lads" who were not his "stile," but added that "we get along without any trouble."

Camp in the Woods 3 miles from Fredericksburg Va May 18th, 1864

Dear Harriet

I seat myself for the 3d time to write you since hearing from you at least you owe me 3 letters. I presume you have not received all of them as the mail has been retained at Washington to prevent people from ascertaining the movements of our army. Gen[eral] Grant seems to wish to be shut out from all the civilized world until he has accomplished his great object—the capture of Richmond which I do believe must fall now or never if we fail now I dont know when we can hope to accomplish the great object we have been striving to gain for the last 3 years. Gen[eral] Grant is an obstinate fighter—victory is his aim. He brings all available troops not needed in other departments to bear on Richmond. We have been continually receiving reinforcements the last 10 days. The 22d Army Corps from the defences of Washington have joined us (the 11th Vt is in that Corps). I am glad to see those chaps that have lain there doing nothing for 2 years brought into the field. There has been no fighting of any acc[oun]t for several days. Lee is falling back & Grant is following we are on what is called Salem heights Guarding the City of Fredericksburg. We are in Burnsides Corps but we are detached from the rest of the Corps under command of Brigadier Gen[eral] Ferrerow we have 2 Batteries of Artillery 1 of them the 3d Vt Battery. I am acquainted with some of the Batterymen. We also have 2 Reg[imen]ts of white Cavalry. So you see it would not be very easy taking us. I am on Picket today with my Company both my Lieut[enan]ts are with me. They have both tendered their resignation & will doubtless be out of the service in a short time. They are smart fellows but they dont like the service & are bound to leave they have been used to living in the City & they being what you would call fast lads, they are determined to go back to their favorite haunts of vice & dissipation. They are not my stile. But we get along without any trouble. They presented me with a beautiful pair of shoulder straps this morning some they bought in Washington a few weeks since while absent there without leave for which they were put under arrest & released providing they would resign. I saw Alex Day before yesterday he was well also saw Oliver Stiles the same day in an old barn where he & his brother who was left to take care of him had been stopping for several days. They left in an ambulance that morn for F[redericks]burg. Oliver will recover I think though he is severely wounded, the reason of his being left was because he could not stand it to be moved at that time. . . . We have not seen any fighting yet nor captured any prisoners as the papers stated. You must not believe all you get in the papers such exciting times as these until it is confirmed. I must now close hoping to hear from you soon. I am well & enjoy myself firstrate most of the time. Give my regards to all the friends accept my best wishes & receive from your lover Dan

Mason then moved with his unit to White House Landing on the Pamunkey River, where he had been two years before during the Peninsula campaign. The sight of Black troops marching through Virginia created an intense backlash among local residents. The *Richmond Dispatch* reported in June that "the most outrageous excesses were committed on the inhabitants by the negro troops. They stole everything they could lay their hands upon, offered indignities to the ladies, and committed excesses that ought to cause the blush of shame to mantle even a Yankee check. . . . The people of Caroline [County] will long remember the passage of the Union 'devils' through their borders."[32] Captain James Rickard of the Nineteenth USCT dismissed such claims as nonsense: "I saw a Richmond paper, and the most scathing language possible was used, heaping abuse on the heads of ourselves (the colored troops) for destroying private property and assaulting defenceless females, reciting not one word of truth. . . . Of course this was for a purpose, to embitter the feeling against us, which was now about as violent as could be."[33]

Mason reported that Alex Davis was ill with the mumps and was "deranged," but cautioned Harriet, "You had not better tell people so that his folks will get hold of it for it will give them a good deal of concern & will do them no good." He then told Harriet that he intended to resign his commission the following winter, since "3 years are enough to serve. Besides I have set that time to be married."

Camp at Old Church Va June 10th [18]64

Dear Harriet

I seize my pen to acknowledge the reception of your ever welcome letter of the 23d which I have delayed answering until now for the reason I had sent you one the day before. I am well since I last wrote you we have been used as train guard. Last Sunday 4 Co[mpanie]s of the 19th went down to White House Landing to guard a train (distance 12 miles). It looked very natural around there I[t] seemed but yesterday since I was there in the days of McClellan. It is a perfect city of canvas. There is a very large Hosp[ital] there where our wounded are well cared for the Christian & Sanitary Commissions are doing a great & good work. They have large tents erected with banners flying where the wounded can hobble up & get almost any kind of drink except (intoxicating) or any thing to eat that they desire. Those confined to beds are furnished by ladies who have been sent on as nurses. Our wounded have never been so well cared for as this campaign. . . . Alex Davis is not very well at this time I go over & see him 3 or 4 times a day. He has had the mumps & taken cold. He now has trouble in his head. He can not remember anything 15 minutes in talking with him an hour perhaps he will ask the same questions half a doz[en] times. He thinks some one is trying [to] steal his money. He says dogs chase him nights. He is not confined he was out to dress Parade last night but he is deranged a good deal of time. But I think he will be all right when his mumps leave him. You had not better tell people so that his folks will get hold of it for it will give them a good deal of concern & will do them no good. There has not been much fighting for several days, except skirmishing & occasionaly a big gun to wake up sleepy heads. They say Grant is mounting siege guns & making all preparation necessary to a siege. It will take several weeks to take Richmond. 3 years of fortifying has made it a very strong place. Harriet—I am glad I came into this service. I intend to resign next winter which [would] be an honorable time when the army is lying inactive. It is concidered dishonorable to tender a resignation in the face of the enemy in the middle of an active campaign. But next winter if spared I shall go home. 3 years are enough to serve. Besides

I have set that time to be married. I am glad your health is improving. Receive from your lover

Dan

After the battles at the Wilderness, Spotsylvania, and Cold Harbor, Grant's Army "moved by the left flank" again, crossed the James River, and approached the city of Petersburg, Virginia. If Petersburg could be captured, then all rail traffic to Richmond would be severed. The armies raced to occupy Petersburg, but unfortunately for the Union cause, the Confederates were able to build a series of strong fortifications ringing the city, thus forcing Grant's federals to besiege the city. Mason wrote on June 19 that "we can see the spires from where we are."

Mason also commented on a move that Harriet made to "a pleasant little village," probably the village of West Glover, ostensibly for health reasons, though it's unclear what Harriet was afflicted by. In Virginia his friend Alex Davis continued to suffer from the mumps. He then chided Harriet, who must have scolded him previously for not writing long enough letters, and complained, "I must fill this sheet or take a lecture in your next."

{ 11 }

"I Say Fight Them" (Summer 1864)

U. S. Grant said that in 1864 his goal was to "hammer continuously against the armed forces of the enemy and his resources, until, by mere attrition, if in no other way, there should be nothing left to him but an equal submission with the loyal section of our common country to the constitution and laws of the land."[1] Grant told George Meade, who was nominally the commander of the Army of the Potomac, "Lee's army will be your objective point. Wherever Lee goes, there you will go also."[2] Union offensives elsewhere were designed to hamper the Confederacy's ability to shift forces along their interior lines. Lincoln, impressed with the plan, remarked, "Those not skinning can hold a leg." In May, as Union forces advanced toward Richmond after the Wilderness and Spotsylvania, the *Orleans Independent Standard* boldly proclaimed, "Grant heads an army of colossal dimensions and as brave and patriotic as ever moved upon the battle field; he has men enough, provisions enough, the hearty cooperation of all his officers, and what is better is backed by all the powers at Washington. We confidently expect that by the fourth day of July our soldiers will be holding high carnival in Richmond, the goal which they have been so anxious to reach for the last three years."[3]

What followed was no carnival. The Army of the Potomac settled in for a siege of the Confederate defenses around Petersburg, Virginia, that would last nearly a year. Both sides dug an elaborate, extensive series of trenches that anticipated the conditions on the Western Front in World War I a half century later. Time was not on Grant's side. A presidential election was looming in the fall. Lee's best hope was to grind down Grant's army and inflict as many casualties as possible, hoping to sap Northern morale and the will to continue the war, empower the Peace Democrats, and seek a negotiated settlement. Meanwhile, General William T. Sherman's forces bogged down outside of Atlanta. The situation for the Union was not bright; even Lincoln predicted that he would lose the upcoming election.

The fighting conditions at Petersburg were grim, demoralizing, and deadly. The romantic characterizations of war that had been common in 1861 were long gone. Wilbur Fisk of the Second Vermont said, "There is nothing desirable about this place. It is all fighting and no fun. We neither whip nor get whipped. It is regular cold blooded duelling, day after day, with no decisive result on either side, and fellows no braver than I am, get tired of it after a while."[4] Each day soldiers died from artillery or sharpshooter fire with no appreciable change in the situation. James Rickard described an incident where "a mortar shell fell nearly in front of a little bomb-proof I occupied and rolled into it; there wasn't room for us both, I thought, so I seized it and threw it over the breastworks before it exploded."[5] Mason and the Nineteenth USCT dug in in front of Petersburg. He told Harriet, "I have conciderable sport with the men they are many of them quite sharp," but he again stated his intention that "I am resolved to leave the service another Winter."

Camp in the field Prince George Co[unty] Va
July 2d, 1864

Dear Harriet

Yours of the 24th arrived today & was read with a great deal of pleasure. . . . We are now about 6 miles from Petersburg guarding the Norfolk Rail-Road. The weather is very warm but we find ice cellars on nearly every Plantation filled with that luxury so we have good cool water most of the time. The siege is progressing a continual skirmishing is kept up night & day with a mixture of cannonading. Since I last wrote you our Divis[ion] was placed in the 2d line of works in front of Petersburg. We had to keep low in the day time as the sharpshooters kept up a continual popping. Stray bullets were constantly whizzing through the air. 2 men were wounded in our Reg[imen]t. The 19th Reg[imen]t went out to the front on fatigue during our stop near P[etersburg] to fill sand bags for breastworks. We were not in sight of rebs but balls came over near us that were fired at our sharpshooters. One man in Co[mpany] H was slightly wounded in the head causing a smart flow of blood for a few moments. . . . I have very nearly $400.00 due me now, being a little more than 3 months pay. I am very well contented most of the time, yet I am resolved to leave the service another Winter. I like this service much better than at first. I have conciderable sport with the men they are many of them quite sharp. They are very willing to do jobs for me in the way of putting up shades & building comfortable quarters. Alex is all right now except he has not much confidence in himself he knows how he has been. It has been very dry weather for several weeks. It is very dusty marching. I think we shall get a Shower tonight—it would seem refreshing. I am getting about run out for news. I shall have to close this dirty sheet by tendering the best wishes of your true lover. Please remember me to all the friends. Write soon & oblige

Dan

In July the Vermont Brigade and the rest of the VI Corps were sent to Washington to safeguard the city against a raid into Maryland by Confederate General Jubal Early. Early's force reached the outskirts of the city, making it as far as Fort Stevens, but eventually was checked by the arrival of the VI Corps and then pursued up the Shenandoah Valley. The siege of Petersburg continued with little movement. As the VI Corps chased Early out of Maryland, Mason wrote to the *Orleans Independent Standard* with an update about his activities outside of Petersburg:

I visited Co. D of the sixth regiment two days before their departure to Maryland; had a fine visit with the few old veterans remaining; it seemed like home. The attachments formed by 29 months association with that band of heroes are not easily broken. Capts. Davis, Dwinell and Joslyn were well. . . . Lt. Nye was also well and seems determined to remain in the service until rebellion is burst up. Lt. Styles, who was wounded in the Wilderness, was expected to return soon. I would like to mention many other scarred veterans, but time and space will not permit.

I am now on picket, have been for four days past; I begin to think we are doing this duty by the season. But we should have to be building forts or slashing trees if we were in camp and I will not complain of this. We have built four large forts within the last ten days and connected them with earthworks; the surrounding forest is now being cut to give range to the artillery. The siege is still going on and constant cannonading is kept up with numerous variations thrown in by sharpshooters, which add beauty and harmony to the dirge which plays many a noble youth to a land where such accursed rebellions are unknown.

But I must close—hoping you and your readers will pardon me for taxing your patience so long. May the time be not far distant when soldiers letters may be reckoned with the things that were, when spears shall be beat into pruning hooks and swords into plowshares, and the people learn war no more.

I remain your ob't serv't,
Dan Mason[6]

Mason worried that his regiment would be assigned to picket duty for the duration of the summer. So did Charles Stinson, a New Hampshire man and fellow officer of Mason's in the Nineteenth USCT, who wrote to his mother, "I think Gen[eral] Grant dont intend to put us in the fight unless he is short of men. Our Div[ision] is guarding wagon trains or on picket all the time where it would take white troops, so we are of service."[7] To many Union officers, even picket duty seemed like too important a task to entrust to Black troops. General Meade was uncomfortable with the Black regiments under the command of General Edward Ferrero performing that task. On July 12 Meade wrote to General Hancock that "I think the best arrangement you can make . . . will be for your corps, while in reserve, to picket Ferrero's front. I do not like relying on the colored troops for this duty in so important a position, and would prefer employing them, on working party."[8] Despite the reservations of Meade and other soldiers in the Union Army, all evidence from the moment that Mason joined the Nineteenth USCT points to his respect and admiration for the Black troops under his command and his belief in their qualities as soldiers. Alex Davis wrote that "for many days until July 30, Dan and I were much together as the Blacks had been trusted in the front line—and were almost constantly under fire—Dan & I losing many men from our companies—by sharpshooters behind breastworks. We were also behind breastworks—and no doubt the Black man 'got in his work some,' for they certainly exceeded for coolness my most sanguine expectations, as they did of Dan's, who so expressed himself to me many times."[9] However, there was no guarantee that the Nineteenth USCT, or the other thirty-seven Black regiments surrounding Petersburg (the most assembled in any one campaign of the Civil War), would ever have the honor of leading an assault. In his next letter to Harriet, Mason wrote of his grim surroundings; the dust was so oppressive that "one can hardly see or breathe."

Camp near Petersburg, Va. July 15th, 1864

Dear Hat,

I will improve these spare moments by writing you a few lines. Yours of the 1st arrived in due season. I have not had a chance to answer the interesting note until now. We have been very busy for several days past building forts & breastworks & strengthening our lines which have been somewhat weakened by taking away some of the army to Maryland. I judge there must be a good deal of excitement all through the North relative to the safety of Bal[timore] & Washington. The last report the rebs were within 3 miles of the former 30,000 strong. . . . Grant is said to be in W[ashington]. If so I don't believe they will get away this time.

I went up to the 6th Vt. Reg[imen]t & staid all day the 7th (the corps started for Md. 2 or 3 days after). I had a good time. Cap[tain] Dwinell will be Major in a few days. Cap[tain] Dwinell & Elbert came over & made me a call the day before leaving for Md. I drilled my Co. in their presence. They were highly pleased with the drill. Alex is well now. I am on picket today in the rear of our army. It is quite cool & breezy compared with many days this season. We have not had any rain at least not enough to lay the dust for 44 days. The roads are very dusty. If you will imagine a few thousand men & several hundred wagons moving on one of our Vt. roads covered 4 inches deep with dry ashes on a windy day you will have a pretty good idea of Virginia dust. One can hardly see or breathe. I am well & hope this may find you fast regaining your former health & vigor. I have not much to write. The siege of P[etersburg] is going on as I write—an occasional cannon is heard or the crack of a sharpshooter's rifle rings out upon the air. I think the scene of strife is changed for a while to Md. But there is no doubt but what Grant intends to hold this position. Our cavalry is said to have gone on another raid to cut the railroads west & south of Richmond. I have just heard that Gen[eral] Wright in command of the 6th corps has defeated the rebs & is following them up. I must now close for I have a chance to send this in to camp & it will go out this eve. My love to all the friends.

Receive from your lover Dan

On July 28 Alex Davis wrote to the *Orleans Independent Standard* to describe the conditions at Petersburg:

> Just now all seems quiet, but within ten minutes some sharpshooter may see a head and discharge his piece; then another will reply—then a dozen—then a whole battalion will rise up and fire.—That is provocation enough for one or two batteries to open; then mortar shells go circling through the air from both lines, which has a cooling effect, as they are most destructive and send the men into their holes. All is again quiet, and judging from the present, you would not think that, two hours ago, lead and iron were whizzing, whistling, screeching and bursting in every conceivable way among our ranks. Thus we spend our time, dodging shells and making the rebels dodge. . . . Every day some of our men are killed while doing fatigue work—but we do not hear any murmuring, or detect any disposition to shrink from duty.
>
> Of the fighting quality of our division I cannot speak, as we have never been brought face to face with the enemy, but I have full confidence in them, as when under fire they have always exhibited true courage, not flinching in the least when duty demanded.
>
> I received a letter from O.T. Stiles last week. He was then at Portsmouth Grove Hospital, R.I. He had nearly recovered from his wound received at [the Wilderness], and I think he is now with his regiment. . . . Capt. Daniel Mason is well and enjoying life, as he always had the faculty of doing. Dan and I were a little homesick when we knew the 6th Corps had gone to Maryland, and we could not go with them; but we are over that now, as we learn the corps is coming back, and had no pleasurable trip to Washington and back on crowded transports.[10]

Two days later Davis, Mason, and the Black troops they commanded would be "brought face to face with the enemy." To break the stalemate at Petersburg, General Ambrose Burnside, commander of the Union IX Corps that the Nineteenth USCT was attached to, approved a plan to undermine a Confederate salient, pack it with four tons of explosives, and blast a massive gap through the rebel lines. The plan was met with great skepticism among many Union officers, who thought the scheme was hairbrained and impractical, though Meade and Grant ultimately approved it. Burnside's IX Corps consisted of four divisions; the Fourth Division, led by General Edward Ferrero, included the Nineteenth USCT. Ferrero's division of Black troops, which had seen little action and was eager to prove its worth, was selected to lead the assault. This was due to several factors: Burnside was far more enthusiastic about the fighting qualities of Black troops than other Union commanders, the white troops in the IX Corps had suffered heavily during Grant's overland campaign, and Ferrero's division was fresh and at full strength. Colonel Henry Thomas, who commanded the Nineteenth USCT, recalled:

> The night we learned that we were to lead the charge the news filled them too full for ordinary utterance. The joyous negroe guffaw always breaking out about the camp-fire ensued. They formed circles in their company streets and were sitting on the ground intently and solemnly "studying." At last a heavy voice began to sing,
>
> "We-e looks li-ike me-en a-a-marchin' on,
> We-e looks li-ike men-er-war." . . .
>
> All at once, when his refrain had struck the right response in their hearts, his group took it up, and shortly half a thousand voices were upraised extemporizing a half dissonant middle part and base. It was a picturesque scene—these dark men, with their white eyes and teeth and full red lips, crouching over a smoldering camp-fire, in dusky shadow, with only the feeble rays of the lanterns of the first sergeants and the lights of the candles dimly showing through the tents. . . . Until we fought the battle of the crater they sang this every night to the exclusion of all other songs.[11]

The mine was scheduled to be detonated at dawn on July 30, but just hours beforehand, General Meade ordered Burnside to withdraw Ferrero's division from the vanguard of the attack. As Meade recalled, he argued that Burnside

> should assault with his best troops; not that I had any intention to insinuate that the colored troops were inferior to his best troops, but that I understood that they had never been under fire; not that they should not be taken for such a critical operation as this, but that he should take such troops as from previous service could be depended upon as being perfectly reliable. Finding General Burnside very much disappointed—for he had made known to General Ferrero and his troops that they were to lead in the assault, and fearing that the effect might be injurious, and in order to show him that I was not governed by any motive other than such as I ought to be governed by—I told him I would submit the matter with his reasons and my objections to the lieutenant-general commanding the armies, and I would abide by the decision of the lieutenant-general as to whether it was expedient and right for the colored troops to lead the assault. Upon referring the question to the lieutenant-general commanding he fully concurred in my views.[12]

The degree to which Ferrero's division had trained for the assault remains an ongoing matter of historical debate. However, when Captain James Rickard of the Nineteenth USCT heard of the change, he commented,

> We were terribly disappointed. We had expected we were to lead the assault, and had been for several weeks drilling our men with this idea in view, particular attention being paid to charging. Only the day before, our regiment was drilled by Major Rockwood in forming double column and charging, which was witnessed by many officers and men of the army. . . . Both our officers and men were much disappointed, as it was an opportunity to show what they could do and there was not an officer but would have staked everything that we would break through their lines and go on to Cemetery Hill, as proposed. When all preparations were made, we lay down for a little sleep, and were awakened shortly

after daylight by the explosion and the terrible discharge of cannon, that made the ground tremble as by an earthquake.[13]

Grant later offered another explanation for his concurrence with Meade that Ferrero's division should not lead the attack: "General Burnside wanted to put his colored division in front, and I believe if he had done so it would have been a success. Still I agreed with General Meade as to his objection to that plan. General Meade said, 'if we put the colored troops in front (we had only one division) and it should prove a failure, it would then be said, and very properly, that we were shoving these people ahead to get killed, because we did not care anything about them. But that cannot be said if we put white troops in front.'"[14]

Regardless of the reasons for the withdrawal of Ferrero's division—racial, military, political, or otherwise—the three remaining white divisions in Burnside's corps drew straws to decide which one would lead the attack. When the mine exploded just before 5 a.m., General James Ledlie's division rushed toward the crater caused by the explosion, not around it. At that same time, 110 cannon and 50 mortars opened fire from the Union line, adding to the cacophony of battle. Charles Stinson, an officer in the Nineteenth USCT from New Hampshire, wrote that "in the morn, we were awakened by the heaviest cannonading I ever listened to & orders came to fall in which we did and proceeded to the place of action well aware that the Colored Troops had got to participate in the great contest."[15] An entire regiment of South Carolinians was buried in a crater that was 30 feet deep, 170 feet long, and 60 feet wide. Ledlie's men were stunned and disoriented by the hellish scene they encountered.

What followed was a confused, disorganized, poorly coordinated attack that cost the Union Army four thousand casualties. Meade and Burnside fired angry telegrams back and forth throughout the day. Generals Ledlie and Ferrero were reported to be drunk, without providing any direction to their divisions. Burnside's three white divisions had been sent forward into the Crater, but over an hour elapsed before Ferrero's division was ordered to advance. In the meantime Confederate forces regrouped and counterattacked. As Ferrero's division moved forward, it came under an enfilading fire as it pushed its way through white troops who were making for the rear. The men of the Nineteenth USCT remained in the Crater for hours, subject to a terrible crossfire, before they were given the order to withdraw. Charles Stinson said that the Nineteenth USCT

> had to charge across a plain to get to the blown up fort exposed to fire from three ways of the enemy. The slaughter was fearful. . . . Men were getting killed and wounded on all sides of me. Well I guess I hugged mother earth if I ever did. I never saw such sights before and hope I never may again. Soldiers were groaning and crying for water which if one undertook to give he would be most sure to get shot. If we tried to carry off the wounded the chances were few to get off with them. The sun poured down on us that we could hardly stand it.

After hours of fighting in the Crater, Stinson wrote that Union troops

> came back pel mel both black and white. We tried to stop them but was like stopping so many sheep. Soon we got orders to fall back, and we did under a terrible fire. I waited until the Col. started then I made tracks well I just flew. The way was completely strewn with dead, dying and wounded. . . . Lieut[enant] Mix . . . got killed just as the rebs came into the fort by a shell! He was very brave fighting with a musket. He shot a reb that tried to take the Colors from the front . . . My best Serg[ean]t was killed instantly. . . . I felt very badly to lose such a good man. We retired from the front at sunset very much fatigued and used up. . . . We have met with great losses in the battle here.[16]

The combat in the 100-degree heat was brutal, intense, and often hand-to-hand. As happened on other battlefields, many Black troops were murdered after they surrendered. A soldier in the Seventeenth Vermont, attached to the Second Division of Burnside's IX Corps, later recalled, "The colored troops . . . fought like heroes and many a rebel bit the dust from their unerring bullets, and as the rebels charged in upon us I heard the order given 'save the white men but kill the damn n——rs.' And I saw them run their bayonets through many a colored man showing him no mercy. I often think of this scene and a cold shudder goes through me as I think of how those poor colored men were butchered in cold blood."[17] Grant called it "the saddest affair I have witnessed in the war. Such opportunity for carrying fortifications I have never seen and do not expect again to have."[18] In his memoirs Grant said, "The effort was a stupendous failure. It cost us about four thousand men, mostly, however, captured; and all due to inefficiency on the part of the corps commander and the incompetency of the division commander who was sent to lead the assault."[19] Mason wrote to Harriet the next day and gave her a detailed account of "the longest day I ever experienced."

Camp near Petersburg Va July 31st 1864

Dear Harriet

You will doubtless be somewhat surprised to hear from me so soon, But as the Colored Troops of the 9th Corps have been engaged you will doubtless feel anxious to hear the particulars. I am all right—I have been once more been preserved & brought safely out of danger. Yesterday the (30th) was the longest day I ever experienced. The night of the 29th we were moved from the left of the army down in front [of] P[etersburg]. We were informed that there was to be a charge made at daylight next morn. The Fort which we had been undermining was to be blown up. We stacked arms within a half mile of our front line behind a piece of woods. It was late before we got camped down our ammunition had to be drawn & issued &c &c. I did not sleep much but I cant say as I dreaded the coming days work very much (I never went into a fight feeling better than the following morn). About daylight a great explosion was heard & then our artillery opened all along the line Such cannonading is terribly grand. We advanced—the 1st brigade in front a white Divis[ion] of the 9th Corps moved in & occupied the Fort before us. We had to pass through a very warm fire to get into the F[ort] which by the way was a perfect crater. The 22 Reg[imen]t South Carolina was nearly all killed or burried in the ruins a great many were dug out by our men & taken prisoners some were all burried but an arm or a leg some with their heads sticking out—4 cannon were blown up 2 of which our men dug out & turned on the rebs. We held the Fort until about 4 oclock in the afternoon when we got orders to evacuate & left under a cruel fire from 3 ways it was not more than 20 rods from the rebel Fort to our front line of works but 20 rods is plenty far to pass over where the air is sizzling hot with bullets & shells. I think I never was under quite as hot a fire. I dont see why I was not wounded. All day we lay under a terrible fire from the front & both flanks. . . . I dont know just how much we lost in the Corps nor Divis[ion] but I know the loss of my Co[mpany] but the reg[imen]ts loss has not been ascertained yet. I lost 1 killed & 15 wounded. Our Reg[imen]t lost our Maj[or] Rockwood a very brave man shot through the head & 3 L[ieutenan]ts killed 1 Capt[ain] wounded 1 L[ieutenan]t supposed taken prisoner. I had a ball put through my coat sleeve just above my elbow of my right arm grazing my arm so that it is purple today. I was once completely covered with dirt so I could hardly crawl out by the explosion of a mortar shell. I saw one man blown up at least 20 feet—he came down in a good many pieces. Alex Davis is all right. Some of our reg[imen]ts lost nearly all of their officers. I think the affair was very poorly managed. I must now close so as to send this out tonight—Remember me to all the friends

from your lover Dan

James Rickard may have described the exact moment when Mason was covered in dirt by the explosion of a mortar shell when he wrote,

> About two o'clock in the afternoon they charged in on our flank at the "crater," and there was a rush of what was left alive for our breastworks, and I think I made good time. A short time before this several officers of my regiment stood partly sheltered by a huge lump of earth that had been rolled out by the explosion, as large as a small room, when a ten-inch mortar shell fell and buried itself in the sand in close proximity, exploded, covering us with dirt and sand. . . . This was at a time when shot and shell were concentrated on this place, and men were being torn and mangled by the hundred every moment. . . . Lieutenant Dobbs of our regiment was also captured. When the captured officers were taken to the rear they were formed in line, and their names and regiments were taken down. None gave their regiment as one of the colored regiments, but

> from some of the white ones known to have been in the engagement, as it had been supposed that they would be executed according to an order issued by the Confederate government, if it was known who they were. Dobbs was indignant, and when they came to him he said, "Lemuel D. Dobbs, Nineteenth N——rs, by ——." They took him by the hand, and said they honored him for his frankness, and showed him more consideration than those whom they thought had lied. No man dodged his position after that.
>
> We attempted under a flag of truce to remove the wounded and bury the dead immediately after the failure to break through their lines, but they would not recognize a flag of truce, and all the rest of that day and night and the next day the wounded lay on the field in the fierce blazing sun, screaming for relief which we could not render, and most of them died. On the second day arrangements were made for a cessation of firing and the burying of the dead, who by this time had become a swollen and putrifying mass, unrecognizable. Long, deep trenches were dug, and by rolling them in blankets the dead were laid in these trenches, several bodies deep. The stench was almost unendurable even after burial, as so much blood covered the ground.[20]

General Meade, unwilling to admit defeat, did not arrange for a cease-fire with Confederate leaders to evacuate the dead and wounded until two days later. One of the wounded men under Mason's command in Company H of the Nineteenth USCT was Corporal John Addison, a thirty-eight-year-old Black man born in Prince George County, Maryland, who was listed on the muster rolls as a "farmer." It is likely that he was one of the wounded men who suffered in the crater with no assistance, as Captain Rickard described. Corporal Addison died of his wounds the next day "without effects."[21] He left a pregnant wife, Charlotte, and a six-year-old son, John, behind. A daughter, Barbara, was born in February 1865 and never knew her father.

In 1866, with the help of the Freedmen's Bureau, Charlotte applied for a widow's pension. Widows and dependents (under the age of sixteen) were eligible to receive a monthly payment if their husbands (or fathers) had died during the war. However, formerly enslaved women like Charlotte Addison faced greater challenges than white women in claiming a pension, since their marriages were not legally recognized, especially before the ratification of the Fourteenth Amendment in 1868, which granted citizenship rights to Blacks. In addition, birth certificates did not exist for children born into slavery, so proving one's status as a widow with dependent children could be problematic as well. In Charlotte's case numerous Black witnesses filed sworn affidavits attesting to the fact that she and John "lived together as husband and wife for the period of seven years previous . . . and that they were so recognized by the community in which they resided." Charlotte was "unable to prove the date of the birth of her two children by any written evidence. . . . She is informed by her former mistress Mary Turner, that the record of the birth of said children has been destroyed, and the said Mary Turner positively refuses to give her sworn evidence in the matter." However, another Black witness issued a sworn statement that "the son of Charlotte Addison was born on the 2nd day of December in the year 1857; that he is positive as to the date from the fact that a son was born to him in the same year, and he has always taken due care to retain the dates of the births of his own children." Charlotte and the other Black witnesses all signed their name with an "X." Charlotte did receive a pension of $12 per month until her death in 1908.[22]

Those Black soldiers who were not summarily executed upon surrendering were not sent to prisoner-of-war camps like their white counterparts. Instead they were sold back into slavery, many of them being sold at Richmond's notorious Shockoe Bottom slave market. The Union prisoners—Black and white—were paraded together through the streets of Petersburg and received a barrage of jeers and taunts from the civilian population. A captured white soldier in the Seventeenth Vermont recalled that when one woman cried out her window that "birds of a feather will flock together," an attack on the racial mixing of the horde of prisoners, "a Lieutenant from the 32nd Maine Regiment who was marching in my front replied, 'yes, but we don't mix in the nest as you do down here.'" Not keen on the Maine soldier's defiant remarks about Southern hypocrisy, "the guard which was on our right cocked and put his gun to his shoulder and said, 'you insult our ladies down here and I will blow you through,' to which the Lieutenant replied, 'shoot down, you, and then boast you have killed a Yankee as you will never kill one by going to the front.'" The guard "took his gun down from his shoulder, marched along, and said no more."[23]

Colonel Henry Thomas of the Nineteenth USCT stated in his after-action report,

> The Nineteenth U.S. Colored Troops . . . remained there unable to strike a blow, but received heavy losses. About 100 of the men of this regiment, with some of the officers, went into the crater and remained there for hours, expending all their own ammunition and all they could take from the cartridge-boxes of the wounded and dead men that lay thick together in the bottom of this pit. . . . Whether we fought well or not, the scores of our dead lying as thick as if mowed down by the hand of some mighty reaper and the terrible loss of officers can best attest. Nearly all the officers who came under my eye were fighting with bravery and coolness.[24]

Captain Alexander Davis of the Thirty-Ninth USCT, who was near Mason during the attack on the Crater, recalled Mason's harrowing near-death experience:

> As the Battle was planned—our Division was to lead—but at the last moment as a matter of national sentiment regarding the slaughter of negros—the three White Divisions went ahead—occupied three lines of breastworks deserted by the Johnnies. When the mine went up—and near two hours after they were in there—we were sent in—"The Blacks!"
>
> The fire from mortars, cannon, and small arms—was something terrible. 1,000 negros fell in passing from our lines to theirs. Then over three lines—before spoken of—filled with white troops—into a field where in a disorganized mass we met Mahone's Div[ision] of Lee's Army and as quick as I can write it, over 500 Blacks were shot, bayoneted & killed by blows from musket balls.
>
> Do not think for one minute that none of Mahone's men went down in the same manner. But the time came when we were so small in numbers that we started out. I [brought] out my 1st Serg[ean]t and when I jumped into the inside of our lines, he came, [got] hold of my coat tail,

and when he could speak, he said “My God! Capt[ain]! Can’t you run! Why! You had me right out straight.”

I took 59 good sable negroes into that fight and never saw but 21 of them again, and only this serg[ean]t for several hours.

I have a printed article now by a southern officer who was there and he says—“The slaughter of these surrounded Blacks exceeded that of Fort Pillow.” . . .

I am going to tell you how I think the life of Dan was spared by my 14 [year] old negro waiter. This morning of July 30, we knew there was to be hot work, and I gave Jim my wallet, diary & watch and told him to find me as soon as the battle was over and bring me a canteen of water and he soon came to me bearing his whole charge & water.

All did not come out where I did—soon after Jim [brought] me my canteen and I was lying on the ground, there came an increased rattle of musketry and soon I heard a heavy foot & all coming nearer & nearer.

I thought as clearly as though it had been spoken to me!

Dan’s coming!

And the next moment Dan jumped over the works & fell within three feet of me. I spoke to him but he could not answer. His face was lurid & his arms twitched like a palsied man—With the aid of my boy, I got him into the shade of a bombproof—bathed him—face, neck, head, & hands and for the remainder of the day I was with him. He talked but was not fully conscious when I found my reg[iment] was gathering together I left him—We was there the next morning, but he was gone. I cannot recall when I saw him again—for his brigade went to the lines at Bermuda Hundred—while my brigade was kept on the firing line front of the Crater for many weeks.[25]

Another account of the fury of the Crater appeared in G. G. Benedict’s history of Vermont in the Civil War:

During the spring of 1864, Dan Mason, the tall orderly sergeant of Company D., and Sergeant Alexander W. Davis of the same company, of the Sixth, were promoted to positions in colored regiments, Mason being appointed Captain in the 19th and Davis in the 39th U.S.C.T., of the

Fourth division of the Ninth Army Corps. On the 30th of July, 1864, these regiments took part in the assault on the enemy's works near the "crater" made by the explosion of the Petersburg mine. In the rout of the division which followed, Lieutenant Davis came back to the Union lines, with the mass of the brigade of which his regiment was a part, while Captain Mason took shelter with others in a bomb-proof within the enemy's lines. When they were driven out by the enemy, Captain Mason made a home run for the Federal lines, passed untouched through a shower of bullets, and sprang over the sandbags of the Union lines, to fall insensible from an apoplectic attack brought on by excitement and over exertion. As it happened he fell at the feet of his old tent-mate, Lieutenant Davis, who was able to render him assistance which restored him to consciousness and probably saved his life.[26]

The failure of Burnside's assault at the Crater was the worst possible news at the worst possible time for Lincoln and the Union. Bitter accusations and finger-pointing followed; a military court of inquiry was established by the War Department days after the battle, and then the Congressional Committee on the Conduct of the War carried out its own investigation. The results of both inquiries did little to help the Union's cause, other than to damage the reputations of the generals involved. Headlines in Democratic newspapers were quick to blame the Black troops for the failure of the assault. The *New York Herald*, nearly expressing sympathy with the rebels, jumped on the opportunity to lambaste Black troops:

> The rebels, exasperated as we know them now to have been at [the] sight of the negroes, fought with the fury of devils, and, reinforcements coming to their aid—our signal officers counted six brigades hurried from a camp beyond the town—the tide of battle turned. The colored troops gave way, broke in confusion, when the rebels, having repulsed their charge, charged them in turn, and then they ran, a terror-stricken, disordered mass of fugitives, to the rear of the white troops. In vain their officers endeavored to rally them with all the persuasion of tongue, sabre and pistol. Whatever of discredit attaches to the troops themselves, their officers are beyond reproach.[27]

The *Argus and Patriot* of Montpelier, which referred to Burnside's IX Corps as "heterogeneous and inferior," printed a statement that read, almost gleefully, "Burnside is now entitled to be called the Emancipator! He 'emancipated' any question of negroes at Petersburg. And not only 'emancipated' the negroes, but he also 'emancipated' a great many people from the idea that the colored troops could fight."[28]

Mason, once again, offered a strong defense of the troops under his command. Employing euphemisms to describe his own brush with death, he wrote to the *Orleans Independent Standard* later that summer:

> The harvest is past, the summer is nearly ended and Richmond is not taken, and we are yet confronting Petersburgh, though our lines have been extended to the left since my last letter. At that time, you will recollect, I was on picket, with a fair prospect of remaining the rest of the season, but as fortune would have it, I was relieved in a few days, and permitted the pleasure of participating in the assault on the enemy's works, July 30th, where Pharaoh, no, Ferrero, and his colored host came very near being swallowed up in the crater. The newspapers that were inclined to be copperish make great ado about the colored troops running, &c. I will admit that a panic got among them, and many of them made good time to the rear, but not until they had been exposed to a terrible fire from three directions.—I did not see a colored man offer to run until the advance, which was composed of white men, came pell-mell over the works, officers and men, very much demoralized. I don't think we ought to blame the colored men for running when the white veterans of many a hard-fought field, whom they have been well taught to imitate, break and refuse to be rallied. But I do know that some of them did stay at the fort and fought manfully, side by side with white men who could not see the point of leaving a position so dearly bought, but were compelled to retreat or be taken prisoners.—The above I know to be a fact. Your humble servant might have been seen about that time making rapid strides to the rear. Gilpin could not have made better time. My go-aheadativeness was excited to such a degree of height that my locomotive powers failed to keep up with the time—consequently I fell down, which was a very natural consequence, though not very agreeable just at that

time, as the climate was very unhealthy, and a sojourn there was sure to end with the loss of time, if not my life.

But enough of this. I managed to get inside our line safe and sound, with no damage except a ball hole through my coat sleeve, which was much better than to have had it through my arm; though it has not healed that, and my arm would have been likely to have been healed ere this; yet I am well satisfied with the arrangement.

Our regiment lost 157 men killed and wounded, and some regiments lost much heavier. Major Rockwood and Lieut. Pennell were killed, and they were gentlemen and scholars—brave almost to a fault. Their loss is deeply felt throughout the regiment and division. Lieuts. Raymore, Dobbs and Nix were taken prisoners, and have lately written to their friends that they were well used as prisoners of war. Capt. Geo. W. Burnell, formerly a lieutenant in the Tenth Vt. Regiment, was wounded, and is now home on leave of absence.

Finally, using language that could be interpreted as racist but was probably intended by Mason as a compliment, he concluded,

I think there is no doubt but that the colored men will make good soldiers, though it will perhaps take longer to discipline and develop their fighting qualities than white men. It is a remarkable fact that not one of them was observed to look *pale* when the missiles of death were falling thickly around and our men continually falling. I think this ought to be enough to satisfy any reasonable man that colored men can't be frightened easy. . . .

I saw Lieut. A.W. Davis yesterday. He was well and in command of Co. E, 39th U.S.C.T. I remain your ob't serv't,

Dan Mason[29]

James Rickard likewise made sure that no blame was attached to the Black troops who assaulted the crater. He said, "The charge of Ferrero's division at the 'crater' at Petersburg, Va., through a broken and demoralized division of white troops, then forming line inside the enemy's works, and temporary capture of their interior works, with awful losses in killed, wounded and *murdered*, is a record to win back the previously prejudiced judgment of the president, cabinet, generals, and officers of the Army of the Potomac, who up to this time had thought negroes all right for service in a menial capacity."[30]

The Battle of the Crater was over. Mason seems to have been shaken by it. His next letter reveals something of his state of mind after the battle. Between his letter of July 30 and his letter of August 10, it appears that he wrote Harriet another letter where he contemplated tendering his resignation or worse, though that letter is not in the Vermont Historical Society collection. Perhaps Harriet thought that it would not reflect favorably upon him. By the time of his letter on August 10, such thoughts had dissipated, and he assured Harriet, "You need not have any fears of me getting under arrest." It is obvious that after the Battle of the Crater Mason contemplated leaving the service on less than honorable grounds. One can only surmise what the contents of his "desperate epistle" were. Regardless, his next letter says much about Harriet's character. Earlier in 1864 she had discouraged Mason from reenlisting, but in her response to the mysterious "desperate epistle" that Mason wrote, she talked him out of any suggestion of his leaving the service on "dishonorable" terms. He thanked her profusely: "Harriet—you are an angel that has called me back to the line of my duty."

Camp in the trenches before Petersburg Va
August 10th 1864

Dear Harriet

Yours of the 3d inst[ant] came to hand this morn or rather last eve. I need not tell you I was very much pleased to hear from you as usual. I was sorry to hear that your health was not improving as fast as we had hoped but it is a season of the year when we cannot expect to improve very much when it is so warm & sultry. I am well in body & much better in mind than when I wrote you that desperate epistle. I dont have such spells very often & I will not write hereafter such days. Harriet—I am ashamed of that letter. I hope it did not make you think I had lost all respect for my honor. I was having the blues that day. I was behind . . . in making my returns to Ordnance Department for the guns & equipments which I am responsible also my Returns of Clothing Camp & Garrison Equipage which have to be sent to Washington at the end of each month. I had not the Blanks to make them then & could not get them until quite recently. . . . So you see there is a good deal of responsibility resting on a Capt[ain]. There has to [be] a great deal of writing to keep all strait. But I have got my blanks & made my returns & am feeling well now. I like the advice in your letter very much. I am glad you did not agree with me in regard to leaving this service dishonorably. I have no doubt you are as anxious to have me come home if I could honorably just as well as I would like to come but your love for my company must not be gratified at any sacrifice of honor [or] virtue on my part. Harriet—you are an angel that has called me back to the line of my duty. You are a precious jewel. I realize the worth of a true woman in the hour of trouble. I dont think I should have done anything to have got dismissed [from] the service dishonorably come to case & hand but now I am feeling very well contented think I am better off than if at home fearing the draft. You need not have any fears of me getting under arrest. Perhaps you may have some fears of me drinking & gambling & getting my morals corrupted but you need not have any fear of that. Harriet—I have something away up in Old Vt that brings me up on the square when these temptations are thrown around me. I have not played a game of cards for more than 2 months. I have lost all love [for] the game.

My love to all

from your lover Dan (I think
your picture quite good)

In July and August 1864, the prospects for Lincoln's reelection looked bleak. His fate was directly correlated to the success of Union military forces, and there was little to celebrate during the summer of 1864. The Army of the Potomac had suffered unprecedented casualties on its march toward Richmond, Grant was stalled before Petersburg after the debacle at the Crater, and Sherman was stalled outside of Atlanta. As the fourth summer of the war dragged on with no end in sight, there was a real question about how much longer the Northern public would be willing to continue the fight. As always Lincoln needed more troops, which would mean another draft, a great political liability in the run-up to the election. The scale of suffering in the summer of 1864 was beyond anything that the Union had experienced before. Northern morale was at its lowest ebb yet. The exhaustion of the war was deeply felt.

The peace faction of the Democratic Party was empowered by this situation and adopted a platform at its Chicago convention in August, which called for an immediate end to the war and a negotiated peace settlement with the South:

> Resolved, That this Convention does explicitly declare, as the sense of the American people, that, after four years of failure to restore the Union by the experiment of war, during which, under the pretense of a military necessity or war power higher than the Constitution, the Constitution itself has been disregarded in every part, and public liberty and private right alike trodden down, and the material prosperity of the country essentially impaired, justice, humanity, liberty, and the public welfare, demand that IMMEDIATE EFFORTS BE MADE FOR A CESSATION OF HOSTILITIES, with a view to an ultimate Convention of all the States, or other peaceable means, to the end that at the earliest practicable moment peace may be restored on the basis of the Federal Union of the States.

Nowhere did the word "slavery" appear in the Democratic platform. Indeed, the platform implied that slavery could continue in the Southern states. Without mentioning the Emancipation Proclamation directly, the platform continued, "That the aim and object of the Democratic party is to preserve the Federal Union and the rights of the States unimpaired; and they hereby declare that they consider the Administrative usurpation of extraordinary and dangerous powers not granted by the Constitution . . . as calculated to prevent a restoration of the Union, and the perpetuation of a government deriving its just powers from the consent of the governed."[31]

The contrast with the Republican platform could not have been more striking. At its Baltimore convention, the Republicans renominated Lincoln, rejected any notion of a compromise with the South, and called for a Thirteenth Amendment to the Constitution that would forever abolish slavery and leave no legal doubt about its status:

Resolved, That we approve the determination of the Government of the United States, not to compromise with rebels, nor to offer any terms of peace except such as may be based upon an unconditional surrender of their hostility, and a return to their just allegiance to the Constitution and laws of the United States, and that we call upon the Government to maintain this position and to prosecute the war with the utmost possible vigor to the complete suppression of the rebellion, in full reliance upon the self-sacrifice, the patriotism, the heroic valor, and the undying devotion of the American people to their country and its free institutions.

Resolved, That as slavery was the cause, and now constitutes the strength of this rebellion, and as it must be always and everywhere hostile to the principles of republican government, justice and the national safety demand its utter and complete extirpation from the soil of the Republic; and that while we uphold and maintain the acts and proclamations by which the Government, in its own defense, has aimed a death-blow at this gigantic evil, we are in favor, furthermore, of such an amendment to the Constitution, to be made by the people in conformity with its provisions, as shall terminate and forever prohibit the existence of Slavery within the limits or the jurisdiction of the United States.[22]

Lincoln's old nemesis, George McClellan, was nominated as the Democratic candidate. Though McClellan was a "War Democrat" who wished to continue the war, the peace faction dominated the convention, as evidenced by the platform the party adopted. As Lincoln's momentum faded, some suggested that he adopt more conciliatory measures toward the South, including renouncing emancipation as a war aim or even returning Black troops to bondage! Some advised him to cancel or postpone the election by declaring a national state of emergency. In a conversation on August 19, Lincoln strongly refused any such notions:

My own experience has proven to me, that there is no program intended by the democratic party but that will result in the dismemberment of the Union. . . . There are now between 1 & 200 thousand Black men now in the service of the Union. These men will be disbanded, returned to slavery & we will have to fight two nations instead of one. . . . There have been men who have proposed to me to return to slavery the Black warriors . . . to their masters to conciliate the South. I should be damned in time & in eternity for so doing. . . . My enemies say I am now carrying on this war for the sole purpose of abolition. It is & will be carried on so long as I am President for the sole purpose of restoring the Union. But no human power can subdue this rebellion without using the Emancipation lever as I have done. Freedom has given us the control of 200,000 able bodied men, born & raised on southern soil. It will give us more yet. . . . My enemies condemn my emancipation policy. Let them prove by the history of this war, that we can restore the Union without it.[33]

Four days later, on August 23, Lincoln told the members of his cabinet, "This morning, as for some days past, it seems exceedingly probable that this Administration will not be re-elected. Then it will be my duty to so co-operate with the President elect, as to save the Union between the election and the inauguration; as he will have secured his election on such ground that he can not possibly save it afterwards."[34]

The *Orleans Independent Standard* was as hostile to "Copperheads" as ever. In an expression of indignation about any discussion of turning back the clock to the 1850s, the editor fumed,

These Peace democrats are forever prating about the "Union as it was." In the name of common sense we ask, why did not their Southern friends stay in the Union as it was? Mr. Lincoln's election did not change the "constitution as it was," or the "Union as it was." This is the cry they love most of all, and is repeated hundreds of times in every copperhead journal in the North—and yet it is the very thing the rebels seek to destroy forever. Before the war they had the fugitive slave law, and a majority in the U.S. Senate. This wicked law virtually made every Northern freeman a *slave-catcher*, an appellation which even southern slave owners would deem dishonorable when applied to themselves. No safer guarantees for slavery could be desired than then existed. But their pride was so great, and their hatred to the Yankees so intense that in seceding they have abandoned the "Union as it was."[35]

The Democrats' Chicago Platform and the upcoming election were hotly debated within the ranks of the Union Army. Wilbur Fisk of the Second Vermont captured the mood of the soldiers in the Vermont Brigade shortly before the election:

> I believe I never enjoyed a discussion better than I did the other day "down to the spring" when the parties concerned were discussing the presidential election and the Chicago propositions for peace. . . . Abraham Lincoln had plenty of defenders, and McClellan had a few. The McClellan men were noisy and defiant, and their arguments were of the old stereotyped order, the sum and substance of which usually is "Damn the n———rs." Two of the loudest talking McClellanites there would vote for him because they were for peace, and because they liked McClellan. . . . One of them would vote for McClellan because he was the best general the world ever produced. . . . The other McClellan man was for peace. All his hopes of our ultimate success had faded out, if indeed, he ever had any. Peace would come if McClellan was elected, and peace was what he wanted. "So I have been out here long enough," he said, "and now I want to go home and so do you." The war had lasted long enough and it was time to have the trouble settled. He had seen all the fighting he wished to see, and let folks say what they would, he should vote to have the war stopped. A fellow by his side said he wanted peace too, but it was no McClellan peace that he wanted. He had served one three years already, and had begun on his second three. He was as anxious to go home as any man could be, but he didn't want to go till the rebels were whipped out clean and smooth. He said he had always stood up for McClellan, was a McClellan man clear to the bone, but he couldn't vote for him on the Chicago platform. Rather than have peace by surrendering to the rebels, he would let his bones manure the soil of Virginia. "Bully for you," was the response all around. One fellow said every man in his company was for Lincoln and Johnson, and several others said it was the same in theirs.

After this initial conversation, a sergeant stepped forward to proclaim, "Every man that would vote for the Chicago platform ought to be made to go in front of the whole length of our army drawn up in a line, with a board strapped to his back marked COWARD in big letters, and every soldier ought to hiss at him as he passed."[36]

In the Nineteenth USCT, of course enlisted Black soldiers could not vote (the Fifteenth Amendment, which granted Black male suffrage, would not be ratified until 1870), but their white officers clearly supported Lincoln as well. Charles Stinson wrote that "Lincoln is the soldier's choice."[37] James Rickard wrote to his mother and said that if McClellan was elected, "what soldiers that have fallen will have fallen in vain." However, he hoped that "Lincoln . . . will defeat them all. I think it will depend altogether on our successes just before election though & something in the nomination at the Chicago convention makes me mad." Rickard railed against "the men at home who have never suffered by the war who are willing to sacrifice anything."[38]

Mason's thoughts on the upcoming election were of a piece with such views. In his letter to Harriet on September 6, he included two newspapers, one of which was the latest issue of *Harper's Weekly*. Mason had much to say about a political cartoon drawn by the famous satirist Thomas Nast, in which Nast suggested that any compromise with the South would mean that all the bloodletting by Union soldiers up to that point would have been in vain. Mason strongly agreed with the sentiments of the cartoon, writing to Harriet, "I say fight them."

He also referred to the recent death of Carlos Dwinell, a Glover officer in the Sixth Vermont. Dwinell had been wounded at the Battle of the Wilderness on May 5, then wounded again at the Battle of Charlestown, Virginia in the Shenandoah Valley on August 21. He died three days later of his wounds at a hospital in Baltimore. The *Caledonian* of St. Johnsbury reported that Major Dwinell's

> wound was not at first supposed to be dangerous, being merely a flesh wound below the knee, but unfavorable symptoms soon appeared, and he died on Wednesday, August 24. His remains were conveyed to Glover, where his funeral services were attended, August 30, by a very large assembly. . . . He shared all the hard fortunes of the 6th regiment, and participated in nearly every battle in which it was engaged, but escaped

> without a scratch 'till the battle of the Wilderness on May 5, 1864, when he received a severe wound near the spine, which disabled him for six or eight weeks. The bullet was not extracted from the wound, and it is probable that the enfeebling effects of that prevented him from rallying against his final wound as he might otherwise have done. He married when at home on a furlough, January 28, 1864, Miss Amanda Smith of Albany, Vt.[39]

The *Orleans Independent Standard* added, "In the battle of the Wilderness he received a severe wound, the ball lodging in his side, which he carried till his death, and at the earliest possible moment of recovery he hastened back to join his comrades in battle only to *die*." A fellow soldier then submitted a statement to the press: "And now to the mourning and weeping brother, sisters, widowed mother and especially to that young and devoted wife, who was left now alone to face the cold and dark future, permit me to extend, in behalf of the officers and soldiers of the 6th Vermont Regiment, our deepest and most profound sympathy. We can truly feel to mourn and weep with you in the sad and almost insupportable bereavement; yet may we feel to exclaim: 'Thy will, O God, not mine be done!'"[40] Dwinell, like so many others, had been married while at home on a furlough, then went back to war, never to return again.

Camp near Petersburg Va Sept[ember] 6th, 1864

Darling Harriet

I take my pen to write you once more to acknowledge the reception of your favor of the 29th Aug[ust]. I am well & enjoying myself very well most of the time. I am Brigade Officer of the Day today have to visit all the Reg[imen]ts in the Brig[ade] & see that everything is in good order grounds policed Slop Holes for waste water around each Co[mpany] Cooking establishments &c &c. Golly you ought to see me swell around in my best suit with my red sash over my right shoulder & around my waist (which is to designate from other officers). You ought to see me step up to a Col[onel] & give him orders. By the way a Brig[ade] Officer of the day is higher in rank for the time Being than any Col[onel] in the Brig[ade]. . . . We get very good news from the Southwest—I think our cause looks more prosperous than ever before. I felt sad to hear to the death of Carl Dwinnell it seemed so bad when he was intending to go home the 15th of next month how his wife must feel. You speak of having curious notions of marriage &c. I think you have changed a good deal in 2 years time. I am sure there is nothing bad in getting married if both parties are agreed & the surroundings are all congenial it is natural for man & woman to unite their destinies in lawfull marriage which is the only true way to carry out the designs of the author of the universe so I think it is best to take a candid & common sense view of the matter & be married this winter if it does vex the Old Ladies. I guess they have forgotten their young days Oh well it will do for them to talk now. They of course feel a good deal of interest in the rising generation. I sent you a paper yesterday that had some good pictures. . . . I also sent a picture taken from another paper which is a great picture. One can meditate hours over it—there is a great meaning attached to some characters represented. The soldier on his crutches The Goddess of Liberty weeping over the graves of heroes sacrificed in a useless war. All combined makes me disgusted with the peace policy. That defiant rebel with his whip in hand with the enslaved around him disgusts me. I say fight them. Please give my love to your mother Aunt Cutler Bell & all enquiring friends

receive from your sincere lover
Dan

{ 12 }

"When Will the Cruel War End?" (Fall 1864)

The Nineteenth USCT hadn't seen much frontline action since the Crater. The term of enlistment of the Sixth Vermont—"the Old Regiment"—was expiring soon, and Mason hoped to go home at the same time as the men of Company D would. Nevertheless, he told Harriet, "I am glad I left the Reg[imen]t when I did. I should have doubtless been killed or wounded ere this." Then, in thinking ahead to wedding preparations, which he had already formulated in his mind in great detail, he added, "I have accumulated some money in 3 years time & if I should die or get killed out here I should rather you would have it than any other one." Harriet's health seems to have been questionable during the summer and fall of 1864. He told her that he wanted to be married the following winter, but added the caveat, "If you should not be able to ride about perhaps it would not be best to be married." Why Harriet's ability to "ride about" was in question is not clear.

Mason also wanted Harriet to know that his letters to the *Orleans Independent Standard* were not designed to flatter his own ego but were the result of the editor's request for them. The relationship was reciprocal; Mason wrote letters and would be sent a copy of the *Standard* in return. Mason's latest letter to the *Standard* contained an optimistic report: "The news from Atlanta and Mobile has a very exhilarating effect upon the soldiers. On receiving the news of the fall of Atlanta, Gen. Grant ordered a salute of the line at the dead of night, which must have surprised the Johnnies. The soldiers nearly all think that if the last quota be filled with good effective men, that Grant will close this wicked and unholy war on terms of justice and equity, and treason laid prostrate in the dust."[1] This was the "October surprise" (or, rather, the "September surprise") that Lincoln had been looking for. Sherman's capture of Atlanta in early September had provided a major boost to Lincoln's reelection chances. So did the capture of Mobile

Bay, Alabama, and another major Union victory in the Shenandoah Valley at the Battle of Cedar Creek (a true October surprise), where Phil Sheridan's Army—with the help of the Vermont Brigade—routed Jubal Early's rebel force and solidified Union control of the Shenandoah Valley once and for all. On September 11 Charles Stinson wrote to his sister:

> I am much encouraged by the election and also the seeming growth of Lincoln's popularity of late. The late victories at Atlanta and Mobile have a great tendency to strengthen our Political party. The rebs must have poor encouragement to fight. . . . I am in favor of a vigorous prosecution of the War until they will declare their allegiance to our Government. Methinks I hear you say, "Charlie you are writing about those things which do not interest the 'peaceful sex.' What do we ladies care about the 'Political world?'" Yet I know you have an interest in the War, perhaps more than if you had no brother sharing the dangers, perils, hardships and privations of the camp and field.[2]

What Mason wanted Harriet to know about was an encounter he and James Rickard had with a Virginia woman who he said "would be called rather plain looking in Vt but women are so scarce here that she looks quite good to us." For some reason, he was out to provoke Harriet.

Camp Near Petersburg Va Oct[ober] 9th, 1864

Dear Harriet

In accordance with agreement—I seat myself to write you though I have but a few ideas to advance that will interest you. I will attempt to chat with you for a few moments. . . . Capt[ain] Pitts Command[er] Co[mpany] D 19th USCT was killed while on a tour of Picket about a week since. I was on the line at the time a sharpshooter shot him through the head. There is no enemy very near us now as we picket in rear instead of the front of the army. I am not on duty today. I am going to tell you something that will make you jealous. Capt[ain] Rickard from the State of Conn[ecticut] now Commands Co G 19th USCT proposed a stroll out to the Picket line this morn. I accepted the proposition & we went to a house & knocked of course we were ushered in by a Virginia lady who was quite agreeable in her manners though not handsome about 22 years of age the Old lady was quite agreeable by the way. There was a younger sister about 18 that was rather dry she is secesh she refuses to take the oath of allegiance the older one is good Union & has taken the oath of allegiance. She is a great lover of flowers she showed the Capt[ain] and myself several very nice specimens in her garden. I will enclose some of the leaves. I had several kinds but they have all got spoiled except 2 the large green leaf is a part of a fig leaf the trees had lots of green figs on them & occasionally a ripe one. This one that resembles sage is a sprig of Lavinder such as perfumery is scented with. There now you are doubtless stomping mad how you will scold me in your next. She would be called rather plain looking in Vt but women are so scarce here that she looks quite good to us. Do you wonder at it? What? But then you know I am virtuous & would not do anything wrong dont you? But I expect to get Hail Columbia in your next. I presume you will not think these flowers or rather leaves of flowers sweet—but you know such things from tiny fingers are sweet—if it is nothing but a Pum[p]kin leaf But—I guess I have lectured you about enough. So I will close by tendering you the best of wishes. You must not get discouraged if you are not quite as well some days you will be all right this winter. My love to your Mother Aunt C[utler] Belle & all the friends who may enquire for me. Yours with much love, Dan.

A week later Mason discussed a wide range of topics: he praised Harriet for her anti-Copperhead views, described his new quarters, lauded his servant Tom for his culinary abilities, and commented on his sister Emily's upcoming marriage.

Camp Near Petersburg Va Oct[ober] 16th, [18]64

Dear Harriet

I received your kind favor of the 7th yesterday. I learned from it that you were still purely patriotic bravely contending for the right & are no sympathizer with copperheads which was very gratifying to your soldier lover. . . . I have got up some good winter quarters viz a log house with tents for roof with a good fire place built in the side of wood chimney ditto topped out with an old flour barrel the whole is lined with a good coat of Clay mud. I have seen many such fireplaces & chimneys in this country that had been in use a great many years. The days are quite warm here but the nights very chilly we have had 2 frosty morns. I suppose you have had some snow. I am living very well these days. My servant Tom has got to be a very good cook. I wish you were here this morn to take breakfast with me. He is baking some very light nice biscuits. He makes very nice apple pies usually have one for dinner. His oven consists of a Sheet iron Mess Pan holding about 4 quarts with a Cast iron Cover made for a regular bake pot. You see the whole oven dont weigh more than 6 or 7 lbs so it is not bad to transport on the March. He bakes very slow & gives the biscuits [a] chance to rise & not burn them. I have plenty of good potatoes & meat frequently boiled apple dumplings for a change. Butter only 80 cts per lb. Coffee Tea with sugar & condensed Milk in them & many other choice viands to[o] numerous to mention. It is Sunday today. Alex staid with me last night—we had a good visit talking over old times, & in regard to the Old Reg[imen]t being mustered out of service yesterday &c &c. Alex Reg[imen]t is encamped but a few rods from ours. I received a letter from Emily yesterday. She said she was going to be married the 11th. Was going to live on Summer St[reet] St Johnsbury. I will close by tendering you all the good wishes of a fond lover. My love to all the friends. Dan

The next week Mason ratcheted up his teasing of Harriet to another level. In response to his description from two weeks earlier about visiting a pair of Virginia sisters in their home with James Rickard, Harriet must have responded in kind by alluding to all of the men back home that were paying attention to her in his absence. Mason stated that Captain Rickard had gone back to the same house and was "picking flowers in the garden" with the Virginia woman they had previously visited, then added, "I expect to go out Tuesday morn & relieve him wont I have a gay time?" Of course, Mason reassured Harriet, "I would not do anything wrong of course not." Not taking Harriet's bait about how she was being wooed by numerous men at home, Mason said that he wasn't concerned about the attention being paid to her, since the only plausible suitor left in town would be "Uncle Sam Hoyt," a seventy-two-year-old Glover man. He concluded, "I am well & hope this will find you improving in health as you doubtless will with such a gay lot of lovers." He still planned to be discharged in January and get married if "Mr. Hoyt dont cut me out" in the meantime.

Near Petersburg Va Oct[ober] 23d, 1864

Dear Harriet

Yours of the 18th arrived in due season & was perused with the usual degree of pleasure. I was happy to learn that your health & symptoms were better than at any time since your ill health. I expected to have gone on Picket today but Capt[ain] Rickard was detailed & went—he was the companion of wickedness that went with me 2 weeks ago today. I presume he is picking flowers in the garden with her today as the Picket Reserve is within a few rods of the house. I expect to go out Tuesday morn & relieve him wont I have a gay time? I find that these Secesh Ladies that dislike colored Soldiers can soon be made to respect & like the officers or in other words be induced to show a due amount of Courtesy & affability. I like to talk with them & draw them out & see what they will say but I would not do anything wrong of course not. I never indulge in any vices of a carnal nature of course I dont cause you know it would make a fuss in the family. O well if I did not talk I should not say anything you know my style of talk. But I have been thinking what gallant it was that paid much attention to your honor called 3 times in one half day & finally took tea with you. Well I declare he is an amorous swain. After deliberate concideration I have concluded that it was Uncle Sam Hoyt—doubtless he is trying to get him a young wife. I am going to be real jealous. It may be some other gay lad perhaps Old Mr Emerson is the chap that is so very attentive. Well I declare that things are coming to a pretty pass. But enough I am well & hope this will find you improving in health as you doubtless will with such a gay lot of lovers. I am going to have some Indian griddle cakes for supper. I usually have an apple pie for supper & splendid warm biscuits & butter. Alex Davis comes up to see me 2 or 3 times a day & I return the compliment. I am enjoying myself very well these days. I intend to go home in January if possible. We are stopping at the same place as when I last wrote you. I wish this cruel war was over but there is no use in wishing. But I intend to fulfill my engagement to you this winter if your health will admit—that is if Mr Hoyt dont cut me out. I must now close for it is [almost] time to send the mail & I wish to have this go out tonight. . . . Please give my love to your Mother & all enquiring friends. Accept these imperfect lines from your lover

Dan

On October 30, just over a week before the election, Mason described an inconclusive skirmish with rebel forces that his division was engaged in: "But I concider it only as a reconnaissance in force to ascertain the position & strength of the enemy & if proper to attack but it was not best to risk very much just before election. I saw Gen[eral] Meade the morn we went out. I learn that he would not allow a general attack on the enemy." Certainly, after the Union successes at Atlanta and Cedar Creek, Lincoln did not want to risk another failed assault on Petersburg days before the election. Mason said he saw General Meade, who confirmed this view, though it is difficult to discern exactly what the nature of Mason's interaction with Meade was.

Writing now with weekly regularity, Mason explained that he had not made another visit back to the "house where the girls live cause I was afraid you would scold & that you know would be a terrible thing for a woman to scold, O deliver me from such lectures. Wonder if I shall always be afraid of crossing you?" As intended his earlier remarks surely raised Harriet's hackles, who fired back with her own scandalous missive.

ABRAHAM LINCOLN WON REELECTION to a second term on November 8, 1864, the first free election held during a civil war in world history. After four bloody years, especially following the unprecedented carnage in the summer of 1864, the election had become nothing less than a referendum on the war itself. The fact that 78 percent of the military vote went for Lincoln, compared with 54 percent of the civilian population, is a remarkable testament to the conviction of Union troops that the war should be vigorously prosecuted to the end. Those who faced the greatest risks and personal sacrifices to continue the war—the troops themselves—were the most enthusiastic about fighting on to ultimate victory. Southern hopes for a negotiated peace evaporated with McClellan's defeat; Lincoln's victory was widely viewed by Southerners as the death knell of the Confederacy. The question was no longer if, but when, defeat would come. As in 1860 the popular vote for Lincoln in Vermont was a whopping 76 percent. In Orleans County Lincoln was even more popular, as 81 percent of citizens there voted to reelect him.[3] These percentages were identical to what they had been in 1860—a stunning degree of approval for Lincoln and his policies, which had become much more radical than they had been in 1860. The *Orleans Independent Standard*, which had often been critical of Lincoln early in the war, now reveled in his victory:

> Abraham Lincoln is re-elected by an overwhelming majority of both of the electoral and popular vote. The free men of the United States have arisen in all their power and majesty, and declare their firm and resolute adherence to the union and the Constitution. They have proclaimed "to all whom it may concern" that the administration will be sustained, the government upheld, and the rebellion crushed. . . .
>
> Thus one by one the bonds of oppression are being loosened and the government of our forefathers is being cleaned and purified of the degrading and polluting stains of human slavery—a glorious work, which Adams and Jefferson supposed would be done, years ago, when they made the constitution and submitted it to the people for their approval. . . .
>
> The patriots and loyal men have great reason for rejoicing in the result of the late election. President Lincoln is no longer the candidate of a minority, but the free choice of an overwhelming majority. Let every Union man take new courage, buckle on his armor, and do his whole duty to his country, for the day is not far distant when we shall again take our place among the nations of the earth, a happy and a prosperous people.[4]

Though they would not be able to vote for over a half century, the women of Derby Center contributed to the war effort in early November by sending to the U.S. Sanitary Commission 29 new shirts, 21 new pillow cases, 11 feather pillows, 23 linen towels, 137 pocket handkerchiefs, 8 arm slings,

86 rolls of bandages, 35 fans, 42 pounds of dried fruit, 17½ quarts of raspberries and currants, 4 bottles of Blackberry wine, 17½ gallons of pickles, 4 barrels of vegetables, and numerous other supplies.[5]

The Confederate situation was growing so desperate that in November, Jefferson Davis even proposed recruiting slaves into Confederate forces and offering them emancipation for loyal service! Defending his suggestion, Davis told the Confederate Congress, "A broad, moral distinction exists between the use of slaves as soldiers in defense of their homes and the incitement of the same persons to insurrection against their masters. The one is justifiable, if necessary, the other is iniquitous and unworthy of civilized people."[6] The day after Lincoln's reelection, the *Richmond Examiner* was aghast with such a proposal: "The negro soldier is incompatible with our political aim and our social and political system. He would be considered by all the world as a compromise to Abolitionism." Davis's suggestion that an enslaved person might earn freedom through military service was "an absurdity; for we hold that the negro as a slave is in a better condition than in a state of freedom. Emancipation, therefore, is a punishment, not a reward."[7] The *Richmond Whig* further explained that Davis's proposal was

> a repudiation of the opinion held by the whole South and by a large portion of mankind in other countries, that servitude is a divinely appointed condition for the highest good of the slave, is that condition in which the negro race especially may attain the highest moral and intellectual advancement of which they are capable, and may enjoy most largely of such comforts and blessings of life as are suited to them. Of this, we have no doubt, and we hold it to be an act of cruelty to deprive the slave of the care and guardianship of a master. If the slave must fight, he should fight for the blessings he enjoys as a slave, and not for the miseries that would attend him if freed.[8]

After the election Mason looked optimistically toward the future and wrote to Harriet, "I hope I shall live to be a citizen once more," though he doubted that the rebels would "acknowledge their Sham Confederacy a failure," even after Lincoln's reelection. Again, he expressed his desire to come home the following winter, get married, go on a "car ride" to St. Johnsbury to visit his sister Emily, and do some "tall visiting."

Camp Near Petersburg Va Nov[ember] 23d, 1864

Dear Harriet

I seat myself this cold morning to chat awhile with you & inform you that I am well though I did not write you Sunday as I intended. . . . I hope I shall live to be a citizen once more. If this Cruel war could be settled up honorably this winter how many happy hearts it would make both North and South it does seem as though the rebels would see the folly of fighting another 4 years which is a sure thing if they court it. How much better to return to their allegiance & acknowledge they were in a great error thereby saving many precious lives which if they persist in their evil must be sacrificed and then acknowledge their Sham Confederacy a failure but they are insane on the subject & hate to because as little children they are truly rebellious such is the human heart prone to evil. I received yours of the 11th in due season. I shall go home, perhaps in Dec[ember], perhaps in Jan[uary] and may be not until Feb[ruary] but I shall be home sometime during the winter if I am well. . . . You may make up your mind to do some tall visiting this winter when I come home. If we are not married you must go to St. Johnsbury with me and visit Emily you know we can take the cars and right there in a little more than an hours time all so nice it will be so gay to take a car ride it will remind us of our Lyndon excursion long ago when peace smiled on our beloved country and then it will make peoples eyes pop out so and and and of course there must be a wedding under contemplation how we will fool them. What? I must close hoping to live to see that wedding at some future day

receive from your sincere lover,
Dan

Mason's "joke" from earlier in the fall that Harriet was being courted by a seventy-two-year-old Glover man, "Uncle" Sam Hoyt, seemed to have backfired. He spilled much ink in his next letter to Harriet backpedaling and defending his integrity.

Camp Near Dutch Gap Va Nov[ember] 28th, [18]64

dier Betzy

You see by the heading I have got out of the Army of the Potomac and now am in the Army of the James under Gen[eral] Butler. We are now between the James and Appomattox rivers about 18 miles to the right of where we were when I last wrote you. I have served 3 years and nearly 2 months in the Army of the P[otomac] and now have gone into the Army of the James the colored troops of Virginia are all now under Butler. Gen[eral] Ferrero commands our Divis[ion] same as before. There are 3 Divis[ions] of Colored Troops here. I have not much news to write you. Yours of the 19th came to hand in due season laden with its lectures for naughty words used in one of my epistles a short time since. Well Hat you gave me a pretty good lecture. I guess you was in earnest some of the time. You intimated that I had become so demoralized since becoming an officer that the language referred to was a natural flow of words which had become a second nature by practice but I will tell you that I used them to carry out the Hoyt Joke and see if I could not get a lecture from you. You seem to think they were wicked words. I dont see it in that light. I will admit they were rather low vulgar terms but I dont see them wicked. You seem to take them rather hard. Harriet I will tell you now that if you flatter yourself that you are courted by [a] pure and spotless lump of perfection you will sooner or later find yourself mistaken. I intend to do about right but like all that is human I am likely to err. I respect a Christian wish I was one myself but I am a sinner. I am glad you are sensitive and anxious in regard to my moral welfare. I trust you may be a sort of an anchor to me (if I am spared to live with you) which will hold me in check as we move down the rapid stream of life and prevent me from being drawn into the numerous whirlpools of vice which present so many dazzling allurements.

I am well. . . . I must now close by tendering you the best wishes of a headstrong lover.

The friction caused by Mason's "joke" continued to plague him in his correspondence with Harriet. Despite all of his assurances that his moral welfare was solid, Harriet must not have been convinced. Beginning with Mason's "vulgar" reference to "Uncle" Sam Hoyt, Harriet appears to have relentlessly questioned his behavior, implying that he was guilty of "taking the name of God in vain," among other offenses. In his usual manner, Mason thanked Harriet for "the earnestness and zeal" of her arguments, which "betoken that yours is a true womans love." Then he offered his strongest defense of his virtue yet, suggesting that he was above the temptations that his fellow troops often succumbed to, including his former tentmates Oliver Stiles and Hobart Bliss. He vehemently denied ever taking the name of God in vain, though he did admit that "in regard to drinking I have taken a little several times this summer for example the day I was in the crater July 30th." He stated that despite an occasional drink every now and then, he still considered himself temperate. Harriet, who would later join the Women's Christian Temperance Union, probably found even this unsatisfactory. Finally, Mason reassured Harriet of his sexual purity amid a sea of wrongdoing: "I never have had improper intercourse with woman since I donned the blue uniform."

Defences of Bermuda Hundred Va
Dec[ember] 4th, [18]64

Dear Harriet

Your affectionate appeal to your demoralized lover came to hand yesterday and was read and reread with much surprise. As it is Sunday I will write you a long letter because I <u>think it my duty to do so under the circumstances</u>.

After mature deliberation I have concluded there is some one playing an underhanded game to make trouble between us or else there is some mistake some misunderstanding between us. I admire your appeal in many respects. The earnestness and zeal with the good arguments used betoken that yours is a true womans love and consequently are deeply interested in my spiritual welfare which is a trait of character which pervades a true womans heart. I cant say that I wonder that you are fearful that I may imbibe some of the many vices thrown around me. But I trust that I have enough principles established in days gone by that

I may never bring my friends to shame on my behalf. I was somewhat shocked to have you accuse me of taking the name of God in vain. I dont know what you mean. . . . I guess we never shall attempt any more fun at Mr Hoyts expense. . . . In response I will say I care not how you got the impression. I deny the charge point blank. I have vices enough but No Man or woman [h]as heard me take the name of God in vain since I have been in the Army. In regard to drinking I have taken a little several times this summer for example the day I was in the crater July 30th. I was almost choked with thrist and suffocated with the heat—one of the Capt[ain]s had a little in his Haversack and I took a swallow twice during the day and I would do the same again under like circumstances. I have refused a great many times during the season and it is known throughout the Reg[imen]t that I am temperate. You need have no fears in that direction for I neither like the taste nor effects of it. I do play a game of cards occasionally but never for money or eatables or anything of the kind. This you knew before. I do miss Capt[ain] Davis. I wish he was here I dont have any good sings as I used to in my Old Reg[imen]t which I enjoyed more than cards or any other Camp amusement. Those were really happy days I sometimes wish I had staid in my Old Reg[imen]t. I would either been a dead Serg[ean]t or a live citizen now. Those are times when I have the blues. Oh Harriet I hope to live to see the time when I can tell you all. It would not be policy nor possible for one to convey by letter my feelings at times. When will the cruel war end? If I could see one ray of hope in the distance of peace and harmony reigning once more. But enough of this I dont see any chance to get out of this until the rebellion is crushed. But we have some cheering reports from the South. . . . Harriet—matters have come to such a state that you will excuse me for being plain spoken. You have many fears in regard to my moral welfare. I dont claim to be anything like perfect—I have many failings. But I am not afraid to call on God as a witness that I never have had improper intercourse with woman since I donned the blue uniform and marched forth to battle for the right. But few soldiers can say that—though you may start at the assertion it is nevertheless true. You ask me to confide in you now if I understand the meaning of the term (it is to have confidence in). I have all confidence in your virtues you dont seem to have confidence in me. I think I should ask you to confide in me rather than you to confide in you. Well I have nearly filled this sheet and must close, hoping that this with the former letters will calm your fears to some extent. Knowing the many temptations thrown around the soldier I dont blame you for having fears. You and the rest of the good people of Glover have but a little ideas of the sin in the world. One has to Marvel to see the monster with 7 heads and ten horns. I think all the more of you for feeling such an interest in me. Indeed I have something to live for if I do get blue sometimes. Alex is well. I learn that Martin Bean is at City Point Va. I think I shall try and go down and see him some day.

receive with much love from Dan

Finally, after all the grief that his reference to "Uncle" Sam Hoyt had caused, the source of confusion was at last clarified. Harriet admitted that she had misread the word "darned" in one of Mason's letters as "damned." Regardless, Mason turned the tables on Harriet again, suggested that she should wear her glasses in reading his future letters, threatened to send one of her "lectures" to the *Orleans Independent Standard* for publication, and expressed great concern over her moral welfare, surrounded as she was by the temptations of "city life" in Glover, Vermont: "It makes my heart ache to think of it surrounded as you are by all the vices of City life do promise me that you will not drink any intoxicating liquors to make yourself popular."

While Mason defended his virtue, sporadic fighting continued in and around Petersburg. His fellow captain Frank Holsinger was wounded on November 28 at Bermuda Hundred while on picket duty. Writing in the present tense, Holsinger later recalled:

> I am struck in the left forearm, though not disabled; soon I am struck in the right shoulder by an explosive bullet, which is embedded in my shoulder-strap. We maintain a spiteful fire. About [noon] I am struck again in my right forearm, which is broken and the main artery cut; soon we improvise a tourniquet by using a canteen-strap, and with a bayonet the same is twisted until blood ceases to flow. To retire is impossible, and for nine weary hours, or until late in the night, I remain on the line. I am alone with my thoughts; I think of home, of the seriousness of my

condition; I see myself a cripple for life—perchance I may not recover; and all the time shells are shrieking and minie bullets whistling over and about me. The tongue becomes parched, there is no water to quench it; you cry "Water! Water!" and pray for night, that you can be carried off the field and to the hospital, and there the surgeons' care—maimed, crippled for life, perchance die. These are your reflections. Who can portray the horrors coming to the wounded?[9]

Mason later told Harriet, "I will enclose a Photo of Capt[ain] Holsinger 19th USCT who had his arm broken last fall at Bermuda Hundred while on picket by a minie ball he has but little use of it now. It was the right one he has to hold his sword in his left."

{ 13 }

"My Future Happiness" (Winter 1864–65)

On Christmas Day, 1864, Mason wrote to Harriet for the last time of the year. He was heartened by recent Union victories in Georgia and Tennessee. He sent her two newspapers: one a *Richmond Examiner* that he must have received from a rebel soldier on a picket line (although he said that "the Johnnies would not exchange papers yesterday they seemed rather sulky they doubtless knew they would contain news of Thomas's victory"), and the other a *Harper's Weekly*, which included a "picture" that Mason described as an accurate one.

Camp of the 19th USCTroops
Dec[ember] 25th, 1864

Dear Harriet

I wish you a "Merry Christmas" I came off picket last eve the Johnnies would not exchange papers yesterday they seemed rather sulky they doubtless knew they would contain news of Thomas's victory.[1] We received orders to fasten a stone to some and throw them over so they could get them if they would not exchange thinking it would encourage desertion. Harriet I feel greatly encouraged I dont think that rebellion can survive long against such Armies and such Generals as we now boast of such brilliant successes have a telling effect upon the exhausted resources of the rebels. I never saw the prospects of a speedy crushing of the rebellion so good no where near as now. Senator Foot of Tenn[essee] made a speech in the rebel Congress declaring the Confederacy to be a failure. With a reinforcement of 300,000 men we will squash this rebellion in 6 months. I dont believe that there will be a great deal of fighting after Savannah Charleston and Wilmington fall which will fall before 3 months. I have strong hopes that we will be spared to enjoy each others

Company after this Cruel War is over. We shall then appreciate the privilege of a free and powerful nation which has been cleansed by blood. I have no news to write. I sent you a couple of papers day before yesterday. The pictures showing the effects of war on Va homes looks very much like houses that I have been in. The one where the young Mother sits watching her Infant is very good representation. The old Clock the Coffee mill with the spiders webb woven over it showing that it has not been used for a long time for want of the material, the old ladies &c &c. The *Richmond Examiner* is one that I got on picket 2 or three days before. I must now close by tendering to you my best wishes.

receive from your lover Dan

As 1865 began Mason's thoughts turned increasingly to getting out of the service, coming home, and marrying Harriet. For months he had written of his desire to tender his resignation during the winter months, as this would be considered more honorable than resigning in the midst of active campaigning. He had formulated a very specific idea in his head of exactly what his return to Vermont would include that he often repeated in numerous letters: an immediate marriage in church in the evening, followed by a dinner at a hotel in Barton with a handful of friends and family members, then a "car ride" to St. Johnsbury, where his sister Emily lived, or to Waterford, where relatives from his late mother's family still lived. He was concerned about Harriet's ability to "ride about" in the winter, suggesting, once again, that Harriet's health was a matter of ongoing concern for him, though what may have afflicted her is not entirely clear. Even if Mason was unable to receive a discharge, he wanted to go home at the earliest possible opportunity, on a furlough. Besides the desire to simply see Harriet and be home, he made it clear that his urgency to be married was due in large part to the looming prospect of death: "If I knew that I should never live to get clear of the army I should feel all the more anxious to unite my destinies with yours." A marriage would give Harriet the legal right to receive whatever "effects" he had, which would allow her a measure of financial independence and security that would otherwise be difficult to obtain as a young, unmarried woman in nineteenth-century America.

Camp of the 19th USCTroops
Jan[uary] 2d 1865

Dear Harriet

I shall be very brief as I am writing by the light of the fire place. I am well. In regard to being married I shall be willing to fulfill my engagement when I can get home which will probably not be until Feb[ruary]. You may make calculations to be married that is if you are able to ride about say as smart as last winter & I judge that you feel as well as last winter. If you are not able to go to Waterford we can go to St. Johnsbury & visit E[mily] & 2 or 3 cousins that I have there & return, but quite probable you may be well enough by the middle of Feb[ruary] to visit at Waterford. What do you say to being married in Church in the eve[ning]. . . . I think that a pretty good way. You may think different. You will please give your views in full in your next. I think we are both old enough to be married & if I knew that I should never live to get clear of the army I should feel all the more anxious to unite my destinies with yours or rather unite with you in the holy bonds of matrimony. If I should live to get out of it I perceive no harm in the act. Alex Davis & his reg[imen]t have got back from their tour after 20 days sail he looks as if he had had a run of fever it did not agree with him very well. I must close hoping to hear from you soon excuse the writing

receive from your true love Dan

Not yet having heard a response from Harriet regarding her views of the wedding arrangements, Mason changed the subject briefly to the culinary prowess of his paid Black servant Tom. It is not clear who Tom was, as Mason never recorded his last name or described anything of his background. Mason clearly enjoyed the comforts that Tom provided and the privileges that accompanied being an officer, though he lamented, "I have not had any apple pies for several days on account of the Commissary not having any dried apple." Charles Stinson similarly wrote that "my boy proves as good as ever. Find it very pleasant to have someone to get my supper and make my bed after a hard days march I live mostly on hard tack and salt pork. Roast pork so very palatable with me now days."[2] Mason enjoyed Tom's services so much that he even suggested to Harriet that "I shall always have to keep Tom he is a jewel, so you may make up your mind to have a third one in the family."

Camp of the 19the USCT
Chapins Farm Va
Jan[uary] 17th, 1865

Dear Harriet

Your kind epistle of the 9th if I am not mistaken in the date arrived in due season & was read do you believe me. I was pleased to hear that your health was improving which was best news you could have written. . . . Harriet—if I should be spared to see the end of this rebellion & peace once more restored I should think I had done something that I could be proud of. I have now served 3 years & nearly 4 months today. I have been wonderfully spared. . . . I am well & enjoying myself very well. I wish you could stop into my house this morning & see me sitting by my table writing. My Tom has got breakfast just ready. I shall have to leave off now & go to do justice to the choice viands. Tuesday eve well Miss Hat—I will now finish out that little chat that I commenced this morn. I will tell you what I had for breakfast. I had coffee, fish balls, & griddle cakes with plenty of sugar & butter perhaps you dont [know] what fish balls are well I will let you into some of the secrets of cooking. They are made of boiled potatoes & fish codfish picked to pieces & made into round balls about the size of warm biscuits & fried in a little grease just enough to prevent burning. They are quite good I assure you. Then dont say that I never learned you anything. Oh yes I had onions boiled & buttered & prepared to suit taste. For dinner I had Potatoes Onions & beef steak also flapjacks. I have not had any apple pies for several days on account of the Commissary not having any dried apple. I <u>assure</u> you it seems very odd to sit down to a table that has not a <u>pie</u> on it but I guess I can stand it until I can get some apple. Well it is [al]most time for Roll Call. . . . I am afraid I shall get lazy if I stay in this service a great while it is so nice to have a Tom run at ones call so gay in the morn to have him come in & build a fire early & Black my boots & then bring a basin of warm water with towel & soap to wash. Oh it is so lovely & agreeable compared with getting up & shivering around & building your own fire & cleaning your own boots & run to the spring & get your own water & then wash in it cold or be to the trouble to warm it & then how easy when the fire gets a little low, Tom more wood & the wood is forth coming & soon blazing on the hearth. Oh I shall always have to keep Tom he is a jewel, so you may make up your mind to have a third one in the family but enough. My love to your Mother & all the friends. I have nothing new to say about matrimony until I get your views.

I am Madam very respectfully
your obedient lover
Dan Mason

Mason again referred to Tom's culinary skills and told Harriet, "Perhaps you would like to take lessons well you can and it will not cost you anything if I take him home with me." But the focus of his attention turned again to wedding preparations. His previous directive that Harriet could invite "another Couple or 2 if you choose" to the post-wedding dinner apparently caused some consternation, as he then amended his original remark and said, "If you have 3 or 4 couples that you would like to invite to accompany us to Barton to take supper you are at liberty to do so." As soon as he arrived home at the depot in Barton, Mason planned to take a team of horses to West Glover to notify Reverend Sidney Perkins of his arrival, then would visit Harriet's house and stop for the evening. The following morning, while Harriet was getting ready for the wedding, he would then proceed to Glover Village to notify his father and his "best man" Elbert Nye of the upcoming nuptials. This would all be done with great speed, and Mason believed that "24 hours notice will be enough to fill the house."

Two days later, as he had been intending to do since the Battle of the Crater, Mason tendered his resignation. He explained his rationale in a letter to the Adjutant General of the Army of the James:

Camp of the 19th USCT
Chapins Farm Va
January 31st, 1865

Sir

I have the honor herewith to tender my resignation as Capt[ain] in the 19th Regiment USCT for the following reasons viz.

Business of a personal nature which demands my immediate and undivided attention as a citizen.

Having served 3 years and 4 months of active service in the field 29 months of it in the 6th Reg[imen]t Vt Vol[unteer]s I now ask to be discharged to enable me to attend to my own private affairs as my future happiness depends upon a proper and speedy adjustment of the same. . . .

With the above reasons knowing it to be utterly impossible (under the existing circumstances) for me to do justice to my Country or command by reason of which my discharge would be beneficial to the service, I do hereby demand an immediate and unconditional acceptance of my resignation.

I am sir very respectfully
Your ob't serv't
Dan Mason
Capt 19th USCT[3]

Mason did not specify exactly what "Business of a personal nature" or "private affairs" he had to attend to, but surely what was foremost on his mind was getting home to marry Harriet. Whether he actually felt that he was no longer able "to do justice to my Country" or if such language was simply designed to serve his purpose of obtaining a discharge (or both) is difficult to ascertain, though what is clear is that he wanted to go home for the sake of his "future happiness." Regardless, his resignation was disapproved at every level from his regiment all the way to army headquarters. General Godfrey Weitzel, commander of the XXV Corps, "respectfully returned" Mason's letter to division headquarters "to know how many officers are on duty in Capt. Mason's Comp[an]y—and in the regiment—also number of officers absent." Joseph Perkins, commander of the Nineteenth

USCT, replied that "there are three (3) officers Co[mmanding] Co[mpany] 'H,' but one (1)—Capt. Mason—on duty with it. The First Lieut[enant] is an escaped Prisoner of War and due here the 11th of Feb[ruary]. The 2nd Lieut[enant] is on duty as Act[in]g Adj[utan]t of the Reg[imen]t. There are 17 officers on duty with the Reg[imen]t and 17 officers absent."[4] The absence of Mason's First Lieutenant Lemuel Dobbs on a leave of absence did not help his situation. Dobbs was wounded in the Battle of the Crater and, when questioned by his Confederate captors, fully acknowledged that he was a white officer in a Black regiment. He was then sent to Confederate prisons in Danville, Virginia, Salisbury, North Carolina, and Charleston, South Carolina, where "he escaped . . . by tunneling November 21, 1864, and after tramping forty-one nights thru the mountains of western North and South Carolina and Eastern Tennessee, much of the way barefoot in snow six inches deep he reached the Union lines at Knoxville, Tenn., January 1, 1865. There he found he had been promoted to first lieutenant while in prison."[5] Without a discharge Mason could only hope for a leave of absence, which would allow him to go home—and then return to the service. He told Harriet that "I tendered my resignation about 3 weeks since it was disapproved all the way up to Army [Headquarters]. Gen[eral] Ord commanding Army of the James indorsed it by saying that the disapprovals at Reg[imen]t, Brig[ade], Divis[ion], & Corps [Headquarters] were the greatest compliments that could be paid me for if I had been a poor officer they would all have approved my resignation—so as to get me out of the service."

Lieutenant Dobbs, who was expected back on February 11, had still not arrived by February 18. Mason, impatient, told Harriet that "my first L[ieutenan]t has not got here yet though I expect him every night & I shall send in my application as soon as he comes to take command of the Company." As such, he told Harriet not to get carried away with making wedding preparations until his return was imminent. He explained, "I have concluded that it is not best to invite any guests at present if you have not already done so, as the precise time of my leave of absence is not known & we can not look far in the future in military life." He again reminded her of his desire to spend their wedding night in a hotel in Barton, "the same as all honest people," then take the "cars" the following morning for St. Johnsbury.

His resignation having been disapproved, Mason then applied for a leave of absence, which was also disapproved. He impatiently waited for the return of other officers so that he could then go home on a leave of absence. After suggesting that Harriet, like Eve, was a temptress—"I should be likely to eat apples that you gave me"—he then hoped that he could still "get home in sugaring" season. Time was of the essence; once the spring campaign began, his chances of going home would plummet further.

CAMP OF THE 19TH USCT
Feb[ruary] 24th 1865

Dear Harriet

Yours of the 18th has just arrived and been perused with the usual degree of pleasure. You speak of the pleasure given you to receive a letter from me, and of the goodness of them. I think mine very dry and uninteresting compared with yours especially your <u>lectures</u> they are <u>right smart</u>. I wonder if you can talk as well to my face what a nice thing it will be to have some one to give me a <u>lecture</u> once in a while to keep me <u>straight</u>. Well you know these men are apt to stray away from the path of duty but women of course they are gems of great price of course they are. Notwithstanding Mother Eve stole apples she was apple hungry of course she was and wanted good ones she wanted the best same as <u>some</u> of her daughters who can <u>blame</u> her? But she had to tempt poor Adam who was such a fine old gent—I think I am some like him dont you? You know I should be likely to eat apples that you gave me without asking any questions, of course I should, but I hope you will never <u>steal</u> any for me. I should <u>feel</u> so <u>mortified</u> of course I should.

Well Miss Hattie I am afraid I shall not get home this month. I have sent up an application for a leave of absence but it went disapproved from Reg[imen]t H[eadquarters] for the reason that so many were absent at that time two officers will be back about the 5th of next month & then 2 more have got to go ahead of me but I shall try to get in an extra one so as to get home about the middle of March. But you must not make to[o] great calculations you see that the time granted is so much longer than in former times that it takes longer for them to get around. I may not be able to get around this winter if the spring campaign should open early but if it should not open until May I can get home in sugaring, but I am in hopes to get home in the month of March if this present one is not granted. First you must always be prepared to receive disappointments. I must close. My love to your Mother and all the friends

receive from your Sincere lover
Dan

Distraught by the delay in obtaining a leave of absence, Mason now told Harriet that he might not be able to return home until April, unless the rebels "evacuate Richmond so that we have to follow up," which could dash any hopes of a return home. He apologized to Harriet for having "disappointed you so much" by continually predicting his return home, only to be delayed further. Despite his dismay over his own situation, a day after Lincoln's second inauguration, he optimistically declared that "the long predicted fall of Richmond & with it the Confederacy is near at hand its days are numbered."

CAMP OF THE 19TH USCT
March 5th, 1865

Dear Harriet

Yours of the 25th was received in due time. You doubtless are feeling disappointed these days so am I but we shall have to yield to the powers that are and call it all right. My application for leave came back disapproved for the present for the reason that so many were absent—we expect 2 officers back tonight from leaves and then I shall give them another call but may not be successful. I feel much more anxious on your account as you have made preparations all on my account. But you must be cheerful and await coming events. I think I shall be able to get leave in the month of April if not before if the rebels dont evacuate Richmond so that we have to follow up. But I have disappointed you so much that I hardly know what to say. I may come home and may not although I think the chances [are] in my favor. I am well. We are having some showery weather here very much like the last of sugaring in Vt—except we have no snow here have not had 2 inches this winter all put together. I received a box from home night before last containing 20 lbs Butter—about 15 lbs Cheese 2 lbs Salaratus & 2 oz. nutmegs. Whew! What cakes and apple pies my Tom will make now. If I get home the middle of April we can be married just the same. . . . Who cares if I can only get a leave of absence I will risk but what we can contrive the matter all right. We have such glorious news from the south that we ought to feel contended & be cheerful the long predicted fall of Richmond & with it the Confederacy is near at hand its days are numbered. Even the papers of that City speak of their Congress skedaddling. When a nation gets so that its Congress deserts it is about played out. . . . I am Brig[ade] Camp Officer of the day today had to go to every Reg[iment] & Inspect the Quarters of the men & see if their blankets were properly folded tents swept Streets policed & things in good shape. I tell you the mens guns have to shine & each man has to have a change of clean clothes in his Knapsack &c &c. You ought to see me strut about. I must now close my love to your Mother & all friends. My regards to Miss Sweeny

receive with much love from Dan

With my red sash over my shoulder how gay to be an officer when you cant help it

{ 14 }

"You Don't Know How I Would Like to See You" (Spring 1865)

Mason's leave of absence was finally approved in March. The Nineteenth USCT furlough book recorded that "Capt Mason started on 25 days leave Mar. 11 to Apr. 8."[1] It is not clear exactly how long Mason's trip home took, but he and Harriet were married on March 20, so it is evident that his plan for an expedited wedding was indeed carried out as intended. The exact details of the wedding—where it was held, who attended, or where the "honeymoon" took place—were not recorded. All one can do is imagine the momentary bliss followed soon thereafter by the anguish of another return to the front. However, the heartache of leaving his newlywed bride may have been tempered by the euphoria of learning that Richmond had fallen upon his return to the front.

Mason was still on furlough when Confederate forces evacuated Richmond. He missed out on the surreal experience of entering the city as it was abandoned. His friend, Captain James Rickard, recorded a play-by-play account of his entry into the city in a letter to his brother:

> Standing in line this morning a little past four o'clock I witnessed one of the grandest sights I ever beheld in the vicinity of Fort Darling. A great heavy column of bright blaze & smoke rose high in the heavens followed by a crash that shook the ground at daylight. . . . Evidently the rebels are blowing up the gunboats and evacuating! A dispatch just received says we have captured 12,000 prisoners & 20 pieces of cannon our left now rests on the Appomattox around Petersburg. We have just got orders to be ready to move immediately. We go for them today I guess. I must stop and eat my breakfast.

7:45 oclock. Moving through the rebel lines they have evacuated our front fires still fanning they have left their tents standing . . . in front of their works.

11. . . . Richmond is in flames constant explosions are taking place continuous roar the rebels are just ahead of us we are after them close. Fine day. One of the most glorious of my life. Caps the climax. Our troops are filled with the greatest enthusiasm.

12 oclock [P]M. In Richmond. We have now entered Richmond the city is on fire. We are going now on board a steamer to cross the river to occupy Manchester, great excitement.

Manchester 2 ½ PM. We are now in the city of Manchester the people very glad to see us. . . . The negroes flock around us in thousands & are in ecstacie. It is thought we may stay here awhile.[2]

Exactly which unit entered Richmond first has been the subject of much debate, though Rickard insisted, "The Colored Troops were the first to enter it—probably as a Reg[imen]t with its colors the 19th was the first in the city a Co[mpany] of the 5th Mass[achusetts] (Col[ore]d) Cavalry were the first troops that entered."[3]

Mason's letters were now addressed to "My dear wife" and included more innuendo than ever. Though he gushed to Harriet, Alex Davis said that Mason "told me of his marriage and showed me the picture of his wife. We held conversation about her, but 'no gush' or needless words were spoken—It would not have been Dan's way."[4] Two days after Lee's surrender at Appomattox, he described his first visit to Richmond and said, "Hattie you dont know how I would like to see you & press my lips to yours. I have made up my mind to leave the service this fall. I must be with you this Winter."

Camp near Bell Isle Va April 11th, 1865

My Dear Wife

I seat myself this evening to chat with my better half. I have been very busy writing all day consequently feel some tired but I will make a commencement this eve & perhaps get time to finish tomorrow. . . . I will give a short rehearsal of my journey from Bal[timore] to this place. I took the boat at 4:30 that afternoon engaged a State room & slept well all night—landed at F[ortress] Monroe at 7 the next morn (Sunday). It was a lovely day peach trees were in full blossom the apple trees were showing some blossoms & all nature seemed gay. At 8 I left for City Point on the Steamer *Thomas Colyer*. It was so warm & pleasant that we could all ride on the upper deck several ladies were aboard & everyone seemed to feel well over the good news after landing at City Point at 12:30. We got some dinner & at 3 we took boat for the great City of Richmond which we have been so anxious to possess for so long a time. I must close for tonight for candle is just burning out. Good night dearest—sweet dreams to you

Saturday April 15th, 1865

Since I commenced this we have moved to the South Side of Petersburg about 25 miles from where we then had to march through P[etersburg] to get here or at least we did so we are now on the Weldon Rail R[oad] occupying the old camps of the 6th Corps it seems very much like home as we were in this vicinity last summer & fall. It is said that we shall stop here sometime & drill doubtless they moved us over here to get us away from the City which is much better for officers & men if one is close by a large place he is not contented unless he can go to all the performances. If he is 3 or 4 miles of course he will not expect it. I went to the Theater in Richmond last Wednesday eve had a good time the performers were the same that used to play to rebel audiences. But now their band discourses Hail Columbia, Star Spangled Banner, Red White & Blue & Yankee Doodle which took well with the audience which was mostly of the Blue uniform, so you see they play for money & not for principle. . . . Hattie you dont know how I would like to see you & press my lips to yours. I have made up my mind to leave the service this fall. I must be with you this Winter & then if prospered I shall have money enough to buy as large a farm as we shall want & pay for it. . . . I must close for the mail carrier is around after letters. My love to all receive from your affectionate husband Dan

While Mason wrote to Harriet on April 11 describing his arrival in Richmond, his friend James Rickard pondered the meaning of the Union's victory in a letter to his sister:

CAMP 19TH USCTROOPS
NEAR MANCHESTER, VA
April 11, 1865

Dear sister,

The war is over, or just the same as over. Lee has surrendered his army & what rebels there are now in arms never have fought any under advantageous circumstances so I do not think they will now when surrounded by so many powerful armies. My impression is that Johnson will surrender without fighting if he has not already. Then comes great points to be settled. What is to be done with the four million negroes set free? They are so ignorant they are not capable of taking care of themselves & if left here among their former masters, they feel they have been so wronged, it will be impossible for them to live together for a long time at least. What is to be done with the leaders in this rebellion, and how are the states to be reconstructed? These are considerations it seems to me are very great & important ones and will be perplexing ones to us for some time.[5]

Though Rickard's characterization of emancipated slaves as "ignorant" is troubling, he expressed the basic fact that the war had not solved the race problem, which would be "perplexing . . . to us for some time." In Vermont the Democratic *Burlington Weekly Sentinel* editorialized about "The Negro Mania" and argued, among other things, that Blacks had done nothing to earn their own liberation:

> Quite an absurd (if not something worse) mania is seizing upon the minds of too many of our people in regard to the negro, and the *status* which he should occupy in [the] future in the political and social relations of American society. He has, for the most part, stood quietly by and seen the whites battle and kill each other for his sake, in order that the shackles

> of slavery may be stricken from his limbs, not raising so much as even a petty village insurrection to help on the work against his old master and for his old abolitionist friends. But now that the work is done for him, he proudly claims to enjoy its fruits, and means, evidently, to be acknowledged as "somebody" in the land.[6]

The newly established Freedmen's Bureau was given the enormous task of facilitating the transition from bondage to freedom for millions of emancipated people. The bureau built schools, helped negotiate labor contracts, offered legal assistance, reunited families separated by the auction block, and provided housing, job training, and other services that made a real difference while it lasted. The creation of the Freedmen's Bureau represented an unprecedented expansion in the scope of the federal government. Its success was short-lived, however—the result of underfunding and a faltering political will to address the race problem directly. If Rickard's statement about the challenges facing newly emancipated people seems problematic, Frederick Douglass expressed identical sentiments:

> Though slavery was abolished, the wrongs of my people were not ended. . . . The Negro, after his emancipation, was precisely in [a] state of destitution. . . . He was free from the individual master, but the slave of society. He had neither money, property, nor friends. He was free from the old plantation, but he had nothing but the dusty road under his feet. . . . The first feeling toward him by the old master classes was full of bitterness and wrath. They resented his emancipation as an act of hostility toward them, and, since they could not punish the emancipator, they felt like punishing the object which that act had emancipated. . . . The freedman had been the friend of the government, and many of his class had borne arms against them during the war. The thought of paying cash for labor that they could formerly extort by the lash did not in any wise improve their disposition to the emancipated slave, or improve his own condition. Now, since poverty has, and can have, no chance against wealth, the landless against the landowner, the ignorant against the intelligent, the freedman was powerless.[7]

After prophesying about the challenges of Reconstruction, like Mason, Rickard expressed his desire to leave the service as soon as possible. Now that the war was over, as was true with Mason, the only remaining motive to stay in the service was economic:

> I have said I would stay in the army as long as the war lasted & it has been a question on my mind whether or not to stay any longer. I have pretty much made up my mind to leave the service if I can, but from what I can observe they do not intend to disband these troops. . . . Mexico has to be rid of the French & I think these troops will be sent there. If I stay I shall endeavor to get a better position, but I would rather commence business life again, as too long service unfits any one for most any other life. I might stay this summer & as officers pay is so increased, could save quite a sum perhaps more than any where else & have a good capital to start with.[8]

The dizzying turn of events in April 1865—perhaps the most turbulent month in the nation's history—reached a tragic crescendo with the assassination of Abraham Lincoln on April 14. Lincoln's death was announced to Union forces by an order from the War Department the day after he died. Grant issued orders that "the officers of the armies of the United States will wear the badge of mourning on the left arm and on their swords and the colors of their commands and regiments will be put in mourning for the period of six months."[9]

The news of Lincoln's death shocked and demoralized a nation that was in the midst of celebrating a momentous triumph four years in the making. James Rickard expressed his despair in a letter to his brother: "The all prevailing topic here, & every where else I guess, is the murder of Abraham Lincoln. A greater loss at this time could not have befallen the nation, but the South will be the greatest sufferers by it—he was disposed to be so very lenient with them. . . . Capt Mason & myself mess together now."[10] Five days later Rickard wrote to his sister that "to day is being observed here according to Gen. Grant's order. . . . Perhaps there never was a more universal mourning through the country than now. Every one weeps as though he has lost a very dear friend. . . . I am almost afraid for our country when I think Abraham is no more. . . . He was known to be so honest wise & faithful. The officers all wear Crape on their arm & hilt of the sword. All reg[imen]tal flags are draped in mourning every one feels so sad."[11]

The *Orleans Independent Standard*, once a critic of Lincoln's, now idolized him with religious reverence:

> Swift upon the heels of victory comes the sad tidings of the death of Abraham Lincoln by the bloody hand of an assassin. What a change in the aspect of affairs during one short week. How eventful the past few days! But one week ago the country was jubilant over our recent glorious successes in the field; the heart pulsated and thrilled with a newer life, and our paths were strewn with garlands of flowers. To day the nation is in tears; our temples and public edifices are draped in deep mourning, and sorrow sits at every loyal hearthstone. . . . All that is left to us now is his memory—rich in sublime works and in noble deeds. . . . Where freedom has a friend, there will the name of Abraham Lincoln. . . . To the Black race will he be held as second only to the Messiah, for he was in truth their great deliverer from bondage. . . . We firmly believe that he was selected and raised up by God to perform the important part assigned him in this great national drama, or tragedy, of the past four years, and that he was chosen by him to be the liberator of that long suffering and down trodden race, as much as was Moses chosen to deliver the children of Israel from the cruelties of the Egyptians. We could not see this two and three years ago. All was then dark and gloomy. But the events of the past few months have made It as clear as the noonday sun.[12]

Encamped outside Richmond in comfortable quarters, Mason hoped that he could remain there all summer and await his opportunity to return home for good. He lamented the generous terms initially given by General Sherman to Joseph Johnston's Confederate force that surrendered in North Carolina. Contrary to Lincoln's wish in his Second Inaugural Address that the nation could be reunited "with malice toward none with charity for all," Mason said, "I want to have some of the Lead men hang for a terror to traitors in future." He then reassured Harriet that although "I do wish I could press you to my heart today & steal a kiss from those dear lips," the "time will soon be around if we are patient."

A certain melancholy or sense of isolation seems to have befallen many Civil War soldiers once the war ended. Enlisted men who awaited being mustered out of the service and officers who hoped to be discharged often felt disoriented by the cessation of hostilities, received less correspondence from home, and grew exceptionally weary of continuing to indefinitely perform the routine, tedious tasks of military life. In late April James Rickard complained that "I dont feel half as contented now as when we were facing an enemy."[13] A few days later he added, "Most of my correspondents have fallen off. I have had no letters from any one at home for some time. I manage to live however."[14] Then the next week: "I am not in the best of humor to day, as they make us move camp every day. . . . Nobody seems to know what to do with us but to keep moving us about. Last night they were not satisfied with something & moved us about three quarters of a mile."[15] Elijah Stone, a private in Mason's old unit of Company D of the Sixth Vermont, wrote to his brother on May 12 and lamented,

> I have not had so many letters lately and have been quite lonsome. I supose my Corespondents think now the war is over that I dont want any letters but I do the time passes a way the slowest now that it has sinse I have bin in the servis. . . . Some say we shall be at home to spend the 4th at home hope it may [be]. Do you think I cold find a girl to go to the selebration with me? I am glad you have got the steers broke but I should think it wold be rather a poor team to draw manure with.[16]

In June Mason similarly complained that "I have not secured a letter from home since I left—father is terrible slack about writing. I expect he thinks the war is over & I am all right—any way but. I think he ought to write."

Like so many others, Mason was preoccupied with the thought of returning home. On May 4, he wrote Harriet one of his most amorous letters yet. He pined for her "precious face" and "honeyed lips," looked forward to being a "Head of a Family," and added that the "Old Ladies" of Glover "will doubtless watch you very close to see if there is any development."

Camp near City Point Va

May 4th, 1865

My Dear Darling Wife

Yours of the 26th arrived in due time and has been read and reread over and over again. I dont know why it is but your letters seem more precious than before we were married if possible though they have always been read with eagerness & reread & then burned, but now I hate to burn them. I keep them 2 or 3 weeks & read them over & over again, then with much reluctance I commit them to the flames. . . . Since my last we have moved down near City Point & gone into camp for instruction. I think we shall stay here sometime. Oh my dear wife you dont know how I do want to see your precious face again & clasp you to my heart again & steal a kiss from those honeyed lips. No it would not be stealing would it—they are mine now aint they darling? I must go home & live with my precious wife this fall. I am so glad we were made one when I was at home. We feel so much freer to express our feelings. We have no secrets to keep indeed we are but one in mind so to speak. Marriage is sacred & why is it that so many become miserable & regret that they were ever united in the holy bonds of matrimony? I think one or both parties did not realize the great & important step they were taking & did not regard the marriage vow with due solemnity. Perhaps pure & spotless love did not cause the connection. I trust that we united our destinies by reason of true unfaltering love which may never forsake us making our pathway one of pleasure & true happiness. We of course must expect trials & disappointments but by true constancy & confidence in each other we shall support & strengthen each and battle successfully the trials and tribulations that flesh & blood are heir to. There is scarcely a moment passes but I think of my dear dear wife precious woman you are mine. I would not take $50.00 for your picture it is so natural & life like. It almost speaks or seems just ready to. . . . I hope I may always try & please you & make you happy. I have a good deal to live for now of course I have. Why just think of it Head of a Family, not but one at present. . . . I hope them old ladies wont worry any more about you nor the road being traveled before. They will doubtless watch you very close to see if there is any development well let them watch & talk they must have something to talk about. I must close. Excuse this blotted dirty sheet for I have labored under difficulties no table tent leaking some have not got fixed up yet. It is showery this morn. My love to all the friends your Mother in particular

Write soon & oblige your true husband

Dan

Soon after the fall of Richmond, the all-Black XXV Corps (the only corps in the war to consist only of Black troops—and their white officers) became mired in controversy. In the chaos surrounding the fall of the city, numerous accusations of misconduct were leveled at Black soldiers. General Edward Ord, who commanded the Army of the James to which the XXV Corps belonged, wrote to General Godrey Weitzel, commander of the XXV Corps, on April 16: "Many complaints have reached me of depredations committed, some of a desperate character, principally by Black and white cavalry. You are authorized to have all or any person found outraging private houses or plundering persons summarily shot . . . post guards and patrols to prevent straggling. Keep your men and officers out of Petersburg. Have your own headquarters with your corps and require all your officers to remain with their men. On account of recent occurrences great care will be taken and proper state of discipline exacted."[17] The next day General Meade likewise reported to General Grant that his troops had captured "a camp with several wagons loaded with plunder. The party consisted of negroes, mostly belonging to this army. Some were killed, and the rest made prisoners."[18] Weitzel defended the conduct of his corps: "I with my two division commanders . . . believe the troops of this corps to be not only as well behaved and as orderly as the average of other troops, but even more so. . . . The behavior of my entire corps during the last month has been most excellent. Only one complaint has been made by the people of the vicinity, and this I traced to troops that did not belong to it."[19] Ord then revised his original assessment somewhat and wrote, "I do not consider the behavior of the colored corps from what I have heard to have been bad, considering the novelty of their position and the fact that most of their company officers had come from positions where they were unaccustomed to command, and this was perhaps the first great temptation to which their men were exposed. In the city of Richmond their conduct is spoken of as very good."[20]

What "depredations" occurred, by whom, and what the nature of these allegations were is hard to pinpoint with exactitude. Of course, as one historian has pointed out, "perhaps the most effective weapons used against Black occupation troops by white Southerners were false accusations that they were guilty of malicious acts. Too often, Union officers accepted such unsubstantiated complaints and initiated punishment without investigation."[21] The highest-profile allegations of misconduct by Black troops were leveled at a number of soldiers of the Thirty-Eighth USCT who were accused of raping two white women near Richmond on the night of April 11, 1865. In a three day court-martial, Sergeant William Jackson of the Thirty-Eighth USCT was charged with rape and with plundering and pillaging. The witnesses at the court-martial were other Black enlisted men of the same unit who were not actually present when the alleged crimes were committed. Their damning and at times graphic statements were based on supposed conversations that took place with the defendants after the alleged crimes took place. The officers detailed for the court proceedings were, of course, all white. Given the nature of these cases and their eventual significance in determining the fate of the XXV Corps, significant excerpts from the courts-martial are worth recording. The first witness called was a Mrs. Fanny Crawford, one of the alleged victims, who was asked about the nature of Sergeant Jackson's entry into her home:

> Answer:—He carried me into the passage. I begged him to let me alone, and he said he would kill me if I didn't hush, and threw me down on the floor, and done me as they chose.
> Did they violate your person?
> Answer:—Yes sir.
> Did they succeed in doing that?
> Answer:—Yes sir. . . .
> Was it dark in the passageway where the Prisoner carried you?
> Answer:—There wasn't any light in there.

How do you know the Prisoner was the soldier who made attempt to ravish your Person if there was no light there?

Answer:—The light was in the dining room, and he made me hold the candle to look in a trunk, and he carried me from there into the passage.—The candle was left in the dining room.

Did you resist him in his attempts to violate your person?

Answer:—Yes sir I begged him to let me alone, but he wouldn't.

Did you offer resistance in any way except "begging him not to touch you?"

Answer:—I tried to push him away and begged him to let me alone, and said if I didn't hush he would kill me.

Did he pull up your clothes after he threw you down?

Answer:—Yes sir.

Did he have sexual connection with you?

Answer:—Yes sir.

Several items were then shown to Mrs. Crawford, including a pair of ladies' hose, a silver thimble, a pair of white kid gloves, a pocketknife, a shirt, a vest, and other articles, all of which she claimed had been stolen by her from the prisoners. Her niece, Eliza Woodson, was called as a witness and offered similar statements about the theft of various articles from the house. She was then asked about the actions of the men toward her.

Question by the Judge Advocate

Do you know where your Aunt Mrs Crawford was during all this time?

Answer:—I know they made her go into the other room, but I dont know where she was after that.

Who made her go in?

Answer:—One of the men about the size of the Prisoner.—I think he was a little darker—might have appeared so in the night.

Can you swear that the Prisoner was the man who forced Mrs Crawford in the other room, or not?

Answer:—No sir I cant.—I think he was rather darker.

What was done in the other room after Mrs Crawford was carried in there?

Answer:—I dont know sir, because the door was shut, and I could not see. . . .

Did you hear anything from that room?

Answer:—No sir. . . .

Question by the Court

Did you hear any screams, or entreaties of Mrs Crawford, begging the Prisoner not to do so, while the alleged crime of Rape was being committed?

Answer:—No sir.

While Mrs Crawford was in the passageway, was the Prisoner in the room with you?

Answer:—Yes sir, if I aint mistaken as to his face. . . .

Question by the Judge Advocate

How many men were in the room with you?

Answer:—Two.

What did they do after that?

Answer:—After one made me get on the bed, then I got on the floor, and then the other man I think it was, made me get on the bed with him.

Question by the Court

Was the Prisoner one of the two who made you get on the bed?

Answer:—No sir—I was mistaken in his face—come to think about it neither of them with me had any beard on his face.

Who told you you made a mistake?

Answer:—Nobody.

Do you think the Prisoner was the man who forced Mrs Crawford from the room in which you were?

Answer:—Yes sir, because that aint the one that forced me on the bed, because he never had any beard on his face.

Mrs. Crawford's brother, a William Woodson, who lived near his sister, was then called as a third witness.

Question by the Judge Advocate
What do you know of a disturbance at Mrs Crawford's house? . . .
Answer:—I heard my sister Mrs Crawford holler, and I heard a shot fired. I run down to the Battery to report them as hard as I could run.
Did you go near Mrs Crawford's house?
Answer:—Yes sir, I went in the field across the road, opposite the house. I did not go into the road. It was very muddy. . . .
Question by the Court
When you were in the field across the road, what did you see or hear, that made you run to the Battery?
Answer:—I saw or heard nothing—that was before I left home.
Question by the Judge Advocate
How near was you to the house, when in the field across the road?
Answer:—I suppose within about seventy-five yards.
Question by the Court
When your sister cried for help, why did you not go to her assistance instead of going away to the Battery?
Answer:—Well sir I was afraid to go. I had nothing but a small shotgun and was afraid if I went, that I would be butchered up.

The prosecution then called its next witness, a private named Edward Berry in Company G of the Thirty-Eighth USCT. The stenographer recorded Private Berry's statements in a "Black" dialect:

Question by the Judge Advocate
What do you know of a Prisoner going to a house outside the picket line on the night of the 11th inst[ant]?
Answer:—We all went to the house, and knocked at the door. Sergeant Brooks he knocked at the door, and told them to open the door—and then the woman she would not open the door, she run upstairs and hollered. Then the corporal or someone, I dont know certain which, fired his pistol—Den after they fired the pistol and the woman screamed, I turned and come away with three of the boys.

Who remained at the house?
Answer:—Sergeant Jackson, Sergeant Brooks, and a Flag Corporal, and one private with them.

Private Berry, who fled the scene, didn't see Sergeant Jackson until the following night, when he reportedly learned some of the details of the previous night's scene.

Question by the Judge Advocate
What did you hear him say concerning what he had done at this house?
Answer:—I heard him say that he had ravished a woman as much as he wanted to, and then got out of the house what he wanted to.—He told me he got some pants, some shirts and a vest.
Who was he talking with?
Answer:—He was talking with me.—I axed him what he did get?
Who did the Prisoner say he had ravished?
Answer:—He said they had ravished an old woman, and the girl too.

After more testimony from another fellow soldier in his unit, Jackson delivered a written statement to the court:

> I did not go in the House at all. I stayed in the rear of the house. When the shot was fired I was in the rear of the house behind the palings of the garden. There I staid till they come out of the house, and we all come away together then. They had I believe two bundles. The corporal had something hanging across his arm, looked like a coat, could not tell what color it was,—it was dark. I never saw no more of that.

The following day the court found Sargeant Jackson guilty of both charges and sentenced him "to be hung by the neck until he is dead, in the presence of the 1st Division 25th Army Corps, at such time and place as the Commanding General may direct." General Ord and President Andrew Johnson approved the sentence.[22]

Three days later the court-martial of Sergeant Danbridge Brooks began. The court called many of the same witnesses that it had in Sargeant Jackson's court-martial. Private Edward Berry offered additional testimony:

Question by the Judge Advocate
Who shot the revolver?
Answer:—I don't know sir who shot it. I never see the one who shot it, I took three of the boys besides myself and come away. . . .
What was the Prisoner doing when you came away?
Answer:—Well I dont know what he was doing.
When did you see the Prisoner next after that, to speak with him, and what did he say?
Answer:—I see him the next night to speak to him, down by the Hospital, most to Richmond, and he told me about his ravishing of the women at the house. He said he went to the old woman, and the young one too. He said he went to the young one first, and then he went to the old one.
What did he say about it?
Answer:—He said he fucked the old woman, and the young one too.

Another witness, Private Anthony Branch, was asked a similar round of questions about the prisoner.

Question by the Court
Did he say he fucked the young gal?
Answer:—He said he got some, from her. He didn't call out fuck.

Eliza Woodson, the thirteen-year-old girl who was one of the alleged victims of the rape, was then subjected to a long round of questioning.

Question by the Judge Advocate
How did he have connection with you?
Answer:—He pulled my dress away.

Question by the Prisoner
Are you sure the Prisoner is the man who put you on the bed?
Answer:—Yes sir. . . .
Question by the Court
Do you remember seeing those stripes on the prisoner's sleeves?
Answer:—I dont remember the stripes on this man's arms.—I didn't notice.
How did he manage to have sexual connection with you, after he threw you on the bed?
Answer:—Well he pulled up my dress, and pulled open my legs.
Question by a member of the Court
What did he enter your person with?
This question was objected to by a member of the court. The court was then cleared for deliberation:—Upon the opening of the court the Judge Advocate announced that the court had decided to overrule the objection and allow the question to be answered, and the witness answered.
Answer:—I should think you might know.
Question by the Court
Did he or did he not enter your person with his penis?
Answer:—Yes sir he did.

Sergeant Brooks was found guilty and sentenced to be hung.[23]

This sensational case raises countless questions: If Mrs. Crawford's brother heard her scream and was armed with a shotgun, why did he not run to her assistance immediately? Why would crossing a muddy road stop him? If Mrs. Crawford screamed when she was being assaulted, why did her niece in the next room not hear her? If only a single candle was burning in the dining room, then how could either of the alleged victims have positively identified their assailants? Where was Mr. Crawford? At the court-martial, General Alonzo Draper said that he followed the tracks of the assailants from the house to their camp and determined that they belonged to the prisoners, but how?

Perhaps the crimes took place exactly as described. Perhaps they didn't take place at all. Or perhaps they took place to some degree, with other details fabricated or exaggerated. Whatever the truth is, the fact is that for centuries, from countless lynchings to the Scottsboro Boys to Emmett Till to the Central Park Five and beyond, allegations of sexual assault by Black men against white women were almost impossible to challenge and often proved fatal to the alleged perpetrators, as they did in this case. During their courts-martial, Sergeants Jackson and Brooks asked numerous questions of the witnesses that questioned the accuracy of their statements. Each denied having been in the house where the events in question took place. The crimes were reported to Union authorities by a white man, Mr. Woodson—the brother of Mrs. Crawford—who was not an eyewitness to the crime. Several Black soldiers who had joined the initial night foray through the picket line had disappeared before any entry into the house took place, though they provided damning testimony based on reported conversations that took place the day following the incident.

Whether Sergeants Jackson and Brooks were guilty or not, their case had profound implications for Mason, the Nineteenth USCT, and the XXV Corps. General Ord, who had already complained about "depredations" committed by the XXV Corps after the fall of Richmond, was anxious to have the corps deployed elsewhere. Just rumors of "depredations," whether founded or unfounded, proved to be a political and military liability for Union authorities who were trying to accomplish the enormous tasks of assisting countless "freedmen" while simultaneously attempting to establish good will with the recently vanquished Southern population. On April 30, days after the courts-martial of Jackson and Brooks concluded, Grant instructed his chief of staff, General Henry Halleck, to "put the Twenty-fifth in a camp of instruction either at Bermuda Hundred or at City Point until some disposition is made of them for defense on the sea-coast. Establish the best labor system you can to employ the idle and prevent their becoming a burden upon the Government." Half an hour later, Halleck responded and said, "On further consultation with General E.O.C. Ord, I am more fully convinced of the policy of withdrawal of the Twenty-fifth Corps from Virginia. Their conduct recently has been even worse than I supposed yesterday."[24] Nobody was yet sure where, but clearly the highest authorities in the Union military wanted the all-Black XXV Corps sent elsewhere.

Where they would be sent did not remain a mystery for long. Confederate forces west of the Mississippi River under General Kirby Smith had still not surrendered, and Union authorities feared a potential Confederate exodus to Mexico. Rumors abounded that Jefferson Davis himself would try to flee to Mexico across the Rio Grande, or that Confederate exiles would coordinate with Mexican leaders to wrest Texas from U.S. control and establish (once again) an independent republic of Texas. General Phil Sheridan, the hero of Cedar Creek, was sent by Grant in mid-May to take command of troops stationed along the Gulf Coast. Grant instructed Sheridan "to restore Texas and that part of Louisiana held by the enemy to the Union in the shortest practicable time, in a way most effectual for securing permanent peace." Grant dispatched tens of thousands of troops to the Rio Grande, including the XXV Corps. Grant told Sheridan,

> You may notify the rebel commander west of the Mississippi . . . that he will be allowed to surrender all his forces on the same terms as were accorded to Lee and Johnston. . . . In case of an active campaign (a hostile one), I think a heavy force should be put on the Rio Grande as a first preliminary. Troops for this might be started at once. The Twenty-fifth Corps is now available, and to it should be added a force of white troops, say, those now under Major-General Steele. To be clear on this last point I think the Rio Grande should be strongly held, whether the forces in Texas surrender or not, and that no time should be lost in getting troops there.[25]

Moreover, Mexico had been embroiled in internal turmoil for years. A civil war between a pro-Catholic conservative party and a secular liberal party had engulfed the country from 1857 to 1860, which resulted in a victory by the liberals and the election of President Benito Juarez. The country was in financial ruin following the war, so Juarez suspended debt payments to European creditors. In response French, British, and Spanish forces landed at Veracruz, though French emperor Napoleon III had greater ambitions than just collecting debts; he hoped to reestablish a French empire in the New World. Napoleon's goal was to install his Austrian cousin Maximilien as a puppet ruler in Mexico. French forces entered Mexico City in 1863, and the Second Mexican Empire was established (the First Mexican Empire under dictator Santa Anna had fallen in the 1850s). The United States, embroiled in its own civil war, officially took a neutral position but sympathized with republican forces who continued to fight against Maximilien and his conservative Mexican allies. Once the American Civil War ended, the United States took a greater interest in the French presence in Mexico, viewing it as a threat to the Monroe Doctrine. The Monroe Doctrine was the guiding principle of U.S. foreign policy in the nineteenth century and stated that the United States would not tolerate any attempt by European powers to reestablish colonial empires in the western hemisphere. Unlike many European nations, the United States never recognized the Second Mexican Empire under Maximilien.

James Rickard welcomed the prospect of a voyage to Texas. On May 19 he wrote, "I hear we are going South (probably to Texas) within forty-eight hours. . . . I dont care how quick we go, for we would get rid of the monotony of this camp & these tedious drills."[26] Before departing for Texas, Rickard also told his sister that "I have got a white boy now for a servant Henry Jones his father & mother are both dead & I took him more out of pity than choice. He is a very bright boy. I only got him yesterday shall keep him awhile & see how I like him."[27] Later Rickard told his father, "I have a little white boy now I like very much & shall take him home with me some time. I think he is a very keen boy. He picks me . . . strawberries every day."[28] Mason likewise had previously told Harriet that he intended to take his Black "boy" Tom home with him, though later acknowledged that he was joking. Rickard was serious about taking his "boy" home with him though. He wrote later to his sister that "my boy Henry got [a] letter from his brother last night which pleases him very much. He likes me & wants to go home with me & I guess I shall take him along as it would be too bad to leave him down here he is a good boy & very smart."[29] His "boy," Henry Jones, actually wrote a letter to Rickard's friends stating his intention to return to Connecticut with Rickard:

> I have been with the Capt eight months I have enjoyed myself very much during this time, but am anxious for him to get his discharge that I may go home with him and see New England which I have heard so much

about. It is very pleasant down here now & also the grass is so green. I was hunting yesterday and killed some birds I go hunting very often. I like my Capt very much. I am well and doing well and am trying to get all the pretty feathers I can. I expect to bring my gun with me when I come. I want to come North so I can go to school. I have been reading [and] writing ever since I have been in the army and I think I have improved some.[30]

Mason was less enamored of the idea of traveling to Mexico; for one thing, it would mean less frequent letters from Harriet. Before leaving, though, he had the opportunity to temporarily assume command of the regiment, as his superior officers were absent on leave or detailed to other duties. In perhaps his most self-promotional letter, Mason boasted of the image he cut at the head of his regiment and the rush he received from giving commands to hundreds of Black men. Hardly his most enlightened letter, he told Harriet, "I tell you I was a big Coon dog." For the moment he was the senior officer in the regiment because his friend James Rickard had received his officer's commission a day later.

Camp near City Point Va May 26th, [18]65

My dear Wife

I am once more permitted to write to you from the sacred soil of Va. We expect to go in a day or two. At the time I wrote you last I expected we would be on our way ere this but it is quite an undertaking to embark so many troops with all the baggage horses waggons rations ammunition &c &c for so long a voyage. Yours of the 13th I think was the date arrived in due season & was devoured in the usual greedy manner. I would rather not go to Texas on account of the distance being so great that letters will be rather old when we get them, but we shall think all the more of them when we get them if we write often. We shall get them just as often as now but they will be about 2 weeks old at least. But dearest we will make the best of it. Well my dear wife the war is over. Jeff Davis & many other leading rebels are in close confinement at Fortress Monroe. Kirby Smith & his rabble in Texas have played out & the armies of the rebels have melted away. It is thought that we shall be scattered along down the Coast to keep order among the people until they legislate & make laws for their own protection. They are now without law or order except Military law which must last for awhile it takes time for all these things to come about. We have 2 women here in camp now L[ieutenan]t Dobbs wife & the Hospital Stewards wife. Many of the officers had sent for their wives when the order for moving came. If we had been put in garrison in Va I should have wanted you to come out if your health would have admitted. Now it will be so far that we shall have to give it up & be content until fall when I must go home to you if prospered with life & health. You dont know how I do want to see you. It dont seem that I can be separated from you 5 long months but suppose I must be content & time will roll on the same steady motion as usual. Oh you ought to have seen me drill the Regiment 2 days in succession a short time since one hour & ¾ each day. Col[onel] Perkins is home on leave Maj[or] Welsh is absent on leave & L[ieutenant] Col[onel] Knorr is sick or detailed Division Officer of the day. I assume command of the Reg[iment] by virtue of my rank & have to drill it. Have a horse to ride & am a big man generally. You ought to have seen me with my white gloves on putting the Reg[imen]t through the different battalion evolutions. What a swell I did cut. You ought to [have] heard me give of[f] the command in thunder tones to their Capt[ain]s & L[ieutenan]ts. I tell you I was a big Coon dog. By the way those ladies were out to witness the drill & of course I done my best. I like to drill the Reg[imen]t it is so nice to ride a horse & make 6 or 7 hundred men do as I order them. Some of their Capt[ain]s that are but one day junior to me in rank you see I was mustered as a Capt[ain] Mar[ch] 30th [18]64 & Capt[ain] Rickard was mustered Mar[ch] 31st, [18]64. But 1 day decides the rank just as much as 10 or 40 days would.

I sent a box by express directed to your father a few days since. I thought I would direct it to your father thinking it might go through more direct than if directed to you. It contained 2 wool blankets which will be very handy when we come to keep house. I have 2 left which is enough for summer. The overcoat Cape will come in play for something.

Receive this with much love. Give my love to Mother & all the friends. Receive from your ever affectionate husband Dan

---

On May 30 the regiment boarded a steamer for Texas. James Rickard wrote that the Black enlisted men "are considerably crowded & we have no windsail & they almost suffocate in the hold where they are stowed. The officers have very good accommodations. We have a stateroom apiece [and] board on the boat with the Captain at $2.00 per day. My boy stays in the room with me & it will cost me nothing for him as the Steward has him help him some enough to pay his way."[31] Mason did not have to share a room with his "boy" Tom, whom he "paid off" before the departure to Texas. He hoped, however, that "I shall have a chance to get a bright little Texas boy to take home with me."

The XXV Corps sailed along the southern coast, rounded the Florida Keys, and docked in Mobile Bay. From there the expedition sailed to the mouth of the Mississippi River to New Orleans, then finally to Brazos Santiago Island at the mouth of the Rio Grande. James Rickard described the transport that he and Mason sailed on as "an iron ship a blockade runner captured I think in sixty-two. . . . If she don't roll too bad I don't see why we can't have a pleasant trip."[32] The ship apparently rolled enough for Mason, who "threw up Jonah several times." While Mason wasn't plagued by seasickness, he enjoyed observing the flora and fauna of the Gulf of Mexico, and he even sent a wing of a flying fish home to Harriet!

On board the Steamer *Everman*

On the Mississippi River 20 miles below New Orleans June 16th, 1865

Dear Wife

I take this opportunity to write you a few lines to inform you of my whereabouts. We left Fortress Monroe June 5th, arrived at Mobile Bay June 15th, stopped a short time & again put out for New Orleans for the purpose of getting a supply of Coal. We expect to get there in about 3 hours it is now about 8 oclock in the eve & thought I would write this eve & mail it tomorrow. We have had a pleasant voyage no bad storms. I was quite sea sick for 2 or 3 days & threw up Jonah several times. We were out of sight of land several days at a time. We are going to Indianola in the Matagorda Bay Texas about 3 days sail from New Orleans as we shall have to run back down to the Gulf of M[exico] as you will see by referring to the map. I have enjoyed the scenery up the river today very much such beautiful residences surrounded by groves of Lemon & Orange trees laden with the precious fruit—ripe & beautiful. I saw 2 Aligaters on a log sunning about 6 feet long. When we were sailing through the Gulf of Mexico one eve just before a shower a flying fish flew on to the deck near me & I caught him he would weigh about half a pound. I put him in a pail of water but he died so I cut of[f] one of his wings which I will send you. You will see that I did not get it spread its full size they fly quite rapid. We expect to stop at N[ew] O[rleans] tomorrow & I expect to look about the City. I am very well since I got over my sea sickness. I think it was a good thing for me. I think I should like this country well if it was not for being so far away & mails will be so long coming & doubtless not very regular but we must make the best of it till fall. I must now bid you good eve for the boat is rather unsteady & it bothers me to write. I may have something to write in the morning. Pleasant dreams to you

June 17th, [18]65

Dear Hattie

We arrived here last eve about 11 oclock. I have been out viewing the city this morn went to the market saw ripe plums watermelons Blackberries Oranges &c &c. As the mail does not leave here for NY until next Sat[urday] I fear this will be rather old ere you get it but dear you must be cheerful & make the best until fall

receive from your true husband
Dan

James Rickard was also impressed with the scenery along the banks of the lower Mississippi River. He wrote that "peaches and plums are ripe here now & we hope to get some. Oranges are not ripe here yet but they are very plenty along the river." He also noted that there were "great plantations of cane corn & cotton all along the river."[33] After his arrival in Texas, Mason then wrote a lengthier description of his travels in a letter to the *Orleans Independent Standard*.

Camp Near Brownsville, Texas
July 14th, 1865

Friend Earle—I am again permitted to trouble you and your readers with army composition, not from the "sacred soil of Virginia," but from the barren sands of Texas. Perhaps a brief account of my voyage from Virginia to this place would interest some of your readers.

June 5th we weighed anchor and steamed out of Hampton Roads on the *J. W. Everman*; the day being pleasant and not uncomfortably warm, the Bay slightly ruffled by a gentle breeze, made our departure quite pleasant. Nothing of importance occurred as we steamed down the coast except many were seasick, which is usually the case with freshwater fowls. Your humble servant done his share toward feeding hungry fish as usual on such excursions, but I can't say that I enjoy the sport of paying 75 cts. for a dinner and then lose it in five minutes after, but of course it is all right to "Cast your bread upon the waters," for the good book says so.

The sea was somewhat troubled in the vicinity of Florida reefs, but nothing serious. We found the weather exceedingly warm at Florida Keys, being nearly far enough South to inhale the atmosphere of the torrid zone. Our sail in the Gulf was very pleasant, the numerous gold colored fish sporting near the surface and the Pelicans and seagulls flitting about added much to the enjoyment of the passengers.

June 15th, we arrived at the mouth of Mobile Bay and cast anchor within a few yards of Fort Morgan, but soon weighed anchor and steamed out, bound for New Orleans, arriving there the morning of the 17th. The ascent of the Mississippi was decidedly the most pleasant part of our voyage, the beautiful Groves of orange and lemon trees glistened with their golden fruit, the mockingbirds and numerous other kinds of songsters warbling sweet melodies, with occasionally an alligator perched on a log with his coat of mail glistening in the rays of the sun all combined to make the scenery interesting. After a sojourn of thirty-six hours in the Crescent city, during which an amount of coal had been transferred to *J. W. Everman*, we again cut loose and made good time down the river; the current being strong our speed was greatly accelerated. In due time we disembarked at Brazos Santiago Island, which is a sand bank without Bush or tree or scarcely a green thing—no water except what is condensed from salt water by steam Engines. The breaking of one of the two Engines with the landing of several thousand thirsty soldiers made the water question quite interesting to all concerned; your humble servant then thought how valuable were the springs of sweet water gushing out from beneath the granite rocks of New England.

After two days stay we left the burning sands of Brazos and struck out for the Rio Grande, which we reached after about six hours March at White's Ranch and drank our fill of the muddy water, which when placed in a pail and settled has one inch of solid mud to seven inches of water, or in other words, a pale eight inches deep being filled at night has one inch of mud in the bottom the next morning, but it is quite good, and said to be healthy after settling. After three days of muddy marching, caused by the overflowing of the Rio Grande we arrived at Brownsville, opposite Matamoros, which is garrisoned by several thousand French and Mexican soldiers. We can hear their bugle and drum calls very distinctly morning and evening from our encampment. Our officers go over there nearly every day some of them, and meet with a kind reception from their soldiers. . . .

There is not much vegetation here, except little stunted thorn bushes from 6 to 8 feet high, no farms, nothing growing except in gardens, which has to be watered; it seldom rains here.—This is a great country for Lizzards, Snakes, Toads, Horned Frogs, Mosquitoes, Spiders, &c. In fact everything, animal and vegetable seems to be armed with a thorn, horn, or spur, ready to wreak vengeance on persecuted man. But enough; Pardon me for wearying your patience so long, but permit me to add

That when all other lands reject us,
This is the land, the land of Texas.

Very Respectfully,
Dan Mason[34]

{ 15 }

"If I Can Get Home This Fall" (Summer 1865)

Mason and the men of the Nineteenth USCT landed at Brazos Santiago Island at the mouth of the Rio Grande in late June. There was no fresh water, no firewood, and little protection from the elements. Mason wrote, "I dont like to be so far away from home. I could have staid in Va quite contended until fall but this is much different."

BRAZOS SANTIAGO ISLAND TEXAS
June 23d, 1865

My Dear Wife

I seat myself on my blanket flat on the ground with my portfolio for a table to write my darling a few lines. We landed here yesterday had a pleasant trip down from New Orleans. We had one man die on the boat & had to commit him to the waves with weights tied to his feet with all the honors of a burial at sea which was impressive. I am well. You will see by referring to the map that we are down near the mouth of the Rio Grande River which separates Mexico from US. We expect to be scattered along the Rio G[rande] to prevent any raids from rebs that may have fled to Mexico with evil intentions. We are now on a sandy Island no wood or water except what we condense by boiling salt water saving the Steam. There are 2 large Steam Boilers with necessary appendages for the business. There are plenty of fish in the Bay near by & I am going out to give them a try soon. . . . I hear that officers are going to have a chance to leave the service soon as we get settled down & the vacancies will be filled from white Reg[iment]s that wish to remain in the service if so I shall embrace the first opportunity—I have now a little better than $2000.00 at my disposal & that is quite a good start for a <u>boy</u> of my age &

with common luck we can get a living. I dont like to be so far away from home. I could have staid in Va quite contended until fall but this is much different. I presume I may feel different when we get back in the country where there is plenty of wood & water. We expect to go to Brownsville in a day or 2 up the Rio G[rande]. You will see on the map. I must close. My love to all the friends.

Accept the best wishes of your
affectionate husband Dan

We have fine sea breezes here it would be very warm but for them

James Rickard was also not impressed with his new surroundings. In a letter to his friends on July 2, he provided a long catalog of the miseries and hardships that he had endured. He wrote that "we are experiencing now some of the hardest soldiering I have ever seen." After leaving Brazos Santiago Island, a "barren sand island without water," he explained,

> we marched that night for a point on the Rio Grande 9 miles & the hardest march I have ever seen . . . & were almost perished for water when we arrived there in the night—the river . . . was very muddy so we could hardly drink it but were glad to get any thing. No grass here & most miserable country. Went to Bagdad on the 27th with Capt Mason a small town in Mexico near the mouth of the river bought a few things but most of the people there are . . . sharpers who have been engaged in running the blockade during the war. . . . This days march beat all I have ever seen or heard of for the first few miles we had to march in mud & water but I thought it would soon be better but we entered a thick "chaparral" & found the water had overflowed its banks & settled in here & so many marching in advance of us slimed it to a thick mud about a foot deep on average & much deeper much of the way, like this for . . . two miles every one nearly gone out, no chance to stop to rest the only way was to keep on though very slowly as it was with great difficulty a foot could be pulled out of the mud by & by we reached a point on the river which was higher & dry where we went into camp for the night—next morning we started again right into the mud for about ½ a mile, then for the first time we crossed a prairie near where the battle of Palo

Alto was fought—then into the water again for about two miles but not much mud my boots had given out by this time & I had thrown them away as they hurt my feet so badly. I have nothing to wear but a pair of slippers. I am barefooted. . . . In the night the wind blew hard next day had a shower which with the wind drove the water onto the point of land where we were & drove us out had to move camp in a furious shower got wet completely through. Slept in the water all night had a big time trying to fix up a tent but it kept breaking down. Next day marched got to Brownsville about noon heavy shower just as we got into camp which covered this floor where we are about six inches deep with water. I went down town just before dark & was so wet & tired did not come back till morning. Went to a Mexican "Fandango" slept in a lounge on some slats pretty hard bed for 75 cts. More rain today . . . this is a desert some call it hell. Almost every one is mad & demoralized here not satisfied with such soldiering in time of peace but we shall like better when we once get settled.[1]

Captain Frank Holsinger of the Nineteenth USCT also remarked that "in our march across the country we had a very severe trial, as the mud exceeded by far anything I saw in Virginia. The river being on a 'bender' overflowed her banks so that we had to march for miles in mud and water to our hips."[2] If the experiences of Rickard, Holsinger, Mason, and the other officers of the XXV Corps were miserable, the Black troops in the XXV Corps suffered even more. A Black soldier in the Forty-First USCT wrote a letter to the editor of the *Christian Recorder*, a Black newspaper published in Philadelphia that was widely read by soldiers in the USCT around the nation, and complained,

I do not think that the government is aware of our situation. Before being detailed to this post, being of the 25th Army Corps, we composed a part of the army of the James.

We have done all that soldiers could do to crush and wipe out this terrible rebellion.

We have been marching for about two weeks, night and day, on half rations. Sometimes we received none at all. . . . White soldiers, in the same corps, are allowed to supply themselves from the enemies farms and store-houses.

While on the March, the white troops were allowed the full liberty and privilege of "helping themselves," while, if we attempted to relieve our appetites at the expense of our enemies, we were immediately punished. Such is the treatment of colored soldiers in Texas. . . .

The white troops have been allowed "liquor," and we have not. We don't care about the "liquor," but we think we should have been allowed our other rations.

We seldom receive fresh meat or fresh bread and molasses. We have received our pay but once in nine months, and consequently our families experience great suffering and distress for the want of the little necessities of life.

If we have the misfortune of being taken sick, we receive only the *poorest* medical attendance.

The men have often called on the doctor for medical instruction, when he told them to go to their duty. Consequently, in a short time afterwards, they were found dead at their posts . . .

Now, Mr. Editor, I'm no scholar, and not being gifted with great educational facilities, I cannot give you such a blazing account as some would. If I only had the education, I would open the eyes of the government, and interest the people, as to the manner in which the poor colored troops are treated.

After doing everything in our power for the country, this is the treatment to which we are subjected to.[3]

White troops were far more likely to be mustered out than Black troops, since their enlistments usually had begun much sooner (most Black units were not organized until 1863 or after). Plus, white civilians back home enjoyed much greater leverage in advocating for the mustering-out of their sons, brothers, fathers, and husbands than their Black counterparts did. It is no surprise, then, that Black units were often given the least desirable assignments in the least desirable places. Just before the XXV Corps left for Texas, Grant's chief of staff, Henry Halleck, pointed out that "there are attached to the Twenty-fifth Corps several batteries manned by white troops. Is it intended to send these with Weitzel? I understand they are very unwilling to go. General Weitzel has plenty of colored artillerymen without batteries. Could not the guns be transferred so as to make his command homogenous?" Grant responded and told Halleck, "The white men connected with batteries may be detached and sent here for muster out, or detained if you have use for them. One gun to 1,000 men will be sufficient for Weitzel to take with him."[4] Simply by complaining that they were "very unwilling to go," the white artillerymen temporarily attached to the XXV Corps avoided service in Texas, while the Black units of Weitzel's corps struggled through mud and chapparal along the Rio Grande with only half-rations of hardtack and condensed water.

While the men of the Nineteenth USCT and the XXV Corps suffered deprivations and fatiguing marches on the Rio Grande, those troops fortunate enough to be mustered out of the service often were greeted by appreciative crowds and a heroes' welcome on their return home. On the Fourth of July, Derby Line, a small village on the Canadian border, celebrated the recent homecoming of its defenders of the Union with great pomp and ceremony. A band from Quebec serenaded the crowd, a flag "was raised upon a beautiful pole erected for the purpose, by thirteen young ladies, amid booming of guns & the deafening shouts of the multitude," and the Declaration of Independence *and* Emancipation Proclamation were read as well as numerous other speeches. In the afternoon, "the returned soldiers who were present to the number of one hundred and fifty, sat down to a bountiful repast, prepared expressly for them in a beautiful arbor, by [the] present proprietors of the Derby Line Hotel, while the crowd were amply provided within the Hotel, with all that an epicure ever might desire." A local reverend then "spoke of the duty we owe our soldiers in caring for them and their families, the duty of introducing into the southern States, the element of northern energy and enterprise, the duty we owe the freedmen in educating them to become citizens and assuming that important right of suffrage which the speaker strongly urge should be granted them, and lastly, of that sterner duty we owe assassins, murderers and traitors, in meeting out condign punishment to those who so richly deserve it." This address was "frequently applauded." In the evening a fireworks display was held and an effigy of Jefferson Davis, dressed in drag, was stripped naked and "hanged amid the cheers of the crowd." Cheers for the flag, the army, and Queen Victoria (Canada still belonged to the British Empire) rent the air. Best of all, reported the *Orleans Independent Standard*, "the number in attendance was variously estimated from five to ten thousand, and what is very surprising for these times there was not to our knowledge, a single instance of drunkenness or a single exhibition of its results during the entire day or evening. It was one of those good old fashioned celebrations, which at these times every man, woman and child, who has left a single patriotic impulse, cannot fail to enjoy. May we as a nation live to spend and enjoy many more anniversaries of this glorious day."[5]

Back in Texas Mason had survived the grueling march from Brazos Santiago Island to Brownsville, which he described as "a hard muddy march." He assured Harriet that "I shall get out as soon as I can. I have soldiered long enough." He also looked forward to purchasing a new horse upon his return in the fall and told Harriet, "We will visit all winter."

Near Brownsville Texas

Sunday July 2d, 1865

My Dear Wife

I seize my pen once more to chat with you awhile. We have at last arrived at this place & gone into Camp expecting to stop here for sometime perhaps all summer. I think I shall like here after we get fixed up comfortable. We are about 1 mile from the village of B[rownsville] on the Rio Grande River which has about 4000 inhabitants. Matamoros Mexico is just across the river. It is no warmer here than in Virginia. The country being level there is a good breeze all the time. . . . I know it will be of no use to tender my resignation yet but you may rest assured that I shall get out as soon as I can. I have soldiered long enough. . . . I went over the river to Bagdad Mexico the same day so you see I have been out of the United States. We had a hard muddy march up here. I wish you to send me some Newspapers every week. We dont get any reading matter at all here. We seem to be out of the world almost. The ground here is covered almost with lizzards toads horned frogs spiders of all shapes & sizes some as large over as a silver dollar. I am well. I hope you are getting along well. I tell you what I intend to do if I can get out this fall. I shall buy a good horse sleigh & harness & we will visit all winter go to Waterford & Littleton, NH & visit all your friends. I intend to visit enough to make up lost time. I dont feel like writing much it dont seem that I have much that would interest you but I do wish you to write all the news anything will be news to me dont be afraid of telling simple news. I must now close. My love to Mother & all the friends with a great ration to yourself

receive from your affectionate
husband Dan

Once in Brownsville Mason had several opportunities to cross the Rio Grande into Matamoras and observe the "ways & customs of the Mexicans," whom he described as "very much like Indians a kind of a greasy Black object." This was hardly the most enlightened sentiment that he ever penned, and it offers a reminder that believing that slavery was a crime and that Black troops should be armed did not necessarily equate to a belief in racial equality. If Mason's racialized language is problematic, his description of the Mexican people was tame in comparison to the language employed by his fellow officers. Frank Holsinger, for example, commented,

> The native Mexican is the laziest creature I ever saw. Gaming and Fandangoes are their chief amusements. They may be seen at all hours loitering around the saloons drinking and carousing. The Fandangoes might bear a passing notice as they are now the peculiar institutions of this country. When one is on the tapis all classes and conditions are admitted upon an equal footing, the only expenses for the evening being what you eat and drink. Thus you ask a senoretta to dance, after which you adjourn to the saloon and quaff a mint julip, a brandy cocktail, or a punch—either of which she can take without wincing. Thus the evenings pass, night after night, and week after week. It is not unfrequently you see the gold laced gentry join in . . . with a slouchy wench of a greaser, who would be kicked out of any northern kitchen on account of her slovenliness.[6]

Holsinger later added, “In manners [the Mexicans] are quite rude as not unfrequently, you see children of both sexes entirely naked. In fact I can see that the greaser is little in advance of the Aborigines on our frontier.”[7] Despite holding Mexicans and Mexican culture in such low esteem, for some reason Holsinger frequently attended fandangoes in Matamoras with “senorettas” who he described as “slovenly wenches” and “greasers” on one hand, but also seemed to be intrigued by them: “The women wear a loose wrapper thrown over their shoulders (very low) without gathering about the waist. . . . I think them a very cool arrangement.” In another letter he added that “the women sometimes appear in the richest costumes, making grand displays of dress and jewelry—others are only about half dressed, making a squalid appearance indeed.”[8]

In July Mason mentioned that Alex Davis had recently been married while home on a leave of absence. Davis had requested a leave of absence in late May because “since enlisting in the service my father has died and as his estate was insolvent my mother and two small children are deprived of a home other than a hovel tenement. On myself rests the responsibility of providing them a home, and I have so far succeeded in my hopes as to have the necessary funds to purchase one. I have no one at home to transact the business for me, and wish to attend to it now in person.”[9] This may have been Davis's primary concern, but he clearly had another objective in mind as well that he did not mention in his request: getting married. Like his friends Fred Kimball, Carl Dwinnell, and Dan Mason before him, he jumped at the first opportunity to come home and be married, even if it meant that he had to leave his new bride behind after a brief honeymoon to return to his unit.

Mason looked forward to renewing his honeymoon as soon as possible. Employing what was possibly the most loving, romantic, and longing language he had yet used, he assured Harriet that he would be home in the fall.

Camp of the 19th usctroops
Near Brownsville Texas
July 15th, 1865

I will chat with you for a few moments but what poor consolation compared with conversing face to face. How I would like to meet you once more & just smother you with kisses if no one was looking how happy we will be if we can ever get us a home by ourselves we shall be so happy & satisfied with each other & no one to laugh & say they act sickish. When we are alone we can act as we please & do many things that some people would call silly but if we enjoy it is no ones business. Oh Harriet my darling how dear you are to me if I can ever get back to you I shall be perfectly happy you are all that I could ask [for]. I wonder if we do love each other so much better than others. Can it be possible that we shall ever injure each others feelings & get angry? I hope not but if we do we must be ready to forgive & do better in the future. My precious darling wife I must be with you. My other friends though dear seem distant compared with you. How can I express my love to you words fail to convey my feelings. It is useless to try. But my precious one if I can get home this fall we will renew the honey moon so suddenly brought to a close last spring & we will just visit & live so happy if we can both be well we will have just as good a time as ever was had in this world. I am so glad that we were married it seems so good to call you my precious wife you are such a treasure. How thankful I ought to feel that I have someone to watch over me & gently correct my failings & short comings. Harriet—my dear wife you are an angel & I am a wayward lad that is frequently led astray & go over the bounds & sometimes use naughty words but I intend to do well & feel sorry afterward but 4 years in the army dont improve ones morals though I think I have held my own very well concidering the many bad examples set by bad men & so completely away from the influence of women. But although you have been many hundred miles away you have been the means of saving me. If I sometimes use bad words I have always been true to you & feel certain that I always shall if I can get home I trust that I may improve by enjoying your society. Oh woman virtuous woman how near an angel you can approximate. I am well & enjoying myself very well. Intend to get home sometime in Oct[ober]. I wish you to write me a good long loving letter it is so much consolation to me not that I doubt you in the least but it makes me so happy. . . . My love to Mother & all the friends

with much love
Dan

Now that he had been settled in Brownsville for several weeks, Mason wrote that "I am well & much better contended than at first but shall leave just as soon as there is any chance to do so." He complained of a lack of available newspapers and told Harriet, "I wish you would send me some papers every week." He lamented that he had only just heard the news of the executions of the conspirators in the Lincoln assassination. James Rickard lodged the same complaint with his sister: "We are still in the same camp near Brownsville, don't hear much from the world very often. . . . I wish you would send me more papers as I have no opportunity here to get any. I got the 'Conn[ecticut] Press.' It was the only paper I have seen from there in a long time." News and letters from home arrived so infrequently that Mason no longer immediately burned letters from Harriet. He instead held onto them and savored their contents until he received the next batch.

Rickard also noted, "We have gone to gardening now. Each Co[mpany] has its garden on the banks of the river, have to water every thing from the river."[10] Captain Frank Holsinger wrote home to his hometown newspaper in Pennsylvania and reported:

> "What are we doing here?" is the all absorbing question. I will tell you, we are *planting gardens*. Yes, sir, the 25th Army Corps have turned "the sword into ploughshares and the bayonet into pruning hooks." If things continue thus for a few months the lower waters of the Rio Grande will be a miniature Egypt. . . . This is, however, a sanitary measure, as scurvey has for some time existed very extensively in our corps. I think it will have a salutary effect in teaching the poor benighted greasers how to garden—or give him an idea of Yankee enterprise.[11]

While the Nineteenth USCT practiced its horticultural skills, Mason also told Harriet that "I went down to Brownsville a few evenings since & went to a Fandango (a dance) the Mexicans & Spanish were the head ones the men & women both smoke on the floor the men wear great wide rimmed hats when they dance the Mexicans look more like Indians than white men long straight Black hair & very red or brown complexion with high cheek bones."

Mason had repeatedly suggested that he would bring "a boy" home with him but then admitted, "I was gassing," and that he could "get a boy" cheaper at home. Before he left for Texas, he had sent an express box home to Harriet with various items, including a cape, that he thought "will be very handy when we come to keep house." After he joked that he could "get a boy" for free after he returned home, he learned that he wouldn't have to wait that long. He received a letter from Harriet, dated July 1, that contained quite startling news. He learned that the cape he had sent home would indeed have a purpose.

NEAR BROWNSVILLE TEXAS
July 27th, 1865

My Dear Wife

I received yours dated July 1st several days since & was much pleased to hear from my dear dear wife precious treasure thou art mine is the proudest boast I can make. I think you were feeling a little crusty when you wrote but you ought to have seen me start & shudder when you commenced telling that you was going to make that cape into a babies cloak &c what a terrible tremor it put me in you was real naughty. . . . I will make you sorry for trifling with my feelings when you know I am so modest you should be careful about dashing my modesty. . . . Well darling if you will be choice of your words in the future & not shock my fine feelings by such shocking language. I have no news to write—I am well & enjoying myself very well but I cant bear to be separated from you much longer. It is so much nicer to have a fine bedfellow than sleeping alone these cold nights, dont you think so? Darling of course you do. . . . I think I shall tender my resignation about the 1st of Sept[ember] & if

I have good luck I would get home the last of the month but you must not expect me until sometime in Oct[ober]. . . . I must close my love to Mother & all the folks receive with the sincerest wishes of your husband

Dan

The Masons had been married on March 20, and only two weeks later Dan had returned to Virginia. In that brief window of time, it is clear that Harriet became pregnant. With remarkable efficiency the Masons seemed to be well on their way to expanding their new family. By the time Harriet revealed this news in her letter of July 1, she would have been through her first trimester. Despite receiving such "shocking" news about the creation of a new life, Mason's next letter focused mostly on a grim tale of the taking of life. Sergeants William Jackson and Danbridge Brooks of the Thirty-Eighth USCT, who had been court-martialed in April for allegedly raping two white women outside of Richmond, Virginia, and were found guilty, now received their sentences in front of the entire division. Their alleged crime certainly played a role in the deployment of the XXV Corps to Texas in June. Mason didn't harbor any doubts in his mind about the verdict. He told Harriet that "they were guilty—it was just to hang them for such a grave offence but it was a solemn sight & I could but feel sorry for the poor fellows." How or why he arrived at that conclusion is difficult to discern. Perhaps he simply assumed, because of the racial dynamics at play, that they were guilty, or he may have heard about the details of the courts-martial and genuinely believed the allegations. After all, the witnesses at the courts-martial had used strong, vulgar language to describe the incident. Mason's fellow officer in the Nineteenth USCT Captain James A. Blakely had been detailed for the court and was present at both courts-martial, so it is possible that Mason had heard Blakely's analysis of the cases and formed his conclusions based on this. Regardless, he seemed to have been somewhat disturbed by witnessing the executions, describing the "solemnity of the scene" in graphic detail to Harriet.

Camp of the 19th USCTroops

Aug[ust] 4th 1865

My Dear Wife

I again set myself to write you a few lines though I have but little news to write. I hope that I may write enough to interest you to some degree. I was disappointed yesterday not to receive a letter from you we get mails at such shocking long intervals that I feel very sad when I fail to hear from my dear wife. I received a letter from father dated July 2d he said that Alex Davis was home and married to Carrie. Well I expect they have gone & done it—strange but they will all do so sooner or later but you & I beat them of course we did but we will just finish out that honey moon in great shape if I can make everything work favorable & I think I shall be able to get home by the 1st of Nov[ember] if not before the[n]. . . . Last Saturday 2 soldiers, Serg[eant]s of the 38th Colored Reg[imen]t were hung in the presence of the Divis[ion] at Brownsville for committing an outrage on the persons of some white women last April soon after our entrance to the City of Richmond. I expect they thought it a good time to get meat for their cats but it proved to be dear enjoyment. They were guilty—it was just to hang them for such a grave offence but it was a solemn sight & I could but feel sorry for the poor fellows when they rode from the jail to the gallows in an army waggon seated on their coffins the band playing a funeral dirge the troops formed on 3 sides of the gallows leaving a few acres square where the guards & some officers stood the citizens filled up the 4th side after entering the square the procession passed clear around inside back to the gallows they then got out & marched on to the fatal drop their arms were pinioned behind them the rope noosed about their necks the bandages placed over their eyes & a prayer offered by the Chaplain. Just before the rope holding the drop was cut one of them asked for water & drank hearty—his last drink the next moment he was hanging in the air with his neck broken. They died with but few struggles nothing but the drawing up of the legs & a sort of quiver that passed over them. They dropped about 6 feet. To add to the solemnity of the scene their graves were dug just in front of them yawning to receive them. I have no more to write. . . . Give my love to Mother & all enquiring friends

receive with much love from
your sincere husband Dan

In his next letter, Mason returned to the subject of Harriet's pregnancy and cautioned her not to overexert herself. As he often did, he expressed great concern about her health, though what exact health conditions he was concerned about are unclear. Apparently Harriet had been seeing a doctor. Mason advised her that she would "gain" more rapidly "if you did not try to do so much." He also cautioned her, "I hope you will not try & get along & do all your work," which he believed was the cause of her illness in the first place. After expressing concern about her health, he concluded on a note of optimism, once again stating his intention to return in the fall, at which point he would buy a farm, a horse, a harness, and a sleigh, do some "right smart visiting," prepare for the arrival of a child, and enjoy fresh apples from his father's orchard. While enduring the scorching heat of a Texas summer, the thought of fresh-pressed apple cider in Vermont in the autumn must have seemed heavenly to Mason: "I shall be ravenous for such things & cider how fine."

James Rickard wrote to his sister in mid-August and complained, "The weather is very hot here thermometer at about 100 [degrees] most of the time. We do not mind it so much as we should but every day is alike." He, like Mason, daydreamed of the "victuals" that he would enjoy upon his return home, but worried that he would not be home in time to enjoy the harvest: "How I would appreciate a good meal of victuals at home, which pleasure I have [been] in anticipation [of], but I shall be too late for all the nice vegetables & fruit, berries &c you are enjoying now."[12] A week later he recorded the temperature as 116 degrees, but said that "I have got more used to the climate & manner in which I have to live here now & get along more comfortably. We begin to get potatoes which are a luxury."[13] In September he also looked forward to the apple harvest, though he wrote to his brother that "I was very sorry to hear that apples were so scarce in New England this season for I had anticipated making up for lost time if I should be lucky enough to get home this winter, which is rather doubtful.

We of course get no fruits here except what is canned & now that is getting scarce & they ask enormous prices for it. The commissaries have kept some kinds but they do not have them half of the time."[14] Since he would not be home in time to enjoy the fall harvest, Rickard gave his sister very explicit instructions about how to preserve the crop.

All the daydreaming about fresh fruits and vegetables back home in New England was likely poor consolation to both men, who each waited for an elusive discharge from the service that seemed like it would never come.

Camp of the 19th usctroops

August 26th, 1865

My Dear Wife

Yours of the 28th July was thankfully received a few days since. I think there must be one between the 14th & 28th that has not got along yet. I learned from your letter that you were gaining slowly or would if you did not try to do so much well there. I did think that my advice was taken some notice of by you but I have concluded that it is of no use to say anything but let you smash about & keep sick. Who cares if that wonderful silk dress aint done just such a time. I hope you will not try & get along & do all your work if your <u>daddy</u> does <u>sweep</u> there is no use in trying any such thing that is the way you got sick in the first place. I am well have not been sick since my sea sickness on the boat. I think I have good reasons to think that I shall get out of the service by the 1st of October which would bring me around the last of the month. I have got a project under way that gives much encouragement although it may fail. We are encamped near Brownsville Texas same as when I last wrote.

In regard to employing the Dr spoken of I shall leave that wholly to you. I wish all done that can be done. If he is certain that he can help you without giving medicines that will otherwise injure you I should think best to try unless you think you are gaining as fast as could be expected. You must act your best judgment. I feel anxious to have you get your natural health as soon as possible. I have not much to write that will interest my darling. We are having a rainy day today the first we have had since we landed in Texas. It seems real queer to have it rain steady as it does in Vt sometimes. I want you to pick out a farm somewhere before I get home about $3000.00 worth will do me. Would like to get it for 2500.00. I dont intend to go away back out of the world to live. I shall buy on a good road where I can get out. I dont mind a few miles from a village if it is easy getting out. I intend to buy me a good horse sleigh Robes & Harness this fall & do some right smart visiting this Winter but there is that baby what a burden that will be. I say that is to[o] bad aint it? Oh well that cape will keep him warm. I guess we can go for all that dont you? What? . . . I expect people are done haying up in Vt & commencing to cut grain. I hope Fathers folks are having a good crop of apples this summer. I shall be ravenous for such things & cider how fine. Well I cant write any more now. Give my love to Mother & all the folks

Good bye darling

Receive from Dan

Harriet had become sick during her first trimester, the cause of which Mason attributed to her continuing her usual pace of work. He worried that she had not been taking his advice seriously. In response to his stern admonition, Harriet must have offered a rebuke of her own. Mason acknowledged her "lecture" but immediately dismissed it and said, "I guess I had better stay down here & keep clear of a scolding wife." Whether he meant this facetiously or not, one can certainly read much into the prevailing gender dynamics of the time. Mason was determined to assert his control over the situation, even if he was over two thousand miles away from Harriet, and wanted to have the last word on the subject. Then, somewhat more cheerfully, he asked how the baby was doing but worried about the impact it would have on his freedom. Though he acknowledged that "those that dance must pay the fiddler," he suggested that Harriet was at fault by having applied her seductive womanly charms against a "virtuous" and "innocent" young man like himself.

Mason received a second letter from Harriet at the same time he received her "lecture," and this letter must have provided him with solace after the first tempestuous one: "I liked your 2d firstrate. It was such a long one & so loving it made me feel so nice." Responding in kind, Mason wrote, "I think of you continually through the day & dream of you nights. Oh how happy we will be together if I can get home this fall." To cap off his sanguinity, he expected that "I dont believe we shall ever quarrel."

CAMP OF THE 19TH USCTROOPS
NEAR BROWNSVILLE TEXAS
Sept[ember] 5th, 1865

Dear Wife

I seat myself to acknowledge myself the recipient of 2 letters from my darling wife day before yesterday. The 1st one was a poor one cause she had the pouts & got angry with her lazy old man down in Texas so she got up on her dignity & thought she would give him a lecture & she done it in her usual style. Well how bad I did feel to have her get so angry at me but then she cant do much to me when away down in Texas. I guess I had better stay down here & keep clear of a scolding wife. But I guess I could bring her to terms if I was there. She wants a little training that is all. I dont believe she is under good discipline but I will fix her all right if I can get home. Well Mrs Mason how do you do? How is the baby? Have you got that cape made into a cloak for him no her? Well never mind the sex. How shall we visit about so much this winter with a little squabler to disturb the quiet of everyone? How I shall hate to be awakened from my midnight slumbers by that little music box. Oh dear. It is terrible [to] contemplate worse than the bursting of bomb shells at dead of night. Well such is life those that dance must pay the fiddler. If a virtuous young man like myself allows himself to be taken in by one of the fair sex he must abide the consequences. But I did think you would set me better examples than that. I did not believe you would let or rather seduce such an innocent boy like I is. But that is the way with women they will do strange things. . . .

The weather is very warm & the mosquitoes are terrible thick & very large. We are situated the same as when I last wrote you. I have nothing new to add about coming home can tell in about 3 weeks if things work around as I expect. It is so warm that I cant write news very well today. I will finish tomorrow.

Sept[ember] 6th, 1865

Good Morning my darling how do you do this morning how is the little one? Well I will try & finish this this morn. . . . I am well. I hope this may find you improving. Harriet—words utterly fail to express my love for you you are all that I could wish. I think of you continually through the day & dream of you nights. Oh how happy we will be together if I can get home this fall. I never knew true happiness until the 20th of last March. I was as near heavenly bliss for 18 days after as mortal man can get in this world. How pleasant the thought that you are mine & I am yours. I do think we were made for each other. I dont believe we shall ever quarrel. I cant think of such a thing of course there will be some little misunderstanding sometimes but we must make it a motto to forgive & forget.

I liked your 2d firstrate. It was such a long one & so loving it made me feel so nice. I shall expect a good long loving one for this. I think I have done real well this time dont you? Darling do praise me. I also received 3 papers which were greedily read advertisements & all. I must close. Give my love to Mother & all the friends. Receive with much love from

Your affectionate Dan

While Mason responded to his "scolding wife," James Rickard complained to his sister of the "awful place" that he found himself in. He said that "we have been having heavy rains of late which have flooded the country & given us a large invoice of mosquitoes. . . . We are tormented almost to commit suicide to get rid of them after dark each night—the air seems thick with them. . . . If it were not for my mosquito net I could not get through a night."[15] Rickard could not wait to escape such a miserable clime and grew more disgruntled with each passing week, waiting in vain for his resignation to be approved.

Mason had tendered his resignation in January, which had been disapproved, and ever since he waited for another opportunity to try again. On August 22 he and four other officers in the Nineteenth USCT submitted their "immediate and unconditional" resignations. Of the five officers who tendered their resignations at that time, only Mason's was endorsed by his commanding officer, who said, "Capt Mason has while in this Reg[i-men]t always done his duty and by his faithfulness and good conduct well deserves any favor that can be granted consistent with the best interests [of the regiment]. Capt Mason will be a great loss to this Reg[imen]t but should receive every consideration in this application." General Weitzel, who commanded the XXV Corps, approved Mason's resignation, but General H. G. Wright, who commanded the Department of Texas, disapproved it "upon the ground that officers should not be permitted, at their pleasure, to leave the service, while enlisted men are compelled to remain." Even Phil Sheridan, who commanded the Military Department of the Gulf, disapproved the resignation. Sheridan's disapproval was not written until September 18, and a month later, on October 17, Mason had still not heard about Sheridan's decision.[16] Although he didn't realize it yet, any hopes of his return home in the fall had been dashed.

{ 16 }

"A Brave and Elegant Soldier" (Fall 1865)

Mason's next letter to Harriet was dated October 9, over a month after the previous letter in the collection from September 6. Surely there were letters written in between. Mason had made it a point to write every five days or so. Why those letters are not in the collection can only be speculated about. Did Mason sink into some form of depression? He had admitted to having "the blues" on several occasions, most notably after the Battle of the Crater. Although Harriet was undoubtedly pregnant, she never had a child, so is it possible that he received news of a miscarriage at this time? Were the contents of his letters in September too personal, troubling, or sensitive to be passed onto descendants, even decades later? It stands to reason that Harriet, who eventually gave the letters to her nephew forty-two years later, wanted to protect her husband's image for posterity and selectively removed any letters that in her view diminished his sterling image as a cheerful, strong, and steadfast soldier who never questioned his duty. This is only speculation, though there must be some reason why certain letters that Mason wrote were obviously not passed on. Mason did come down with dengue fever in September, so perhaps that is part of the explanation for the absence of letters during that time.

In his next letter, he spoke of having witnessed several reviews of troops in the weeks prior with his friend James Rickard and expressed the opinion that "the unbleached Americans beat the white Troops all to pieces. I expect it was because the darks have so much better Officers." Rickard agreed that "our Brig[ade] did the best of them all. It takes a great while to get a Div[ision] into position for review, & then there is a great deal of waiting always & then a long march & then to stand again which is very, very tiresome; after the review a number of medals were presented for gallant & meritorious conduct in action, which took until after dark. Quite a large number of ladies were present, mostly officers wives."[1] Mason, who was unhappy because he was not able to enjoy the company of his wife due to their separation, sighed, "Oh if I had a certain young Mrs with me how happy I should be."

Camp of the 19th USCTroops Near
Brownsville Tex[as]
Oct[ober] 9th, 1865

My Darling Wife

I will now do what I intended to have done yesterday viz write to my darling. You will excuse me. I know you will darling when I tell you all about it. Yesterday after the usual Sunday morning Inspection I went to church at B[rownsville] heard quite a good sermon helped sing the choir being mostly Officers of the different Reg[imen]ts one presiding at the Melodeon. There were 2 or 3 fair damsels that sang of course. I did not dare look at them being extremely modest & bashful (as you well know) but their voices sounded sweet—of course now dont you get jealous will you darling? Well in the afternoon we (Capt[ain] Rickard & myself) went down to the 7th Vt to witness a review of the white Troops (5 Reg[imen]ts) you may think strange their having it on Sunday but such is army custom. Well we had several reviews about 2 weeks since & the unbleached Americans beat the white Troops all to pieces. I expect it was because the darks have so much better Officers. . . . I am well & enjoying myself much better than in the heat of the summer. The weather is going to be beautiful for 4 or 5 months now just warm enough for comfort. Nights just cool enough to sleep lovely. Oh if I had a certain young Mrs with me how happy I should be. I have no news to write. We are having some rainy weather now days. . . . I must close please send the Stamps before mentioned. Give my love to Mother & all the friends.

Receive with much love from
your Dan

On October 6 Major General Giles Smith issued orders to the First Division of the XXV Corps that stated, "Serious depredations having been committed within the limits of this town, by soldiers who are usually armed, and under the pretext of searching for liquor &c, intimidate and rob the stores and dwellings of citizens, Commanding officers of Brigades and Regiments will at once increase the guard of their respective commands to such strength and adopt such measures as will effectually prevent the men from leaving camp, and visiting the town after sunset."[2] As had been the case in Virginia after the fall of Richmond, white civilians who claimed that they were the victims of "depredations" exerted political leverage that often resulted in the reassignment of Black units to different locations or disciplinary crackdowns in the ranks. On November 5 another order came from Division Headquarters that stated, "The General [Commanding] directs me to inform you that the owner of the land on which the 19th USCTroops is encamped has made a demand for it as he [has] intent to plant on it. You will please give orders to have the 19th USCTroops removed to [an]other camping ground."[3]

These orders prompted a shakedown in the Nineteenth USCT. Company commanders were routinely reprimanded for not reporting roll call, for which they had to explain their delinquency to regimental headquarters. On October 6 Captain W. C. Bryant wrote to regimental headquarters, "I have the honor to report that I have no good reason to offer for not reporting roll call this morning. I slept soundly until an orderly came with a note not hearing the reveille." Bryant admitted that his actions amounted to "a serious failing and I must ask the leniency of my Commanding Officer."[4] A week later James Rickard explained his failure to report roll call: "The only reason I have for not reporting my Co[mpany] this morning is I was not well which kept me awake a part of the night & was asleep at roll call, did not hear the bugles at dawn."[5] Two weeks later he missed roll call again and said, "The reason for not reporting my co[mpany] at roll call this morning [was that] I was not awakened by the 'Reveille' & was not awakened until it was too late to report."[6] The next day Captain Frank Holsinger also failed to report roll call and wrote, "I have the honor to report as my reasons for not reporting company at Reveille roll call this A.M. to be; that until I received your communication, I was not aware that there had been anything of the kind—having slept soundly and not hearing the 'call.'"[7] Earlier, Captain Marion Patterson had offered a similar explanation for his failure to report roll call and received a stern rebuke in return from headquarters: "The excuse given for not reporting tattoo roll call is trivial, disgraceful, and entirely unsatisfactory."[8] There are no records of Mason ever being chastised for a dereliction of duty, though it is obvious that the esprit de corps of the Nineteenth USCT was in rapid decline as unit after unit was mustered out except theirs. Mason hinted once again at rumors that his unit would be mustered out but didn't place much stock in them. He desperately wanted to go home and told Harriet, "Oh my darling wife how I do hope we shall be mustered out this fall or the first of winter how I do want to see you how happy we shall be when I get home for good."

CAMP OF THE 19TH USCTROOPS
NEAR BROWNSVILLE TEXAS
October 17th, 1865

My Darling Wife

I am again obliged to write you before receiving a letter from you well I have got used to it so it does not seem so bad as formerly but I expect you have just the same troubles. I was very much disappointed not to get one in the last mail but am in hopes to get a double portion in your next or rather in the next mail. I am well & enjoying myself very well the weather is cooler & I feel well & hearty. I think we shall have 4 or 5 months of pleasant weather they say that it never snows here but have some frosts in the course of the winter. The coldest weather ever known here freeze[s] water standing in a pail ½ inch thick so you see we are in a moderate climate. The Reg[imen]ts being mustered out are leaving every day. We hear many rumors that all the colored troops are to be soon mustered out & what every one thinks must be true. Oh my darling wife how I do hope we shall be mustered out this fall or the first of winter how I do want to see you how happy we shall be when I get home for good how I shall hug & carress you we will act just as loving as we please when we are alone & no ones business is it—darling we are one how happy to think that you are mine & I am yours no one has any claim on us may we both strive to promote each others happiness & always be ready to forgive & forget when little jars may be excited though I trust we may not be troubled very much with such unpleasant things. I have not sent the last $100.00 spoken of yet. I am keeping it until I get a final decision from Gen[eral] Sheridan in regard to my resignation. Gen[eral] Weitzel sent them all back again & though it is very doubtful about their being approved there is a possibility of it. It is said that Gen[eral] S[heridan] dont like Weitzel very well & takes such way to snub him which is as much as to say that Weitzel is not competent to tell how many officers can be spared from his command without injury to the service. Well I must close the flowers are in full bloom here now growing wild all kinds nearly.

Give my love to Mother & all the friends

receive with much love from
your Dan

Black soldiers, of course, were also anxious to reunite with their families and suffered declining morale along with their white officers as the long-awaited order to muster out proved elusive. Owing to poor literacy rates and uncertainty about the whereabouts of their families, given the transient nature of postemancipation Black communities, they often lacked the means to correspond with their loved ones at home, though somehow wives often found their way to their husbands' camps and were usually employed as laundresses. Each company was allotted several laundresses who were allowed to travel to Texas at government expense.[9] Black women were not always welcomed by white officers, however. An interesting example of the emotional strain that the deployment to Texas wrought on the enlisted men of the Nineteenth USCT (and their families) involved Private Zachariah Butcher of Company C. On November 16 he wrote to regimental headquarters, "I have the honor to request a furlough of (60) days, to go home to Maryland, for the purpose of attending my wife hither, who is now a laundress in this company, and who joined me at Fort Monroe when en route to Texas. Children were left behind and my wife is in poor health now from pining for them. It was not my intention to bring my wife hither and I would most respectfully ask that transportation be recommended on her final return to Maryland." Mrs. Butcher couldn't be in two places at once and must have regretted her decision to accompany her husband to Texas. For some reason her influence upon the troops was not appreciated by Captain W. C. Bryant of Company C, who heartily endorsed Butcher's application and wrote that he "firmly believe[ed] that the return of the unhappy woman . . . would be a measure to the highest interests of the service and remove a serious cause of evil in our companies." Butcher's request was approved, though once he returned to Maryland, he never came back to Texas. He was officially listed as a deserter. Apparently the thought of returning to the Rio Grande after having been reunited with his family was too much for all involved.[10]

While the men of the Nineteenth USCT experienced declining morale in the fall of 1865, they also observed fighting in Matamoros, awaited being mustered out (which didn't happen until 1867), and sometimes enjoyed other leisurely pursuits. James Rickard described the following form of recreation to his sister on October 29:

> Pigeons are quite thick out in the chapparal. Capt Mason, Henry & myself have been out twice. The first day I killed 8 & Capt Mason 6. The last time we were not as fortunate. We started early in the morning for an all day hunt. There was a heavy dew which nearly ruined my shoes. We had to go about 3 miles to get where the hunting ground is, the sun came out very hot & all the birds of course were hid in the swamps in the shade. [In the] afternoon a very heavy thundershower, accompanied by a heavy wind, came up. We got drenched of course. We built a fire & made coffee. During the day Capt M[ason] shot one pigeon, Henry 5 & I 4. It was awful walking to get back to camp. I had to take off my shoes & go barefooted. A tornado passed over the camp while we were gone. . . . I don't think we shall go out so far again soon. I shot a bird for some beautiful feathers but put it in the bag with the others & it got all bloodied & I do not think they are good for anything. I will get some if I can.[11]

The declining morale of the men of the Nineteenth USCT was significantly worsened by the outbreak of illnesses as winter approached. As a whole Black units received inferior medical treatment to their white counterparts. Reports from Texas of the despicable treatment of Black troops were common. Stories abounded of Black patients being neglected, gagged, chained, kicked, sworn at, whipped, and even mutilated after they had died. Medical care was comparatively better in regimental hospitals, where greater oversight from commanders and closer proximity between sick soldiers and their regimental surgeons resulted in higher quality care. General hospitals, or post hospitals, by comparison, were notorious for poor care and higher mortality rates.[12] The spread of illnesses within the Nineteenth USCT had reached a level that on November 16, Colonel Joseph Perkins wrote a lengthy letter to division headquarters with the following plea:

> I have the honor to respectfully request permission to erect a [Regimental Hospital] and that I be furnished with the necessary means to do this. I have now in my [Regiment] over twenty men who are suffering from ulcers, the result of a Scorbutie state of the system, who would, in the opinion of my surgeon, be entirely cured with a little treatment in a [Regimental Hospital]. Some of these men have been sent to the Post [Hospital] and were at once sent back to the [Regiment]. If something is not done for them at once, their disease may become malignant and lead to serious consequences. I would also request that all the men of my regiment now at the Post [Hospital] be at once returned to the [Regiment]. I have twenty-seven men thus performing guard duty, and a great number claimed as patients but employed as nurses &c who are frequently in my camp and apparently as well as the men who are doing duty in the [Regiment], and who have desired their company commanders &c endeavor to have them returned to the regiment. As a matter of justice to my men, and as a means of increasing the effective strength of my command, I earnestly request that this be granted.[13]

Two days later Perkins's request was returned by the division adjutant with the explanation that it "should have been addressed to the [Headquarters] of the District which has sole jurisdiction of the matters in question. As a matter of opinion however, I should not think it expedient to establish a regimental hospital in the 19th USCT."[14]

Perkins then wrote a lengthier plea to the headquarters of the Department of the Gulf and registered an even more impassioned complaint about his situation:

> The men doing guard duty there have been selected by the Officer of the Guard, and comprise the very best men of my Reg[imen]t. If the men cannot all be returned I would most earnestly request that the guard be changed for I have noticed with extreme regret that since these men have been on duty there they have been losing all those soldierly qualities which it has been my pride, aim, and ambition to instill in them during the last two years. I consider it [a] great injustice to myself and to the officers of my command, after taking these men from a state of perfect ignorance, teaching them all the qualities of soldiers, enforcing strict discipline and obedience, to have the pride of all our hard labor taken from us to suffer gross neglect from persons who can not or at least do not, perform their duties. It is common talk among the officers who have visited the Hos-p[ita]l recently that all the salutes and ceremonies, which are so essential in a well disciplined command, seem to be, and are, entirely neglected.
>
> If I may be allowed to change the officers and men of the guard occasionally, so that they may be under the eye of their immediate responsible commander, I am confident that the appearance and discipline of the guard will be greatly increased. . . .
>
> While I feel called upon to make this request and statement, I do not wish to be considered at all personal, for although I have the greatest respect for Surgeon Radmore as a gentleman, and confidence in him as an officer, yet I consider it my imperative duty to my command and to the Gen[eral] commanding to make this request.[15]

A week later Perkins received a stern, unsympathetic reply from the chief medical examiner of the Department of the Gulf. Perkins's request was

> respectfully returned with the opinion that a "Regimental Hospital" is impracticable in the extreme, especially when Col. Perkins Reg[imen]t is not stationed five hundred yards from the Post Hospital. The Com[-mandi]ng General is respectfully invited to inspect the Post Hospital and see for himself, if the sick of the command can be treated in a Regimental Hospital to any better advantage. . . .
>
> Lieut[enant] Dobbs of Col. Perkins own Reg[imen]t is in charge of the undisciplined guard. As far as my own knowledge goes the discipline

> is good, and as far as good men are concerned, a Hospital containing some 4 or 500 patients, need good men to be on duty. It is to[o] often the case that Colonels of Reg[imen]ts want to give us all their old beats, both for duty in Hospitals, Ambulance Corps &c, and then complain if these men are not treated properly.[16]

Perkins seemed to have been concerned with a variety of factors: a genuine desire to seek better medical care for his men, a concern about the reduction of his force from having so many of his "best men" detailed as guards or nurses at the post hospital, and a breakdown in discipline among those who were acting as guards. He even invoked a racist, paternalist argument to lobby for the return of his troops, who, without his guidance, might lapse backward into a "state of perfect ignorance." Perkins's poor assessment of his troops' discipline was challenged by the chief medical examiner, who denied any breakdown in discipline and added that a large hospital with a significant number of patients needed "good men" to be on duty, not "beats." The term "beat" (or "deadbeat") originated in the Civil War to describe an individual who frequently "shirked" their duty.

The end result of this clash was that there was no regimental hospital established. Mason, who was in Texas to begin with in part because of racial politics and whose resignation had been disapproved in part because Phil Sheridan believed that Blacks preferred military service to civilian life (and therefore their white officers had to remain in the service), was now admitted as a patient to the post hospital in Brownsville, Texas. The fact that there was no regimental hospital was itself partly a result of the army's lack of interest in devoting more resources toward the medical treatment of Black troops. The surgeon in charge at the post hospital in Brownsville was Charles Radmore of the 114th USCT. Despite Colonel Perkins's praise of Surgeon Radmore, James Rickard wrote of the hospital: "It is a bad place to be sick in, none of the doctors . . . here or elsewhere have I any confidence in at all."[17] Several weeks later, after recovering from his own illness, Rickard wrote, "I am so disgusted with our doctors they do not know but very little, & are too lazy to apply what they do know."[18]

While Perkins complained of the number of sick men he had at the post hospital, Mason began to suffer the effects of dysentery, a disease that he most likely contracted by drinking water contaminated with human fecal matter. The symptoms of dysentery included severe abdominal cramps, chronic bouts of bloody diarrhea, fever, dehydration, and delirium. On November 20, 1865, Colonel Perkins received the following letter from Surgeon Radmore:

Post Hospital Brownsville, Texas
November 20th 1865

Commanding Officer
19th usctroops

Sir
It becomes my painful duty to inform you that Captain Mason of your command died in this hospital this afternoon and I most respectfully request that you will as soon as possible inform me of what disposition you wish to make of his remains.

Very Respectfully
Your obedient Serv't
CC Radmore
Surg[eon] in Charge[19]

Later that day Colonel Perkins issued the following orders announcing Mason's death:

[Headquarters] 19th usctroops
Brownsville Texas Nov[ember] 20th 1865

General Orders No. 18
It becomes the painful duty of the Col[onel] [Commanding] to announce to the officers and men of this Reg[imen]t the death of Capt. Dan Mason 19th usct. By the sad event we lose a pleasant friend and

companion in arms, and the Government a brave and elegant soldier. For him we may with perfect trust leave him in the hands of his creator.

It is hereby ordered that the usual badge of mourning be worn by the Officers of this Reg[imen]t for thirty days [from] the date hereof. The funeral event will be performed by Co[mapnies] H and K formed in two platoons to be commanded by Capt. F. K. Fletcher assisted by Lieut[enants] Mix and Patterson. The time of the funeral will be announced in orders from these [headquarters].

By order of
Col. J. G. Perkins[20]

The most detailed, heart-rending account of the circumstances surrounding Mason's death comes from a letter that James Rickard wrote the following day. He poured out his grief to his mother, who of course had never met Mason.

Camp 19 USCT
November 21st 1865

Dear Mother,

I have not written you for some time, although I have written home often but will write you this time. I am very well. We are all feeling very sad however today caused by the death of Capt. Dan Mason yesterday. He died at the hosp[ita]l of dysentery. Had been there only three or four days & sick about a week. It is sudden & so unexpected. He has been one of the most healthy men in the Reg[imen]t. Has been in the army for more than four years through all the hard battles of the "Army of the Potomac" & never was hit by a ball or been sick a day. He married a beautiful young lady last spring when he went home on a leave of absence. He was one of the best friends I ever had, "faithful and true to me." We have been together most of the time, he either at my tent or I at his when not on duty. He has messed with me most of the time for a year. He seemed as a brother to me & I shall probably miss him more than any one else here. I went to see him at the hospital but he had passed a "miserable" night been out of his head & was so wasted I was alarmed & was satisfied if he had another such a time he would not live & he had become so weak I thought it very doubtful if he recovered. He wanted me to take his money & keep for him which I did. $160.00. He had been saving it expecting his discharge. He wanted me to write to his wife when I went to see him Sunday, but I did not as I thought he would be better or worse & he was a little wild though he had been sick a long time. The officers met last evening to take measures to send his body home & appointed a committee to see to it. We had his body embalmed last night & are having a coffin made lined with galvanized iron. We shall pay the expenses & pass resolutions expressing our appreciation of his worth & words of condolence also &c. I have written thus lengthy about my friend for he was a friend, blessed with a disposition which never would give him an enemy. He was beloved by all who knew him.[21]

Rickard's account reveals much about the sad, grim final days of Dan Mason's life. He was "miserable," "out of his head," "wild" with delusion, and aware that he was dying. He asked his friend Rickard to write to Harriet for him, but Rickard wasn't fast enough. If only he had—what would his parting words to his newlywed wife have been? Would they have been coherent? How would he have characterized his condition? What was going through his mind? One can only guess.

Rickard was still distraught a week later, when he wrote to his brother, "We feel sad now on account of the death of Capt. Dan Mason. He died quite suddenly of dysentery. I miss him very much as he was with me most of the time. We have had his body embalmed & put in a metallic coffin & sent by express to his friends in Vt. The officers sent a copy of resolutions to his wife signed by each officer they were very elegantly copied by a clerk at Div[ision] [Headquarters]. I drew up the resolutions. Enclosed please find them. How do you like them?"[22]

It is not known how exactly Harriet learned of her husband's death. Surely a fellow officer—perhaps Rickard himself—wrote to inform her of the terrible news. The last letter that Mason wrote that is in the Vermont Historical Society collection was dated October 17, but as is obvious elsewhere, Harriet did not pass every letter along. It is highly unlikely that this was his final letter. But given how quickly he died after becoming sick, and because he was not able to write to Harriet from his deathbed, the news of his death must have seemed like it came out of nowhere. Whatever initial correspondence that she received was probably too raw and painful for her to include in the collection, which she eventually gave to her nephew. The news of his death had arrived in Glover by mid-December, just before Christmas.

All one can do is imagine Harriet's grief as she mourned the loss of her handsome twenty-six-year-old soldier husband during the holiday season in West Glover, Vermont. Whether she was still pregnant or not is also unknown, but she never gave birth to a child, so at some point later in her pregnancy she had a miscarriage. Whether she lost her child or her husband first is not clear, but either way, she lost them both in close succession. After years of separation, her husband was finally on his way home as an embalmed corpse in a galvanized casket. How she managed to function that first winter as a widow is beyond comprehension. She had experienced a double loss that defies belief. Perhaps the resolutions sent by the officers of the Nineteenth USCT offered some minor consolation. Mason was clearly viewed by his fellow troops, both during the war and for decades after his death, as the quintessential citizen-soldier, a true patriot and gentleman who was the essence of a brave, noble, and honest man. The praise from Rickard and his other fellow officers could not have been higher:

CAMP OF THE 19TH REGIMENT USCTROOPS
1ST BRIGADE 1ST DIVISION 25TH ARMY CORPS
Near Brownsville Texas November 21st 1865

At a meeting of the officers of the 19th Regiment USCTroops called on the occasion of the death of Captain Dan Mason 19th USCTr. November 20th 1865, the following preamble and resolutions were adopted, viz:

Whereas, It has pleased God in his wise and mysterious Providence, to take from us, our much esteemed, honored and well beloved friend, companion and comrade in arms, by the hand of disease, after having passed unharmed through most of the sanguinary conflicts of a four years terrible war, therefore, be it

Resolved, That by his death we lose one whose sterling qualities as a soldier and a gentleman made him dear to us, his associates, enlivening our most gloomy hours by his brilliant genius and sparkling wit, by his wise counsels, congenial disposition and even temper, endearing himself to all who knew him, and one whose rare abilities as an officer, made him valuable to his country, which he has served so long and so faithfully.

Resolved, That we do deeply sympathize with his bereaved wife and family in mourning him, thus cut down in the prime of his manhood, and while with keen anguish we submit to the will of heaven, we feel that he has made a happy exchange of worlds.[23]

Word of Mason's death also stunned his former comrades in the Sixth Vermont when they heard the startling news. Fred Kimball, who was visiting his wife's family in Cabot, recorded his disbelief in his diary on December 13, 1865: "A letter from father stating that Dan Mason is dead—Can it be possible. I cant realize I cannot. He was one of our brave boys. Probably died in Texas. Is Dan dead?"[24] A month later Kimball penned a tribute to Mason in a local newspaper that expressed further anguish: "He passed through the whole war without a wound, and almost without a sickness, till the last sickness which terminated his life. His friends were wholly unprepared to receive the shocking news of his death, being in daily expectation of hearing that he was discharged and coming home. He leaves a young wife to mourn that he is gone. Captain Mason was a brave, faithful and intelligent officer, and one who held the respect and esteem of all his friends and acquaintances. His remains are expected home, to be interred in the land of his nativity."[25]

Alexander Davis, perhaps Mason's closest friend throughout the entire war, had just been mustered out of the Thirty-Ninth USCT. He did not learn of Mason's death until his arrival home. Davis later wrote, "My reg[imen]t was mustered out in December 1865. I arrived home at Glover, Vt. January 3, 1866. The 1st I knew of Dan's death was in passing the cemetery at Glover, I saw a burial party and learned by inquiry that it was the friends of Dan. It may be a matter of sentiment but I was touched. Dan and I had much in common."[26]

Mason's remains did not come home immediately though. Harriet corresponded with Major William Welsh of the Nineteenth USCT after Mason's death, who told her the following news on January 4, 1866:

ST JAMES HOTEL
NEW ORLEANS LA
January 4th 1866

MRS CAPT D. MASON
WEST GLOVER VT

Madam,

I presume you are almost frantic on account of the delay of the remains of your husband. They were delayed at Brazos. I found it out by a mere accident—and at once ordered them to be put on board the U.S. steamer *Crescent* and came with them to this place. The Agent says he will forward them by sail to you tomorrow. I was surprised to see that the company had been so dilatory as I supposed there would be no delays made under any circumstances. I write this that you may not be uneasy as they will surely reach you soon. The only difficulty we had was to get them [past] quarantine on the Mississippi. This has been done, and now there is nothing to stop them. His personal effects are packed in a box and came down here on the same ship with his remains. If it was in my power I would take charge of the remains and take them to you but I can not. Be as easy as the circumstances under which you are placed will allow as I feel confident there will be no more delays made.

I sent you the following receipt—1 for the remains and 1 for his effects—and 1 for some money. I also sent you a list of his effects—attached there is a receipt. As soon as received please sign your name thereto and return to me as I have to make a report to the Adj[utan]t Gen[era]l at Washington in order that you may receive the back pay and allowances due your husband at the time of his death. I am pleased to inform you that the standing of your husband as an Officer and a gentleman was such that he was beloved by all of us. The expenses of the express &c have been paid by the Officers of the reg[imen]t. You will pay no express charges, though if you have received the receipts you can present them. I am particular in telling this as some persons have had to pay the same bill twice.

Should you wish any information relative to his accounts with the U.S. write me I will give it.

I remain

Very respectfully
Your ob[edien]t serv[an]t
Will Welsh
Major 19 USCT
Brownsville Texas[27]

Mason's death was announced in the *Orleans Independent Standard* two weeks later:

> DEATH OF CAPT. DAN MASON.—Capt. Dan Mason of the 19th Colored Regiment, died in Brownsville, Texas, Nov. 20th, aged 25 years. He was the son of Moses F. Mason of Glover, and enlisted in the service of his country in September, 1861. He became a member of Co. D, 6th Vt. Reg't; and perhaps no company from Vermont deserved or won more praise than this. Many of its members distinguished themselves as brave and accomplished officers. . . . Having participated in the taking of Richmond and the overthrow of rebellion in the north, he was sent with a colored troops to Texas and remained there till the time of his death. He was seized with dysentery and died after a short illness. He was a young man of ability and promise; At home he won the esteem of all by his manliness and integrity; in the army he obtained promotion and distinction by faithfulness and valor. He died loved and esteemed by all, leaving a large circle of friends and a young amiable wife to lament his loss. Upon another tombstone may be inscribed, "He died for his country."[28]

Mason's funeral was held in Glover on February 4, 1866, and was conducted by General William Wallace Grout of Barton, a veteran of the Fifteenth Vermont Infantry who later became a U.S. congressman. After readings from Lamentations ("And I said my strength and my hope is perished from the Lord"), Jeremiah ("All ye that are about him bemoan him, and all ye that know his name say how is the strong staff broken, and the beautiful rod"), and Psalms ("I will say of the Lord he is my refuge, in him will I trust") were finished, Mason's pastor and former schoolmaster at the Orleans Liberal Institute, Sidney K. Perkins, delivered the sermon.

Reverand Perkins enumerated the qualities that young *men* should possess in a republic. Notwithstanding his exclusion of young *women* in his message and his insistence that true patriots should be *Christian*, he offered a timeless meditation on the meaning of citizenship and patriotism:

> Under no form of government in the world do young men exert greater influence than under our own, for soon after attaining the age when they should leave the schools *so* wisely provided by the public, each becomes a sharer in the government and helps to determine what the destiny of his country shall be. . . .
>
> Then she calls upon them to leave the peaceful pursuits to which they have been accustomed, to buckle on their armor and to go forth to endure the hardships of war with a purpose to persevere till the last foe is subdued. In time, they are the nation's right arm to bear the sword in its defense. Such then are the relations in which young men stand to their country.—They are her hope as to the future, they may be her present efficient aid, and her protectors in time of war.
>
> We consider secondly, the characteristics which render them equal to the trust to be reposed in them.
>
> 1st. They must be intelligent. I would not argue that everyone must pursue the full course of study required in the college or university, but every young man should receive an education to the extent afforded by our public schools, and there should be added there to the influence of reading for information as to affairs of interest in general. This is necessary in order that the Excellency of our government as compared with other forms may be appreciated, and that no more may be dazzled (as some have been) with the show and splendor of the courts of kings and emperors and thus be led to covet them.
>
> Besides, without this, what hinders them from becoming the dupes of designing and wicked men?

An *education is necessary* that they may think independently, exercise the elective franchise wisely, and may fill places of trust with honor to themselves, and with profit to the state or country.

2dly. They must be virtuous. A man whose ruling or habitual principle of action is, a sense of duty or a regard to what is right may be properly denominated virtuous.

It is men of this character who can be trusted in an emergency and who will be faithful when away from under the eye of their superior in office.

Without such men among its subjects a government is in a condition threatening its speedy fall, but if it has such men for its pillars, clouds may darken its horizon and storms may fall upon it, but it will be secure. . . .

3d. They must be patriotic. Providence has so arranged that the earth instead of being inhabited by one nation only should be possessed and occupied by a variety of people speaking different languages, and having peculiar characteristics. . . . A country like ours will demand patriotism in her young men because *true patriots* are desirous that the broadest freedom consistent with the existence of a good and sufficient government should exist, and if the tendency of the existing government is in that direction, will take a manly position to maintain it.

They will also, being possessed of a love of humanity, do all in their power to secure the rights of *full citizenship* to all classes qualified: for has not God made of one blood all men to dwell upon the face of the earth? . . .

4th. A country is highly favored when many of its young men manifest that what they do is prompted by the influence of pure religion reigning in their hearts.

Were the young men of any nominally christian nation, to reject the Holy Scriptures and refrain from prayer to the God of Heaven, what a gloomy future would be before it, for it is true that nations as well as families that dishonor God are soon despised or lightly esteemed.

I now in the *third* place proceed to such application of the discourse as may appear appropriate on this solemn occasion. . . .

How generously and freely did the young men of the North respond to the call of the executive, the moment the hostilities had become open. By thousands they left their homes and went forth to the conflict. . . . A goodly number of the volunteers of the first year survived to see the difficult task they had undertaken perfected, and while all honor the noble dead, who perished for their country, those who survive, may justly be proud that they helped achieve the greatest triumph of Liberty and humanity, that the country has witnessed. Among the first to volunteer for this noble object, in this community, was the beloved young man whose Funeral services we attend this day.

After chronicling Mason's four years of service and the numerous campaigns he fought in, Perkins concluded his sermon with this consolation:

> To you especially, dear Madam who are by this bereavement left desolate, the chosen partner of your youthful hopes and joys having been taken from you, let me present the promise of our heartfelt sympathy and of our prayers, that you may be sustained under your affliction and enabled to submit to the holy will of God. As one well says: "Affliction properly borne, not only purifies but elevates. Its tendency is to strengthen religious feeling, and to increase that devout trust by exercise which teaches us that all is in God's hand and assures us that the end will be right."
>
> There are present also, some who were associated with Capt. Mason, in the noble service in which he engaged and in which he laid down his life, his comrades in arms.
>
> Today you add another name to your role of departed heroes. It has upon it the name of Dwinell, Gray, Williams, Wright, Phillips, and of others, and now you add that of Mason.
>
> Let me urge you to emulate his virtues, and to follow his example.—Still love your country saved, as you loved it in its hour of peril and of need. Cherish and guard ever in your hearts those motives which your country can approve, and let their influence be manifest in your lives.
>
> Above all, regard the demands of the religion of Christ, become soldiers of the Prince Emmanuel here, that you may glorify him in heaven, and may participate in his glorious victories for ever. Amen.[29]

The press also noted that "the bearers were veteran soldiers. Several other soldiers were also present."

Thus was twenty-six-year-old Captain Daniel Mason, Company D, Sixth Vermont Volunteer Infantry and Company H, Nineteenth U.S. Colored Troops, a flower of American manhood who had helped save his nation and redefine its democratic aspirations, laid to rest in his native hills in the snows of midwinter Vermont.

Epilogue

"Let Us Not Mock Our Honored Dead"

At some point in late 1865 or early 1866, Harriet Mason lost her child. Whether she had a miscarriage or stillbirth is not known. In the 1870 census, twenty-eight-year-old Harriet was listed as a "domestic" who lived with her fifty-seven- and sixty-two-year-old parents.[1] Harriet became known as the "Widow Mason," as recalled by a contemporary who later reminisced about her memories of West Glover (and included a not-so-subtle feminist message in her verse):

Across the road a few old houses stood
In the long days of little memories.
Has Old Time chopped them into kindling-wood,
I wonder?
I think that Hattie Mason lived in one,
A bonny dark-eyed woman, young, admired,
Who wedded and then lost Captain Dan Mason–
The Widow Mason called; for it transpired
That with these folk as so with many other,
Instead of, She has genius; or another Is artist,
Or We hope will be,
With the authority almost of pure religion,
They named each woman's matrimonial relation.[2]

Another contemporary poet from West Glover, Celestia Stevens, expressed the grief felt by the community at Mason's loss. It was given to Harriet in an attempt to console her.

Suggested by the Death of Capt. Dan Mason
He sleeps, a nobleman of earth,

He sleeps, the gifted and the true,
A man of virtue, sterling worth,
Ever true, to the red, white and blue.

And many grieve, his head laid low,
The valued, loved, in life's young bloom,
That he, from earth's dear ones,
Should go, to slumber in the lovely tomb.

Ne'er acted he the coward part,
Leaving his post in direct need,
But with a brave, and faithful heart,
He won the patriot's well earned meed.

On whom has burst the darkest cloud
Round whom the sable garb is thrown,
Fit emblem of thy heart's dark shroud,
In sadness sittest thou alone.

No way of life, doth darkened seem
In widowhood while yet in youth,
But seest though no cheering beam,
from the great fount of love and truth?

Thou sorrowing, and stricken know,
That many prayers ascend for thee,
As through deep waters, thou dost go
And stern affliction's surging sea.

O may this mighty arm sustain,
E'en the great shepherd of his flock,
Thy earthly loss, be endless gain,
Though the "dark valley" thou dost walk.
May'st hear the Saviour's warning voice,
Be ready whenso'er I come,

Look upward, and by faith rejoice,
Till death is conquered, victory won.[3]

A month after Mason's funeral, Harriet applied for a widow's pension from the federal government. In 1867 she began to receive $20 per month, retroactively dated to the time of Mason's death on November 20, 1865.[4] She was remarried on April 29, 1873, to a local man, John Borland, who had been born in Strathaven, Scotland, and came to Glover when he was eighteen years old. After her remarriage Harriet's widow's pension payments ceased. It was the second marriage for each, and Harriet became a stepmother to John's son (also John) from his first marriage. It was later said that "she gave him the best of care and was a wonderful mother to him."[5] Harriet gave birth to her own son, Clark Mason Borland, on December 9, 1876, making her a relatively old first-time mother by nineteenth-century standards, at the age of thirty-four. Clark was her only biological child.

Harriet, her husband, and their children lived and worked on a farm in West Glover that still exists today. In 1900 the Borlands had fifty head of cattle on their dairy farm, which was considered to be "one of the best in town." In addition, Mr. Borland was a "noted sugar maker" whose sugar bush of two thousand trees produced sugar that was "always first class."[6] On June 16, 1902, John Borland, who had been in poor health for two years, died. His obituary reported,

> On the day of his death he was out about the premises more or less until nearly 4 o'clock in the afternoon, when he was taken with severe pain, and passed away at 9:20. . . . Mr. Borland was a man who always took the right of every moral question. He was exceedingly benevolent, kind hearted, neighborly and conscientious. . . . He was more than ordinarily intelligent, well informed in current events and history, a close student of the Bible, which he read daily and made the rule of his life. As a farmer he had few superiors, and being a great worker he brought his farm to a state of superior cultivation. . . . His buildings and everything about his premises gave evidence to the fact of his thrift, industry, and wise management.[7]

Apparently his qualities were of a piece with Harriet's first husband.

After John's death Harriet reapplied for a widow's pension, which she received again in the amount of $20 a month. In 1920 the payment was increased to $30 a month.[8] In the half century after the end of the Civil War, she attended several reunions of Company D. Harriet then moved to Barton to live with Emily Mason Blake, Dan's sister, and her husband, Albert, a Methodist preacher. Around 1917 she moved in with her niece in West Glover, in the same house where she grew up. In the early 1920s, her health began to decline, as she suffered from "senile dementia." In November 1924 the *Orleans County Monitor* reported that Harriet was living with her niece "in very poor health and is confined to her bed much of the time." At the same time that Harriet was bedridden, "a cross was burned on the hill west of Barton on the evening of November 3, and also in practically every town up and down the line from Derby Line to Wells River, which shows that the Knights of the Ku Klux Klan are increasing rapidly."[9] Three weeks later, on November 27, 1924, Harriet died. Her obituary reported, "She was a woman of character and ability who had a wide circle of friends." The funeral was held in West Glover, in her childhood home. Her stepson, John Calvin Borland, "was called home from deer hunting last week by the death of his mother, Mrs. Harriet Borland."[10] Harriet Clark Mason Borland was buried with her first husband in Westlook Cemetery in Glover, Vermont.

In 1907 Harriet wrote a letter to her "nephew," Dan Owen Mason, who was actually the son of Dan's younger half-brother. It is the only surviving letter written by Harriet.

Barton July 11, 1907

My dear Nephew,

I was looking over some of your Uncle Dan's letters last night. I send you a few of them feeling you will know him better and also it brings one in touch of times that tried mens souls.

I send you his Sash. Am so sorry that I forgot to bring his sword. It would be such a good opportunity to send it to you, his namesake. Am glad you want it & pray that you may be as noble a man and do your part as bravely as did he is the earnest wish of Your Aunt Harriet[11]

Harriet's advice was heeded by future generations of the Mason family. Dan Owen Mason, after graduating Middlebury College in 1917, served in World War I in the newly created Chemical Warfare Service. He passed his namesake's letters along to his son, John Owen Mason, who served in World War II. Like Dan Mason, John fought in an army of liberation and recalled years later a memory from the war:

> In late April of '45 I was a young soldier in Troop C of the 92nd Reconnaissance Squadron of the 12th Armored Division. At the time we were operating in the general area of Munich, Germany. Part of our Recon. Squadron was rolling down a road which ran parallel with a railroad line. As we pulled to a halt next to a stopped train of maybe a dozen European freight cars we spotted several very nervous looking German soldier types and quickly had them lined up with their hands on top of their heads. From the freight cars came sounds, weak and pitiful but human.
>
> Our platoon sergeant told the German who seemed to be in charge to open the cars but at first he refused. Our sergeant quickly changed his mind with an offer to shoot him on the spot and a sharp jab in the belly with the muzzle of his carbine. The chief guard complied. "Open them all," shouted our man and several of the guards scurried to comply.
>
> Inside the cars were men—grey, thin, wan and not sure at all of what to expect. At first they hung back but in a few moments they recognized that we were no Wehrmacht—different uniforms, different vehicles and then they literally came tumbling out.
>
> We were engulfed in a stumbling, shambling flood of striped uniforms, gaunt faces and waving hands and arms. They sobbed and cried. They kissed our hands, they kissed our uniforms which were not much cleaner than what they were wearing, if any. They stank to high heaven. They treed me on top of my jeep. We could not deal with their emotions, their gratitude. We were embarrassed for what had we done, but our duty?
>
> When things quieted a bit we passed out whatever rations we could spare and further encouraged them as best we could to forage freely upon the neighborhood. I assume and hope that a Military Government Unit was notified by radio.

In the confusion the train engineer and fireman managed to detach the engine and coal car and took off down the line. Bad luck for them as the road ran parallel to the tracks for some way. One of our armored cars pursued them and exploded the boiler with gunfire. Whether they survived I knew not nor at the time did we much care.

To this day I can still see the faces, the striped jackets and pants and remember the cries and sobs. I cannot forget.[12]

In 1989 John Mason and his wife, June Wardell Mason, donated Dan Mason's letters to the Vermont Historical Society.

The town of Glover never recovered from the upheaval of the war. Aside from those who died in the service, there was an exodus of other veterans to points south and west. The town's population, which had grown steadily during the first half of the nineteenth century, peaked in 1860. Glover lost 5 percent of its population in the 1860s, then another 10 percent in the 1870s, and even by 2020, its population had not recovered to the level it was in 1860. The war's toll became evident immediately. In 1868 a town history lamented that "Glover is affected by the rebellion not only because some of her choicest sons laid down their lives on the altar of their country, but because others travelling have made new acquaintances and have established themselves in business far from their native town. But do we not receive adequate compensation by means of the name acquired by our soldiers and especially as we view the results of the contest in the advancement of justice and liberty throughout the land?"[13]

Only a handful of men of Company D of the Sixth Vermont remained in Orleans County after the war, and of Mason's close friends who he tented with, all of them moved out of the area. Oliver Stiles moved to Kansas after the war and worked for the Santa Fe Railroad for four years before becoming a cashier in a bank in Florence, Kansas. He died suddenly at thirty-four years old of a "hemorrhage of the lungs." He had been wounded at the Battle of the Wilderness in May 1864, where he received "a gunshot wound, the ball entering just in front of the right shoulder, and passing in an oblique direction through his body, either struck or seriously injured his right lung."[14] Stiles "never fully recovered" from his wound, "which was the immediate cause of his death."[15] He and his wife had conceived a child before he died, though he did not live to see her birth. His daughter, Carrie Stiles, only lived ten months.

Hobart Bliss, wounded at Banks's Ford, moved to Lebanon, New Hampshire, after the war, where he farmed on Poverty Lane, had three children with his first wife, who died at forty-eight, then remarried and had another child with his second wife. On July 18, 1916, Bliss, "who had been out of health for some months," committed suicide "by shooting himself through the temple."[16] His son, Arthur Bliss, died two years later at twenty-six years old while serving in World War I.

Captain Martin Warner Davis, wounded at Lee's Mills and the Wilderness, auctioned off his farm in Brownington in 1866, then moved west to Wisconsin, where he lived until his death in 1923. Elbert Nye, Mason's "best man" at his wedding, moved to Iowa in 1871, then to Chicago, then eventually back to Vermont. Alexander Davis, wounded and captured at Savage's Station, became a postmaster in White River Junction, Vermont. He, too, moved back to Glover in 1910 but died a month later.

Fred Kimball, twice wounded, became an agent in the Freedmen's Bureau after the war. He was responsible for overseeing labor contract negotiations, supervising elections, and constructing schools in multiple counties in Virginia. In his annual report in 1867, he lamented that "the recent exercise of [the freedmen's] political rights, conferred upon them by the General government, has intensified the innate prejudice of the white race toward them into absolute and bitter hatred, because they would not exercise this privilege to reenslave themselves, but in opposition to their old masters."[17] Kimball and his wife became targets "in the midst of a people so recently in rebellion. His life was a number of times in jeopardy. . . . He was shot at several times, and received KuKlux letters ordering him to leave the country under pain of death. His noble wife stood by him through it all. . . . They were ostracized from society and subjected to many indignities by the ex-Confederates."[18] A particularly harrowing incident occurred in 1869 at a political meeting where "several rebels interposed, drew pistols, and attempted to break up the gathering. . . . The colored men at once arose and drew pistols, when a riot seemed imminent, but by the prompt interposition of Lieutenant F. M. Kimball and others the danger was averted, order was restored and the rioters withdrew." Later that night four white men entered the Kimball residence and assaulted both Kimball and "a Mr. James W. Jones, a Union citizen of the county." In the scuffle that ensued, "two of them beat Mr. Jones over the head with a cane very severely, while the other two caught and held Kimball, who, however, as soon as he could liberate himself from them, started to the assistance of Jones, when he in turn was assaulted. Mrs. Kimball hearing the affray rushed to the assistance of her husband and presented a pistol at the head of one of the rebels who was fighting him, and was about firing when the pistol was seized. Assistance arriving the assailants retreated."[19]

After the Freedmen's Bureau fell into oblivion, Kimball and his family moved to Missouri, then Colorado, then Kansas, and, finally, to California. After six decades as a correspondent to the local press, he wrote his final letter to the *Orleans County Monitor* in 1920, describing a reunion he had in California with a fellow member of Company D, William Snell. The two former soldiers, along with their wives, enjoyed "a most delightful auto trip from Los Angeles to Bakersfield . . . zigzagging over the mountains at every point of the compass amid the surroundings of nature in its most inspiring grandeur." They saw a huge oil field outside of Bakersfield, "under control, of course, of the Standard Oil Company," the monopolistic corporation founded by John D. Rockefeller. Snell, originally from Derby, Vermont, had lost an arm in the Wilderness, but as Kimball noted, "Comrade Snell with only a left hand drives his car like a veteran."[20]

In 1879 the surviving members of Company D began holding annual reunions in Orleans County that continued for over thirty-five years. The old veterans often traveled across the country to meet with their former comrades, share a meal, appoint "officers," offer toasts to the Union, listen to reminisces, prayers, and songs, and pledge to meet again the following year. Those who could not attend often wrote letters to be read aloud at the gatherings. Several wives of the living and the dead—including Harriet—attended as well.

In 1880 Fred Kimball penned a letter to be read at the annual reunion of Company D. Frustrated by the failed promises of Reconstruction, which had officially ended in 1877 following a contested presidential election the previous year, he offered a tribute to those "honored dead" who had given their lives to the Union's cause and implored his audience not to forget what the war had been fought to achieve:

CAMERON, MO., Sept. 24, 1880

Old Friends and Comrades of Co. D, 6th Vt. Vol.: Learning by invitation of our friend and comrade, Capt. A. W. Davis, that you are to hold a reunion on the 5th of October, it but tamely gives expression to my feelings to say that nothing could afford me greater pleasure than to be with you on that occasion, that I might grasp the hands of old comrades, renew acquaintances formed nearly twenty years ago, in times that tried men's souls, recount old war scenes, of long and weary marches, of the bivouac and the battle, and to renew again our vows of allegiance and fidelity to the old flag the honor of which we had an humble past in helping to defend through those dark years of intestine war, when armed hordes were seeking its dishonor and disgrace. But this great pleasure is denied me, as I find myself separated from you by mountains, forests, rivers, lakes and almost boundless prairies, a distance of nearly two thousand miles, which would make the journey almost impossible. Hence, I can only be with you in thought and spirit, and as, in imagination, my eyes run over the company, I see that all are not there. There were Hale, Phelps, Dwinell, Bailey, Mason, Gray, Stiles, Abbott, Bickford, Page, Livingston, Williams and many others, whose names I cannot now recall, who are now sleeping in soldiers graves. Brave, noble men! May we never have to feel that they died in vain! They gave their lives for their country, and while we would pronounce their eulogies and bedew their graves with our tears, let us not be unmindful of the fact that the sacred cause for which they died is still imperiled, that upon us, the living, rests the responsibility of reclaiming and preserving the liberties of the people of our common heritage, transmitted to us by our sacred dead. Let us never forget that "eternal vigilance is the price of liberty." When we see the Congress of the United States controlled by rebel brigadiers, and the poor maimed soldier, crippled in defending our country's flag, turned out of positions in the departments of the government, to be succeeded by rebels, and the freed people of the South turned over to the slave oligarchy, and even now virtually disfranchised and reduced to a condition little better than that of absolute slavery, may we not feel, and justly too, that the loyal North has been hushed into a lethargy by the sophistry of the South until the government, saved at such a fearful cost, is almost captured by its enemies, and the fruits of that terrible contest in danger of being overthrown? Let us not mock our honored dead by speaking eulogies to-day, but rather let us bow our heads in shame above their hallowed graves and swear by the Great Eternal, upon the altar of our country that we will never lay off the armor until these wrongs shall be righted, until the liberties of the people shall be made secure, until the rights of every citizen shall be respected and protected, until life and property are safe wherever our flag flies; until every citizen can cast a vote expressive of his honest sentiments, without fear of molestation, and have that vote honestly counted, and until loyalty, at least, shall be made respectable, if not treason odious. . . . Yes, Vermont is truly the "star that never sets," and she may indeed be termed the polar star in the galaxy of states. You remember the order of Gen. Sedgwick when a forced march was to be made: "Put the Vermonters ahead and keep well closed up." The same order is again applicable in the great political struggle now before us. We are called upon to contend at the ballot box for the same cause and for the same principles for which we fought.

The country is told by confederates, high in authority, that they are fighting for the same (lost) cause for which Lee and Jackson fought for four years. Hence it behooves every loyal state, now that Vermont is in the lead, to keep the columns well closed up. If this is done, victory will again be ours, and the enemies of this, the best country the sun ever shone upon, will be put to flight.

Believing that every one of my old comrades is as true as the needle to the pole, to the sacred cause for which he imperiled his life, I subscribe myself your old friend and comrade.

F. M. Kimball[21]

Lieutenant Kimball understood, as did other veterans of Company D of the Sixth Vermont Volunteer Infantry, that "the new birth of freedom" that Lincoln spoke of at Gettysburg would ring hollow if the "Lost Cause" narrative triumphed. Unless the nation recognized that Black lives did indeed matter, those who had given "the last full measure of devotion" to the cause of Union and freedom may have done so in vain. It would be for the living to "take increased devotion to that cause" to make sure that "government of the people, for the people, and by the people" would not perish from the earth.

NOTES

ABBREVIATIONS

AAS American Antiquarian Society
CWL *Collected Works of Abraham Lincoln*
NARA National Archives and Records Administration
OIS *Orleans Independent Standard*
OR *The War of the Rebellion: A Compilation of the Official Records of the Union and Confederate Armies*
VHS Vermont Historical Society

INTRODUCTION

1. "Governor's Message," OIS, May 3, 1861, 1.
2. CWL, 8:332–33.
3. CWL, 8:332–33.
4. Vermont Election Returns, 1860 Presidential Election, Vermont State Archives and Records Administration.
5. "Orleans War News," OIS, May 3, 1861, 2.
6. "Orleans War News," OIS, May 3, 1861, 2.
7. "Orleans War News," OIS, May 3, 1861, 2.
8. "Union Meeting at Newport," OIS, May 17, 1861, 2.
9. "Orleans War News," OIS, May 3, 1861, 2.
10. Grout, *Memoir of Gen'l William Wallace Grout*, 219.
11. Corwin Amendment, House Joint Resolution 80, National Archives.
12. "Peace by War," OIS, June 7, 1861, 1.
13. "No More Compromise with Slavery," OIS, June 14, 1861, 2.
14. "To the Ladies of Orleans County," OIS, June 28, 1861, 2.
15. "Local Items," OIS, September 27, 1861, 2.
16. Catton, *Stillness at Appomattox*, 851.
17. Churchill, *History of the English-Speaking Peoples*, 263.

1. "THE WILDEST ENTHUSIASM PREVAILS"

1. "A Sermon, Preached at Glover," OIS, February 21, 1866, 2.

2. 1860 U.S. Census, Population Schedule, Census Place: Glover, Orleans, Vermont, Roll M653_1322, 936, Image 241, NARA.
3. Nonpopulation Census Schedules for Vermont, 1850–70: Agriculture and Industry, M-1798, Roll 4, 1860, Glover, Orleans, Vermont, NARA.
4. McPherson, *Battle Cry of Freedom*, 19–20.
5. Hemenway, *Vermont Historical Gazetteer*, 200, 203–5.
6. Catalog of the officers and students of Orleans Liberal Institute, Glover, Vermont, for the academic year 1856–57, *School Student Lists*, Worcester, Massachusetts, AAS.
7. Nonpopulation Census Schedules for Vermont, 1850–70: Agriculture and Industry, M-1798, Roll 4, 1860, Glover, Orleans, Vermont, NARA.
8. Unless otherwise indicated, all quotes from Dan Mason are from the Mason letters in the Vermont Historical Society collection.
9. Benedict, *Vermont in the Civil War*, 1:210
10. Phelps, "From the Sixth Regiment," *OIS*, November 15, 1861, 2.
11. Benedict, *Vermont in the Civil War*, 1:211.
12. Kimball, "From the Sixth Regiment," *OIS*, December 13, 1861, 2.
13. Phelps, "From the Sixth Regiment," *OIS*, December 20, 1861, 2.
14. Earle, "Emancipation," *OIS*, December 6, 1861, 2.
15. "Anti-Slavery Convention," *OIS*, December 27, 1861, 2.
16. Stiles, "From the Sixth Regiment," *OIS*, January 3, 1862, 2.
17. Kimball, "From the Sixth Regiment," *OIS*, January 10, 1862, 3.
18. Kimball, "From the Sixth Regiment," *OIS*, January 10, 1862, 3.
19. Moodie, "From the Sixth Regiment," *OIS*, January 10, 1862, 3.
20. Kimball, "From the Sixth Regiment," *OIS*, January 10, 1862, 3.
21. Kimball, "From the Sixth Regiment," *OIS*, March 7, 1862, 2.
22. Benedict, *Vermont in the Civil War*, 1:240.
23. "Anti-Slavery Convention," *OIS*, March 7, 1862, 2.

2. "THE FINAL BLOW TO SECESSION"

1. *CWL*, 5:185.
2. *OR*, ser. 1, vol. 11, pt. 2, 363.
3. *OR*, ser. 1, vol. 11, p. 2, 366.
4. Benedict, *Vermont in the Civil War*, 1:249.
5. Benedict, *Vermont in the Civil War*, 1:212–13.
6. Kimball, "From the Sixth Regiment," *OIS*, May 2, 1862, 2.
7. Benedict, *Vermont in the Civil War*, 1:266.
8. *OR*, ser. 1, vol. 11, pt. 2, 363.

9. Stiles, "From the Sixth Regiment." *OIS*, May 30, 1862, 1.
10. Bickford is buried at Yorktown National Cemetery.
11. Sir John Moore was a British officer killed in 1809 during the Peninsula campaign of the Napoleonic Wars. Mason quoted from "The Burial of Sir John Moore After Corunna" by Charles Wolfe.

3. "We Had a Pretty Rough Time"

1. *OR*, ser. 1, vol. 11, pt. 1, 51.
2. *OR*, ser. 1, vol. 11, pt. 3, 259.
3. Mason, "From the Sixth Regiment," *OIS*, July 11, 1862, 1.
4. *OR*, ser. 1, vol. 11, pt. 1, 61.
5. *OR*, ser. 1, vol. 11, pt. 3, 269.
6. Benedict, *Vermont in the Civil War*, 1:289.
7. Davis, "The Old Sixth Vermont—A Chapter of Reminiscences," *Valley Sun*, October 1, 1886.
8. Benedict, *Vermont in the Civil War*, 1:310.
9. Benedict, *Vermont in the Civil War*, 1:310.
10. Kimball, "From the Sixth Regiment," *OIS*, August 1, 1862, 2.
11. "War Meeting in Troy," *OIS*, August 22, 1862, 2.
12. Earle, "Character of Our Cause," *OIS*, August 8, 1862, 2.
13. Kimball, "From the Sixth Regiment," *OIS*, August 1, 1862, 2.
14. McClellan to Ellen McClellan, August 10, 1862, McClellan Papers, Library of Congress.
15. Earle, "A New and Baser Base," *OIS*, September 12, 1862, 2.

4. "The Next Flop"

1. Kimball, "From the Sixth Regiment," *OIS*, November 21, 1862, 2.
2. Stiles, "From the Sixth Regiment," *OIS*, November 28, 1862, 2.
3. Kimball, "From the Sixth Regiment," *OIS*, November 21, 1862, 2.
4. Earle, "Change of Commanders," *OIS*, November 28, 1862, 2.

5. "The Manner the Machine Is Handled"

1. "Summary of News," *Burlington Weekly Sentinel*, January 2, 1863, 2.
2. Kimball Diary, January 1863, Kimball Collection.
3. Kimball Diary, January 21 and 26, 1863, Kimball Collection.
4. Martin Warner Davis Diary, February 25, 1863, Old Stone House Museum.
5. Martin Warner Davis Diary, February 5, 1863, Old Stone House Museum.
6. Bliss Diary, February 20, 1863, VHS.

7. Kimball Diary, March 8 and 29, 1863, Kimball Collection.
8. "The Sixth Vermont on Copperheads," *Green Mountain Freeman*, March 31, 1863, 2.
9. Mason, "From the Sixth Regiment," OIS, March 20, 1863, 3.

6. "THE THRILL OF JOY"

1. "Treason and Loyalty," *Burlington Weekly Sentinel*, March 20, 1863, 2.
2. Kimball Diary, March 15, 16, 17, 20, and 21, 1863, Kimball Collection.
3. Kimball Diary, April 15, 1863, Kimball Collection.
4. Martin Warner Davis Diary, April 8, 1863, Old Stone House Museum.
5. Stiles, "From the Sixth Regiment," OIS, April 24, 1863, 3.
6. Kimball, "From the Sixth Regiment," OIS, April 17, 1863, 2.
7. Martin Warner Davis Diary, April 28, 1863, Old Stone House Museum.
8. McPherson, *For Cause and Comrades*, 39–41.
9. Kimball, "From the Sixth Regiment," OIS, May 22, 1863, 2.
10. Davis, "From the Sixth Regiment," OIS, May 24, 1863, 2–3.
11. OR, ser. 1, vol. 25, pt. 1, 601.
12. OR, ser. 1, vol. 25, pt. 1, 605.
13. OR, ser. 1, vol. 25, pt. 1, 609.
14. Bliss Diary, 1863, VHS.
15. Stephen Bliss obituary, OIS, May 15, 1863, 3.
16. Davis, "From the Sixth Regiment," OIS, May 24, 1863, 2.
17. Bliss Diary, 1863, VHS.
18. Martin Warner Davis Diary, May 5 and 6, 1863, Old Stone House Museum.
19. Earle, "A Severe Disappointment," OIS, May 15, 1863, 2.
20. Kimball Diary, May 4, 5, and 6, 1863, Kimball Collection.
21. Morrison and Sharples, *History of the Kimball Family*, 2:852–53.
22. Martin Warner Davis Diary, June 15, 1863, Old Stone House Museum.

7. "PUTTING DOWN REBELLION"

1. Martin Warner Davis Diary, June 28, June 29, and July 30, 1863, Old Stone House Museum.
2. Martin Warner Davis Diary, July 3, 1863, Old Stone House Museum.
3. "Victory," OIS, July 10, 1863, 2.
4. OR, ser. 1, vol. 27, pt. 1, 539.
5. Kimball Diary, July 5, 1863, Kimball Collection.
6. Kimball Diary, July 7, 1863, Kimball Collection.
7. Martin Warner Davis Diary, July 7, 1863, Old Stone House Museum.

8. Kimball Diary, July 11–15, 1863, Kimball Collection.
9. Kimball Diary, July–September 1863, Kimball Collection.
10. *CWL*, 6:328.
11. Stiles, "From the Sixth Regiment," *OIS*, August 21, 1863, 4.
12. "The Draft," *OIS*, August 7, 1863, 2.
13. Stiles, "From the Sixth Regiment," *OIS*, August 21, 1863, 4.
14. "The Election," *OIS*, September 4, 1863, 2.
15. McPherson, *Battle Cry of Freedom*, 606.
16. "The Draft and Riots," *Argus and Patriot*, July 23, 1863, 2.
17. Stiles, "From the Sixth Regiment," *OIS*, October 9, 1863, 2.
18. *OR*, ser. 1, vol. 29, pt. 1, 156.

8. "TREACHEROUS WALLS OF SLAVERY"

1. Martin Warner Davis Diary, October 3 and 6, 1863, Old Stone House Museum.
2. A reference to Hamlet's soliloquy contemplating death: "For in that sleep of death, what dreams may come, / When we have shuffled off this mortal coil, / Must give us pause. There's the respect / That makes Calamity of so long life."
3. Benedict, *Vermont in the Civil War*, 1:221.
4. Stiles, "From the Sixth Regiment," *OIS*, October 9, 1863, 2.
5. Webster, "From a Conscript," *OIS*, September 25, 1863, 2.
6. Stiles, "From the Sixth Regiment," *OIS*, October 23, 1863, 3.
7. Peck, *Revised Roster of Vermont Volunteers*, 141.
8. Benedict, *Vermont in the Civil War*, 1:221.
9. Benedict, *Vermont in the Civil War*, 1:400.
10. Kimball Diary, October 1863, Kimball Collection.

9. "SOMETHING WILD AND EXCITING"

1. Benedict, *Vermont in the Civil War*, 1:410.
2. Benedict, *Vermont in the Civil War*, 1:221–22.
3. Martin Warner Davis Diary, December 16, 17, and 20, 1863, Old Stone House Museum.
4. John Clark, Harriet's father. "Sugared off" may refer to the processing of maple sugar, a springtime task, or there may be some innuendo implied.
5. Mason, Application for Officer's Commission, Entry PL-17 360-A, Colored Troops Division, Letters Received 1863–88, Record Group 94, NARA.
6. James Rickard to sister, January 10, 1864, AAS.

7. James Rickard to brother, January 17, 1864, AAS.
8. James Rickard to brother, February 2, 1864, AAS.

10. "I WAS REALLY PROUD OF MY COMMAND"

1. *CWL*, 5:357.
2. Not until the Korean War would Blacks and whites fight alongside each other in integrated units.
3. Wilbur Fisk, *Anti-Rebel*, May 20, 1862, 29.
4. "Employment of Negro Soldiers." *Burlington Weekly Sentinel*, February 19, 1864, 2.
5. *OR*, ser. 3, vol. 3, 860–61.
6. Rickard, *Service with Colored Troops*, 9.
7. Compiled Military Service Record of Samuel Adams, NARA.
8. *OR*, ser. 3, vol. 3, 862.
9. *OR*, ser. 3, vol. 3, 882.
10. Compiled Military Service Record of Benjamin Brown, NARA.
11. "Local Matters," *Baltimore Sun*, July 28, 1863, 1.
12. "Correspondence of the Baltimore Sun," *Baltimore Sun*, October 22, 1863, 4.
13. *CWL*, 6:529–32.
14. Quoted in Dobak, *Freedom by the Sword*, 317.
15. "Correspondence of the Baltimore Sun," *Baltimore Sun*, October 22, 1863, 4.
16. "Maryland Legislature," *Baltimore Sun*, January 12, 1863, 4.
17. Mason to A. F. Rockwell, Assistant Adjutant General, March 23, 1864, Entry PL-17 360-A, Colored Troops Division, Letters Received 1863–88, Record Group 94, NARA.
18. Rickard, *Service with Colored Troops*, 11.
19. Mason, "Letter from Harpers Ferry," *OIS*, April 22, 1864, 2.
20. "Departure of Colored Troops," *American and Commercial Advertiser*, April 19, 1864, 1.
21. Alexander Davis, letter written in memory of Dan Mason, 1906, Borland Collection.
22. "General Burnside's Command," *American and Commercial Advertiser*, April 26, 1864, 1.
23. "Important from Annapolis," *Chicago Tribune*, April 28, 1864, 1.
24. *Fall River Evening Daily News*, April 27, 1864, 2.
25. Mason, "From the 19th Colored Regiment," *OIS*, June 29, 1864, 2.
26. Quoted in Dobak, *Freedom by the Sword*, 338–39.
27. Nineteenth USCT Circular, December 29, 1863, Order Books of 19 USCT, NARA.

28. Davis, "In Memory of William S. Livingston," *OIS*, June 15, 1864, 2.
29. Davis, "From the Sixth Regiment," *OIS*, June 27, 1864, 2.
30. Elijah Stone to Samuel Stone, May 13, 1864, Stone Papers, Glover, Vermont, Historical Society.
31. Davis, letter written in memory of Dan Mason, 1906, Borland Collection.
32. "Outrages of the Enemy in Caroline," *Richmond Dispatch*, June 22, 1864, 1.
33. Rickard, *Service with Colored Troops*, 19.

11. "I SAY FIGHT THEM"

1. *OR*, ser. 1, vol. 46, pt. 1, sec. 11.
2. *OR*, ser. 1, vol. 33, 828.
3. Earle, "The War News," *OIS*, May 20, 1864, 2.
4. Wilbur Fisk, *Anti-Rebel*, December 15, 1864, 287.
5. Rickard, *Service with Colored Troops*, 24.
6. Mason, "From the 19th Colored Regiment," *OIS*, June 29, 1864, 2.
7. Charles Stinson to mother, May 19, 1864, Stinson Papers, Army Heritage and Education Center.
8. *OR*, ser. 1, vol. 40, pt. 3, 187.
9. Davis, letter written in memory of Dan Mason, 1906, Borland Collection.
10. Davis, "From the 39th Colored Regiment," *OIS*, August 5, 1864, 2.
11. Thomas, "The Colored Troops at Petersburg," in Johnson and Buel, *Battles and Leaders of the Civil War*, 4:563–64.
12. *OR*, ser. 1, vol. 40, pt. 1, 46.
13. Rickard, *Service with Colored Troops*, 26–27.
14. Rickard, *Service with Colored Troops*, 26–27.
15. Charles Stinson to Dear Ones at Home, August 1, 1864, Stinson Papers, Army Heritage and Education Center.
16. Charles Stinson to Dear Ones at Home, August 1, 1864.
17. Frank Kenfield, "Captured by Rebels: A Volunteer at Petersburg, 1864," *Vermont History*, 36:233.
18. *OR*, ser. 1, vol. 40, pt. 1, 17.
19. Grant and Marszelek, *Personal Memoirs*, 2:315.
20. Rickard, *Service with Colored Troops*, 28–30.
21. Compiled Military Service Record of John Addison, NARA.
22. Widow's Pension Application of Charlotte Addison, NARA.
23. Frank Kenfield, "Captured by Rebels: A Volunteer at Petersburg, 1864," *Vermont History*, 36:234.
24. *OR*, ser. 1, vol. 40, pt. 1, 598.

25. Davis, letter written in memory of Dan Mason, 1906, Borland Collection.
26. Benedict, *Vermont in the Civil War*, 1:227–28.
27. "The Charge of the Colored Division," *New York Herald*, August 2, 1864, 1.
28. "The Petersburg Disaster," *Argus and Patriot*, August 11, 1864, 1.
29. Mason, "From the 19th Colored Regiment," *OIS*, September 23, 1864, 2.
30. Rickard, *Service with Colored Troops*, 31–32.
31. Democratic Party Platform, 1864, Library of Congress.
32. Republican Party Platform, 1864, Library of Congress.
33. *CWL*, 7:506–7.
34. Abraham Lincoln Papers, Series 3, Memorandum on Probable Failure of Reelection, Library of Congress.
35. "What Peace Democrats Want," *OIS*, August 5, 1864, 2.
36. Wilbur Fisk, *Anti-Rebel*, October 12, 1864, 264–65.
37. See King, *Desperate Courage*, 5.
38. James Rickard to mother, August 25, 1864, AAS.
39. "Major C. W. Dwinell," *Caledonian*, September 23, 1864, 1.
40. "Death of Major C. W. Dwinell," *OIS*, September 9, 1864, 2.

12. "WHEN WILL THE CRUEL WAR END?"

1. Mason, "From the 19th Colored Regiment," *OIS*, September 23, 1864, 2.
2. Charles Stinson to sister, September 11, 1864, Stinson Papers, Army Heritage and Education Center.
3. Vermont Election Returns, 1864 Presidential Election, Vermont State Archives and Records Administration.
4. "Result of the Election," *OIS*, November 18, 1864, 2.
5. "Derby Sanitary Commission," *OIS*, November 18, 1864, 2.
6. Richardson, *Compilation of the Messages and Papers of the Confederacy*, 1:495.
7. As quoted in the *Richmond Whig*, November 9, 1864, 1.
8. "The President's Message," *Richmond Whig*, November 9, 1864, 2.
9. Holsinger, *War Talks in Kansas*, 304.

13. "MY FUTURE HAPPINESS"

1. A reference to Union major general George Thomas's victory at the Battle of Nashville, Tennessee, on December 15–16, 1864.
2. Charles Stinson to mother, May 19, 1864, Stinson Papers, Army Heritage and Education Center.
3. Dan Mason to Acting Adjutant General of the Army of the James, January 31, 1865, 41, Compiled Military Service Record of Dan Mason, NARA.

4. Dan Mason to Acting Adjutant General of the Army of the James, January 31, 1865, 41, Compiled Military Service Record of Dan Mason, NARA.
5. "Encampment Visitor Dead," *Chanute (KS) Daily Tribune*, May 21, 1918, 2.

14. "HOW I WOULD LIKE TO SEE YOU"

1. Regimental Guard Report and Furlough Book, Nineteenth USCT Infantry, NARA.
2. James Rickard to brother, April 2, 1865, AAS.
3. James Rickard to sister, August 6, 1865, AAS.
4. Davis, letter written in memory of Dan Mason, 1906, Borland Collection.
5. James Rickard to sister, April 11, 1865, AAS.
6. "The Negro Mania," *Burlington Weekly Sentinel*, May 26, 1865, 2.
7. Douglass, *Life and Times of Frederick Douglass*, 458–59.
8. James Rickard to sister, April 11, 1865, AAS.
9. General Orders No. 66, April 16, 1865, in Richardson and U.S. Congress, *Compilation of the Messages and Papers of the Presidents*, 3487–88.
10. James Rickard to brother, April 20, 1865, AAS.
11. James Rickard to sister, April 25, 1865, AAS.
12. Earle, "Our National Calamity," *OIS*, April 21, 1865, 2.
13. James Rickard to sister, April 25, 1865, AAS.
14. James Rickard to brother, April 30, 1865, AAS.
15. James Rickard to sister, May 6, 1865, AAS.
16. Elijah Stone to brother, May 12, 1865, Stone Papers, Glover, Vermont, Historical Society.
17. *OR*, ser. 1, vol. 46, pt. 3, 797.
18. *OR*, ser. 1, vol. 46, pt. 3, 811.
19. *OR*, ser. 1, vol. 46, pt. 3, 1160.
20. *OR*, ser. 1, vol. 46, pt. 3, 1160–61.
21. Trudeau, *Like Men of War*, 467.
22. Court Martial of Sergeant William Jackson, Thirty-Eighth USCT, NARA.
23. Court Martial of Sergeant Danbridge Brooks, Thirty-Eighth USCT, NARA.
24. *OR*, ser. 1, vol. 48, pt. 2, 1016.
25. *OR*, ser. 1, vol. 48, pt. 2, 476.
26. James Rickard to sister, May 19, 1865, AAS.
27. James Rickard to sister, April 11, 1865, AAS.
28. James Rickard to sister, May 24, 1865, AAS.
29. James Rickard to sister, September 3, 1865, AAS.
30. Henry Jones to Dear Friends, November 21, 1865, AAS.

31. James Rickard to father, May 30, 1865, AAS.
32. James Rickard to sister, June 4, 1865, AAS.
33. James Rickard to sister, June 17, 1865, AAS.
34. Mason, "Letter from Texas," *OIS*, August 11, 1865, 2.

15. "IF I CAN GET HOME THIS FALL"

1. James Rickard to friends, July 2, 1865, AAS.
2. Holsinger, "Letter from Texas," *Bedford Inquirer*, September 8, 1865, 3.
3. M. R. Williams, "Letter from Texas," *Christian Recorder*, July 29, 1865, 3.
4. *OR*, ser. 1, vol. 48, pt. 2, 1168–69.
5. "The Fourth at Derby Line," *OIS*, July 14, 1865, 2.
6. Holsinger, "Letter from Texas," *Bedford Inquirer*, September 8, 1865, 3.
7. Holsinger, "Texas Correspondence," *Bedford Inquirer*, January 26, 1866, 2.
8. Holsinger, *Bedford Inquirer*, September 8, 1865, 3, and November 16, 1865, 1.
9. Alexander W. Davis to J. A. Campbell, May 31, 1865, 32, Compiled Military Service Records of Alexander Davis, Thirty-Ninth USCT, NARA.
10. James Rickard to sister, August 6, 1865, AAS.
11. Holsinger, "Letter from Texas," *Bedford Inquirer*, September 8, 1865, 3.
12. James Rickard to sister, August 17, 1865, AAS.
13. James Rickard to brother, August 25, 1865, AAS.
14. James Rickard to brother, September 18, 1865, AAS.
15. James Rickard to sister, September 3, 1865, AAS.
16. Nineteenth USCT Regimental Letter and Order Book, August 22, 1865, NARA.

16. "A BRAVE AND ELEGANT SOLDIER"

1. James Rickard to brother, September 18, 1865, AAS.
2. General Orders No. 64, October 6, 1865, Nineteenth USCT Regimental Papers, NARA.
3. Letter to Colonel Thomas Bayley, November 5, 1865, Nineteenth USCT Regimental Papers, NARA.
4. W. C. Bryant to Acting Adjutant, Nineteenth USCT, October 16, 1865, Nineteenth USCT Regimental Papers, NARA.
5. James Rickard to Acting Adjutant, Nineteenth USCT, October 12, 1865, Nineteenth USCT Regimental Papers, NARA.
6. James Rickard to Acting Adjutant, Nineteenth USCT, October 28, 1865, Nineteenth USCT Regimental Papers, NARA.

7. Frank Holsinger to Acting Adjutant, Nineteenth USCT, October 29, 1865, Nineteenth USCT Regimental Papers, NARA.
8. Acting Adjutant to John Patterson, July 8, 1865, Nineteenth USCT Regimental Papers, NARA.
9. For an explanation of the employment of laundresses in the XXV Corps, see Dobak, *Freedom by the Sword*, 423–24.
10. Zachariah Butcher to Acting Adjutant General of the Army of the James, November 16, 1865, 24, Compiled Military Service Records of Zachariah Butler, Nineteenth USCT, NARA.
11. James Rickard to sister, October 29, 1865, AAS.
12. For an analysis of the medical treatment of USCT units, see Glatthaar, *Forged in Battle*, 185–97.
13. Joseph Perkins to Acting Adjutant, First Division, Twenty-Fifth Army Corps, November 16, 1865, Nineteenth USCT Regimental Letter and Order Book, NARA.
14. Acting Adjutant of First Division, Twenty-Fifth Army Corps to Joseph Perkins, November 18, 1865, Nineteenth USCT Regimental Papers, NARA.
15. Joseph Perkins to Adjutant General District of the Rio Grande, November 21, 1865, Nineteenth USCT Regimental Papers, NARA.
16. Chief Medical Examiner of the District of the Rio Grande to Joseph Perkins, November 29, 1865, Nineteenth USCT Regimental Papers, NARA.
17. James Rickard to sister, December 7, 1865, AAS.
18. James Rickard to sister, December 22, 1865, AAS.
19. C. C. Radmore to Joseph Perkins, November 20, 1865, 44, Compiled Military Service Record of Dan Mason, Nineteenth USCT, NARA.
20. General Orders No. 18, November 20, 1865, Nineteenth USCT Regimental Letter and Order Book, NARA.
21. James Rickard to mother, November 21, 1865, AAS.
22. James Rickard to brother, November 26, 1865, AAS.
23. Resolutions passed on the death of Captain Dan Mason, Nineteenth USCT, November 21, 1865, Borland Collection.
24. Kimball Diary, December 13, 1865, Kimball Collection.
25. Kimball, "Our Martyred Dead: Captain Dan Mason," *Vermont Record*, January, 12, 1866, 6.
26. Davis, letter written in memory of Dan Mason, 1906, Borland Collection.
27. William Welsh to Harriet Mason, January 4, 1866, Dan Mason Papers, VHS.
28. "Death of Capt. Mason," *OIS*, January 17, 1866, 2.

29. "A Sermon: Preached at Glover, Feb. 4. at the Funeral of Capt. Dan Mason," *OIS*, February 21, 1866, 2.

EPILOGUE

1. 1870 U.S. Census, Population Schedule, Census Place: Glover, Orleans, Vermont, 127A, NARA.
2. Phebe Estelle Spalding, *Little Memories in Silhouettes and Other Lines*, 1872, Glover, Vermont, Historical Society.
3. "Suggested by the Death of Dan Mason," Celestia C. Stevens, West Glover, Vermont, February 1866, Borland Collection.
4. Widow's Pension Application of Harriet Mason, NARA.
5. "John Calvin Borland," *Orleans County Monitor*, April 12, 1950, 3.
6. "Glover," *Orleans County Monitor*, December 3, 1900, 5.
7. "West Glover," *Orleans County Monitor*, June 23, 1902, 5.
8. Widow's Pension Application of Harriet Mason, NARA.
9. "Barton," *Orleans County Monitor*, November 5, 1924, 1.
10. "Harriet B. Borland," *Orleans County Monitor*, December 3, 1924, 1.
11. Harriet Borland to Dan Owen Mason, July 11, 1907, Dan Mason Letters, VHS.
12. Memory of John Owen Mason, Mason Family Collection.
13. "History of Glover: Eighth Paper," *Orleans County Monitor*, March 6, 1868.
14. *Daily Commonwealth* (Topeka KS), October 17, 1865, 1.
15. "Sudden Death," *Harvey County News* (Newton KS), October 13, 1875, 8.
16. "Suicide of Aged Veteran," *Barre Daily Times*, July 18, 1916, 1.
17. Fred Kimball to Brevet Brigadier General O. Brown, December 31, 1867, Kimball Collection.
18. Morrison and Sharples, *History of the Kimball Family*, 1:853.
19. "Affairs in Brunswick County," April 26, 1869, Kimball Collection.
20. "Comrades of Sixth Vermont Tour in California," *Orleans County Monitor*, July 21, 1920, 1.
21. Letter of Fred Kimball to Old Comrades, September 24, 1880, Kimball Collection.

BIBLIOGRAPHY

ARCHIVES AND MANUSCRIPT MATERIALS

1860 U.S. Census, Population Schedule, Census Place: Glover, Orleans, Vermont, Roll M653_1322, National Archives and Records Administration.

1870 U.S. Census, Population Schedule, Census Place: Glover, Orleans, Vermont, Roll M593_1623, National Archives and Records Administration.

Abraham Lincoln Papers, Library of Congress.

Alexander W. Davis Papers, Borland Collection.

Case Files of Approved Pension Applications of Widows and Other Dependents of Civil War Veterans, ca. 1861–ca. 1910, Record Group 15, National Archives and Records Administration.

Charles Stinson Papers, Army Heritage and Education Center.

Colored Troops Division, Letters Received 1863–88, Entry PL-17 360-A, Container No. 194, Record Group 94, National Archives and Records Administration.

Compiled Military Service Records of Volunteer Union Soldiers Who Served with the United States Colored Troops: Infantry Organizations, 14th through 19th, Publication No. M1822, Record Group 94, National Archives and Records Administration.

Dan Mason Papers, Vermont Historical Society.

Elbert Nye Papers, Mohrman Collection.

Elijah Stone Papers, Glover, Vermont, Historical Society.

Frederick M. Kimball Papers and Diary, Kimball Collection.

George McClellan Papers, Library of Congress.

Hobart Bliss Diary, Vermont Historical Society.

James Rickard Papers, American Antiquarian Society.

Martin Warner Davis Diary, Old Stone House Museum.

Martin Warner Davis Papers, Old Stone House Museum.

Nonpopulation Census Schedules for Vermont, 1850–70: Agriculture and Industry, M-1798, Roll 4, 1860; Schedule 4, Agriculture; Lamoille—Windsor; Glover, Vermont; Washington DC; National Archives and Records Administration.

Order Books of the Nineteenth USCT, Record Group 94, National Archives and Records Administration.
Records of the Office of the Judge Advocate General, Court-Martial Case Files, 1809–1938, Record Group 153, National Archives and Records Administration.
Regimental Descriptive, Consolidated Morning Report, and Order Book, Book Records of Volunteer Union Organizations, Sixth Vermont Infantry, Entry 112-115, PL-17, Record Group 94, National Archives and Records Administration.
Regimental Guard Report and Furlough Book, Book Records of Volunteer Union Organizations, Nineteenth USCT Infantry, Entry 112-115, PL-17, Record Group 94, National Archives and Records Administration.
U.S. Colored Troops, Regimental Papers Nineteenth–Twentieth U.S. Colored Infantry, Office of the Adjutant General, Box 20, Record Group 94, National Archives and Records Administration.
William Welsh Papers, Grand Valley State University.

PUBLISHED WORKS

Benedict, George G. *Vermont in the Civil War*. Vol. 1. Burlington VT: Free Press Association, 1886.
Berlin, Ira, Joseph Patrick Reidy, and Leslie S. Rowland. *Freedom's Soldiers*. Cambridge: Cambridge University Press, 1998.
Billings, John D. *Hardtack and Coffee: Or, the Unwritten Story of Army Life*. Boston: George M. Smith, 1888.
Blight, David W. *Race and Reunion: The Civil War in American Memory*. Cambridge MA: Harvard University Press, 2002.
Bonner, Robert E. *The Soldier's Pen: Firsthand Impressions of the Civil War*. New York: Hill & Wang, 2007.
Brownlee, Peter John, Sarah Burns, Diane Dillon, Daniel Greene, and Scott Manning Stevens. *Home Front: Daily Life in the Civil War North*. Chicago: University of Chicago Press, 2013.
Catton, Bruce. *Bruce Catton: The Army of the Potomac Trilogy (LOA #359)*. Washington DC: National Geographic, 2022.
Churchill, Winston S. *A History of the English-Speaking Peoples*. Vol. 4. New York: Dodd, Mead, 1958.
Clarke, Frances M. *War Stories: Suffering and Sacrifice in the Civil War North*. Chicago: University of Chicago Press, 2012.
Coffin, Howard. *The Battered Stars: One State's Civil War Ordeal during Grant's Overland Campaign*. Woodstock VT: Countryman, 2002.
———. *Full Duty*. Woodstock VT: Countryman, 1992.

Dobak, William A. *Freedom by the Sword: The U.S. Colored Troops, 1862–1867*. Washington DC: U.S. Army Center of Military History, 2011.

Douglass, Frederick. *The Life and Times of Frederick Douglass, from 1817–1882*. London: Christian Age Office, 1882.

Egerton, Douglas R. *Thunder at the Gates: The Black Civil War Regiments That Redeemed America*. Philadelphia: Basic Books, 2016.

Faust, Drew Gilpin. *This Republic of Suffering: Death and the American Civil War*. New York: Vintage, 2009.

Fisk, Wilbur. *Hard Marching Every Day*. Edited by Emil Rosenblatt and Ruth Rosenblatt. Lawrence: University Press of Kansas, 1992.

Gallagher, Gary W., and Caroline E Janney. *Cold Harbor to the Crater*. Chapel Hill: University of North Carolina Press, 2015.

Glatthaar, Joseph T. *Forged in Battle: The Civil War Alliance of Black Soldiers and White Officers*. Baton Rouge: Louisiana State University Press, 2000.

Grant, Ulysses S., and John F Marszalek. *The Personal Memoirs of Ulysses S. Grant: The Complete Annotated Edition*. Cambridge MA: Belknap Press of Harvard University Press, 2017.

Grout, Josiah. *Memoir of Gen'l William Wallace Grout and Autobiography of Josiah Grout*. Newport VT: Bullock, 1916.

Hemenway, Abby. *The Vermont Historical Gazetteer*. Burlington VT: A. M. Hemenway, 1867.

Johnson, Robert Underwood, and Clarence Clough Buel. *Battles and Leaders of the Civil War*. Vol. 4. New York: Century, 1888.

Jordan, Brian. *Marching Home: Union Veterans and Their Unending Civil War*. New York: W. W. Norton, 2015.

Kalmoe, Nathan P. *With Ballots and Bullets: Partisanship and Violence in the American Civil War*. New York: Cambridge University Press, 2020.

King, John. *Desperate Courage: Raising a New Army of United States Colored Troops*. Harpers Ferry WV: Harpers Ferry National Historical Park, 2014.

Kinsley, Rufus, and David C. Rankin. *Diary of a Christian Soldier: Rufus Kinsley and the Civil War*. New York: Cambridge University Press, 2004.

Levin, Kevin M. *Remembering the Battle of the Crater: War as Murder*. Lexington: University Press of Kentucky, 2017.

Lincoln, Abraham, and Roy P. Basler. *The Collected Works of Abraham Lincoln*. New Brunswick NJ: Rutgers University Press, 1953.

Luke, Bob, and John David Smith. *Soldiering for Freedom: How the Union Army Recruited, Trained, and Deployed the U.S. Colored Troops*. Baltimore MD: Johns Hopkins University Press, 2014.

Marshall, Jeffrey D. *A War of the People*. Hanover NH: University Press of New England, 1999.

McPherson, James M. *Battle Cry of Freedom: The Civil War Era*. New York: Oxford University Press, 2003.

———. *For Cause and Comrades: Why Men Fought in the Civil War*. New York: Oxford University Press, 1997.

Mitchell, Reid. *The Vacant Chair: The Northern Soldier Leaves Home*. New York: Oxford University Press, 1995.

Morrison, Leonard Allison, and Stephen Paschall Sharples. *History of the Kimball Family in America, from 1634 to 1897*. Boston: Damrell & Upham, 1897.

Peck, Theodore. *Revised Roster of Vermont Volunteers and Lists of Vermonters Who Served in the Army and Navy of the United States during the War of the Rebellion, 1861–66*. Montpelier VT: Press of the Watchman, 1892.

Richardson, James D. *A Compilation of the Messages and Papers of the Confederacy*. Nashville TN: United States Publishing Company, 1905.

Richardson, James D., and U.S. Congress, Joint Committee on Printing. *A Compilation of the Messages and Papers of the Presidents*. New York: Bureau of National Literature, 1897.

Rickard, James H. *Service with Colored Troops in Burnside's Corps*. Providence: Rhode Island Soldiers & Sailors Historical Society, 1894.

Silber, Nina. *Yankee Correspondence: Civil War Letters between New England Soldiers and the Homefront*. Charlottesville: University Press of Virginia, 1996.

Smith, John David. *Black Soldiers in Blue: African American Troops in the Civil War Era*. Chapel Hill: University of North Carolina Press, 2004.

Sodergren, Steven E. *The Army of the Potomac in the Overland and Petersburg Campaigns*. Baton Rouge: Louisiana State University Press, 2017.

Summers, Robert K. *Maryland's Black Civil War Soldiers*. N.p., 2020.

Trudeau, Noah Andre. *Like Men of War: Black Troops in the Civil War, 1862–1865*. Edison NJ: Castle, 2002.

Walker, Aldace Freeman. *The Vermont Brigade in the Shenandoah Valley, 1864*. Burlington VT: Free Press Association, 1869.

The War of the Rebellion: A Compilation of the Official Records of the Union and Confederate Armies. Washington DC: Government Printing Office, 1888.

War Talks in Kansas. Kansas City MO: Franklin Hudson, 1906.

Wickman, Donald. *A Very Fine Appearance: The Civil War Photographs of George Houghton*. Montpelier: Vermont Historical Society, 2010.

Willis, Deborah. *The Black Civil War Soldier*. New York: New York University Press, 2021.

Wilmer, L. Allison, James H. Jarrett, and George Vernon. *History and Roster of Maryland Volunteers, War of 1861–65*. Baltimore MD: Guggenheimer, Weil, 1898.

INDEX